DATE DUE

MR 29 01			
AP 25 06			

ONE OF A KIND

ONE OF A KIND

A COMPENDIUM OF UNIQUE PEOPLE, PLACES, AND THINGS

BRUCE FELTON

Illustrations by Kimble Mead

Quill
WILLIAM MORROW
NEW YORK

It is the policy of William Morrow and Company, Inc., and its imprints and affiliates, recognizing the importance of preserving what has been written, to print the books we publish on acid-free paper, and we exert our best efforts to that end.

Library of Congress Cataloging-in-Publication Data

Felton, Bruce.
    One of a kind: a compendium of unique people, places, and things
  / by Bruce Felton.
        p.   cm.
    Includes index.
    ISBN 0-688-10815-6
    1. Curiosities and wonders—United States. 2. United States—
  History—Miscellanea. I. Title.
  E179.F34   1992
  973—dc20   91-32893
                                                                    CIP

Printed in the United States of America

First Quill Edition

1 2 3 4 5 6 7 8 9 10

BOOK DESIGN BY BERNARD SCHLEIFER

FOR BEN,
WITH LOVE

CONTENTS

8　　**C O N T E N T S**

ACKNOWLEDGMENTS

I MAY BE the only person listed on the title page of *One of a Kind*, but that doesn't mean I'm the only person who had anything to do with writing it. A number of people helped, and to them I extend my heartfelt thanks.

Among them: Hunter-gatherers Richard Friedman, Elihu Sussman, Bill Haney, and "Research Ed" Kagen; editor Randy Ladenheim-Gil, for her support and encouragement, and her deft hand at sanding the rough edges from the manuscript; usage maven Michael Goodman, who added a large measure of factual accuracy and syntactical precision; my longtime cotrivialist, Mark Fowler, who inspired several items described in these pages; Anna Benadon, who was always there to lend a hand; Jay Acton, my agent since 1977; and Stacey Woolf, whose support and persistence quite literally made this book happen.

To my family, I owe a special kind of thanks. It was my son Ben who goaded me to write this book in the first place, suggested several entries ("the only major automobile company to manufacture edible cars" and "the only president sworn in on an airplane," among others), and endured far too many dadless evenings and weekends while I wrote. All the while, my wife, Judith, kept the demons at bay and made a place for me to work—in every sense.

▉NTRODUCTION

BACK IN THE 1950s, *The New York Times* conducted a six-month survey of advertising in its pages and counted no fewer than 58 products and services billed as "the only . . ." God knows how many they'd find today. *The only full-service tanning salon in central Montana . . . The only place to go for all your bathroom remodeling needs . . . The only solid-waste-management handbook endorsed by the Twin Forks Sanitation Department . . .*

I suppose a collection of advertising "onlies" wouldn't make for edge-of-the-seat reading (though it probably would be the only collection of its kind). But their sheer number do reflect an ancient and universal fascination with anything that can legitimately claim to be sui generis.

Even Aristotle was into it—and he probably never saw a tanning salon in his life. "The two qualities which chiefly inspire regard and affection," he wrote, "are that a thing is your own and that it is your only one." See?

One of a Kind is a compendium of stand-alone phenomena in an improbably broad range of categories, from the arts and sciences to crime and punishment. In it you'll learn that King Louis XIV was the only European monarch to be eaten at a formal dinner. . . . that Alaska is the only state without houseflies. . . . that *Incu-*

bus was the only feature film spoken entirely in Esperanto. . . . that Abraham Lincoln was the only president to be cloned.

You'll also meet such overlooked luminaries as Alkan, the only composer crushed to death by a plummeting Talmud . . . Plennie L. Wingo, the only person ever to walk backwards from Santa Monica to Istanbul (He wore eyeglasses equipped with a rearview mirror to help him see where he was going) . . . and Jackie Mitchell, the only woman ever to strike out Babe Ruth. Every one is certifiably unique—a true "oner" in crossword parlance.

But don't take my word for it. Ask the Twin Forks Sanitation Department.

Of course, some "onlies" are easier to pin down than others. It's a fairly easy matter to establish beyond question that Jimmy Carter was the only president to report seeing a UFO, or that Venus is the only planet to spin counterclockwise, or that the Sovereign Military Order of Malta is the only country small enough to have a street address.

But other items might be more accurately described as "the only *known* . . ." I'm not aware of a *second* movie made in Esperanto, or a *second* woman to fan the Babe, and all efforts to uncover one turned up negative. Early in the writing of *One of a Kind,* I celebrated the daring of one Owen J. Quinn, the only person to parachute safely from the roof of New York City's World Trade Center. He did it in 1975, but in 1991, while I was still at work on this book, a *second* jumper made the descent. Quinn's place in the "Overachievers" chapter was invalidated.

So was that of Armand Hammer, the late chairman of Occidental Petroleum. At ninety-two Mr. Hammer was to be bar mitzvahed in Los Angeles—and to be enshrined herein as "the only nonagenarian bar mitzvah boy to run a *Fortune* 500 company." Regrettably, he died on the eve of the grand event. He too was expunged.

The great Gummo Marx is here, though—the only non-funny Marx Brother. Gummo once attributed his siblings' success to his early retirement from their act. He may have been right. But he's an indispensable player in the cast of characters of *One of a Kind*, along with such other singular personae as St. Wilgefortis (the only female saint to sport a full beard and mustache), Fred Newton (the only person ever to swim the length of the Mississippi River), and Hessie Donahue (the only woman ever to knock out John L. Sullivan). If *One of a Kind* proves a winning book, the credit belongs to them far more than to me.

And in books as in pro football, to quote Vince Lombardi, "Winning isn't everything. It's the only thing."

—BRUCE FELTON
New York City

ONE
OF A
KIND

PRESIDENTS

The only president to be cloned

If the idea of cloning a president unnerves you, take comfort in the fact that the cloners cared enough to clone only the very best—Abraham Lincoln. The last thing the world needs is a half dozen carbon copies of some third-rater like Millard Fillmore or Warren Harding running loose.

The Lincoln cloning project was conceived in 1990 by a team of researchers who planned to duplicate DNA samples from Lincoln's hair, blood, and skull. Their objective was to verify whether the sixteenth president suffered from Marfan's syndrome, a disorder of the connective tissue that can play havoc with the heart, skeleton, and eyes.

The cloners obtained the requisite tissue samples from Washington's National Museum of Health and Medicine. An ethics committee concluded that smearing bits of the Great Emancipator on a microscope slide did not constitute a violation of his privacy, given that he'd been dead for 125 years and had no living descendants. But others weren't so sure.

"Lincoln spent his whole life trying to teach the nation to transcend biology," said University of Minnesota bioethicist Arthur Caplan. "Now he winds up being reduced to his own biology."

The only president to elope

Six months after his first wife died in 1842, President John Tyler proposed to Julia Gardiner, the twenty-four-year-old socialite daughter of New York State senator David Gardiner. Though flattered, she turned him down—partly because Tyler was thirty years her senior and the father of eight children.

But the president was smitten and popped the question three more times over the next year and a half. Each time Julia said no. Then, on February 28, 1844, she and the president were among a party of high-society types sailing on the test run of the world's first propeller-driven frigate, the USS *Princeton*. During the trip, the breech of the ship's main gun exploded, and six people, among them Julia's father, were killed.

Julia fainted, and the president himself carried her off the ship. She grieved for weeks and suffered nightmares; Tyler was very attentive and a source of great comfort and compassion during this time. When he proposed a fifth time, she said yes.

Because of the age difference, and of the eyebrows that might be raised at the prospect of a widowed president remarrying in office, John and Julia married in secrecy. Without a word to the press or to anyone outside the family, they sneaked off to New York City and tied the knot at a quiet ceremony at the Church of the Ascension on June 26, 1844. Rev. Benjamin Threadwell Onderdonk presided.

Word leaked anyway, and while tongues wagged, no real scandal ensued. During her White House years, Julia

Tyler proved a gracious and admired hostess. She threw boffo parties, became the first First Lady to hire a full-time press agent, and bore seven children—the last when Tyler was seventy, years after he left office. She died in 1889, outliving her husband by twenty-seven years.

The only president to report seeing an unidentified flying object

"I don't laugh at people anymore when they say they've seen UFOs, because I've seen one myself," Georgia governor Jimmy Carter mentioned at a governors' conference in 1973. The sighting had occurred in Leary, Georgia, four years earlier, before he became governor. Carter was chatting in front of the Lions Club with several other men after a business dinner. According to accounts he gave to two UFO sighting organizations, all the men watched a shining "bluish . . . then reddish" saucerlike object move across the night sky, shrinking from the size of "a planet" to "the apparent size of the moon.

"It seemed to move toward us from a distance,

stopped and moved partially away," the future president stated. "It returned and departed. It came close . . . maybe three hundred to one thousand yards away . . . moved away, came close, and then moved away."

Carter was not the only elected official to see a flying saucer. In October 1973, a month after the future president went public with his 1969 sighting, Ohio governor John Gilligan told reporters he'd seen a UFO while driving with his wife on a darkened highway near Ann Arbor, Michigan.

"It was a vertical beam of light, amber colored, and we watched it for about 35 minutes," he said. "It would fade out and get bright. I frankly don't know what it was. I'm absolutely serious. I saw this. It was not a plane, it was not a bird, and it didn't wear a cape."

The only female president

Officially, Edith Wilson, Woodrow's First Lady, was never president of anything. She was only the president's wife.

But from the time Wilson suffered a massive stroke during a speaking tour in Colorado in 1919 until he retired from office seventeen months later, Edith, not Woodrow, ran the country.

And why not? Vice-President Thomas Marshall, who ordinarily would have been expected to step in, publicly confessed that the thought of being president terrified him. Edith Wilson may have had little formal education and even spoken out against women's suffrage, but she knew as much about foreign policy and domestic politicking as anyone. Even before the stroke, Edith was her husband's confidant and most trusted adviser. She was even privy to secret codes used by the White House to communicate with U.S. emissaries abroad.

With the exception of Wilson's physician, F. X. Dercum, no one knew how incapacitated the president was. Despite daily bulletins that he was recovering, he remained paralyzed and partially blind for many months. Meanwhile, Edith stood guard at his bedroom door, barring even Cabinet officers and trusted aides, and deciding what matters were worth bothering him about.

Sometimes she brought official documents for him to sign, guiding his writing hand on the paper; it's not certain that he always knew what he was signing or that she didn't simply forge his signature. She often emerged from closed-door conferences with her husband to convey his views to the press. Most likely, she made up the words herself.

Edith Wilson's presidency—or what she preferred to call her stewardship—got mixed reviews. Republican journalist Dolly Gann broke ranks with her own party to praise Edith's grit and good sense. The London *Daily Mail* spoke admiringly of her presidency in its editorial pages. But others snidely referred to her as "the presidentress" and the "Iron Queen," and Senator Albert Fall banged on his desk in the Senate chamber and shouted, "We have a petticoat government! Mrs. Wilson is president!"

The only president to make more sense backwards than forwards

The utterances of politicians are always open to multiple interpretations. But one Texas researcher believes he has found a foolproof way of deciphering polspeak for once and for all: Listen to it backwards.

According to David J. Oates, originator of "reverse speech technology," people often give voice to unconscious thoughts in reverse: All it takes is a trained ear and a tape recorder that plays backwards to figure out what they're *really* saying.

In 1990, C. B. Scott Jones, a staff assistant to Rhode Island senator Claiborne Pell, thought Oates was on to something and ran a bunch of speeches by President George Bush and his top aides through a tape player in reverse. To a layman, it all sounded like dialogue from an Ingmar Bergman film, but Oates said he repeatedly heard the name, "Simone." Could it have been a secret code word?

In a memo to Secretary of Defense Dick Cheney, Jones urged him and the president to watch their mouths, especially if Simone stood for something covert. There is no record of Cheney's response to Jones. But Senator Pell fired him.

Oates, meanwhile, had decided it wasn't "Simone" the president was saying, but "simoom"—Arabic for "desert dust storm." When the Persian Gulf War broke out in January 1991, "and they called it Operation Desert Storm," he said, "I got chills down my spine."

Throughout the Gulf War, Oates claimed he knew about planned strategic initiatives long before the public—or even the press. "I'd get news hours or days before it was released," he said. "James Baker would announce that Egypt was going to join the coalition, but when I played the statement back, I heard 'a problem is left.'"

When a CNN newscaster reported, "Saudi Arabia has no further information," Oates heard otherwise: "War is here. Ashamed of me." Correspondent John Holliman's "We've seen these bombs come down before" became "Bomb them often. I must love in Hebrew."

CNN derided Oates's claims, noting that "we broadcast in straight speak, not back talk." President Bush, however, had no comment—not even a terse "spil ym daer."

The only president to have hanged a man

In the early 1870s, several years before he was elected president, Grover Cleveland served a term as sheriff of Erie County, New York. In that capacity he was twice called upon to serve as hangman—for Patrick Morrissey, who had been convicted of murdering his mother, and for John Gaffney, who had killed a man in a poker game.

Both times, Sheriff Cleveland placed and tightened the noose, slipped the hood over the prisoner's head, and sprang the trapdoor. Deeply upset by the experience, he declined to run for reelection.

The only president born on the Fourth of July

Calvin Coolidge came into the world on July 4, 1872.

Interestingly, three former presidents *died* on the Fourth: Thomas Jefferson and John Adams in 1826 (that's right—the same day); and James Monroe in 1831.

The only divorced president

Nancy Davis was the second Mrs. Ronald Reagan; the first was actress Jane Wyman, who married Ron in Hollywood on January 26, 1940. They had met three years earlier at the Warner Bros. studios and acted together in three movies: *Brother Rat, Brother Rat and a Baby,* and *An Angel from Texas.*

Hollywood columnists depicted the Reagans as the perfect couple, and during the war, *Modern Screen* magazine published Captain Ron's moving "Letters to Button Nose"—his nickname for Jane—which made it seem as if he was stationed overseas and under heavy fire. In truth, Reagan's eyesight ruled out combat duty; his military service consisted largely of doing voice-overs for Army training films at the Hal Roach Studios in nearby Culver City. He was home for dinner every night.

After the war, the couple's marriage began to unravel, in part due to Ron's growing obsession with politics. They were divorced in 1948—not long after Jane won an Oscar for her performance in *Johnny Belinda*. When Reagan ran for president in 1980, he was occasionally greeted by derisive placards reading, "Jane Wyman was right."

The only president to take the oath of office on an airplane

It all happened so fast: Barely two hours after the assassination of President John F. Kennedy in Dallas on November 22, 1963, Vice-President Lyndon B. Johnson succeeded him as the nation's 36th president. Normally the Chief Justice of the Supreme Court administers the oath of office on the steps of the Capitol. But these were hardly normal circumstances, and the new president was sworn in by federal judge Sarah T. Hughes aboard the presidential jet, *Air Force One,* as it sat on a runway at Love Field. Johnson's wife, Lady Bird, and a stunned, blood-spattered Jackie Kennedy were at his side. Nine minutes later, the plane took off for Washington.

The only remaining tooth of George Washington

George Washington's teeth began falling out with distressing regularity around the age of twenty-two, and by the time he was inaugurated as president, he retained only one of the teeth he was born with—a lower-right bicuspid.

It's hard to say which was the greater affliction—Washington's diseased teeth or the succession of horrendous dentures he wore to replace them. Typically carved from ivory or elk's teeth (not wood, rumors to the contrary), they were hinged with tautly wound steel coils that required him to bear down just to keep his mouth shut. Eating and speaking were difficult, and he was in almost constant pain. Portraitist Gilbert Stuart stuffed cotton under Washington's lips to give him a more natural appearance but only succeeded in making him look puffy-mouthed. The results are visible in the portrait of Washington on the one-dollar bill.

Eventually, Washington switched to a New York City dentist, John Greenwood, who fashioned his first presidential dentures in 1789; a hole in the plate fit over Washington's surviving bicuspid. Washington marinated his choppers in port wine each night in a futile effort to deodorize them. The only effect of the soaking was to soften the teeth and turn them black.

In 1796 Greenwood extracted Washington's last natural tooth, which he kept in a gold locket that he wore on his watch fob and inscribed thusly: "In New York 1790, Jn Greenwood made Pres Geo Washington a whole sett of teeth. The enclosed tooth is the last one which grew in his head." Tooth, locket, and watch were donated by Greenwood's descendants to The New York Academy of Medicine in 1937, where they repose today.

Washington wasn't the only president with bad teeth. In *The Strange Story of False Teeth*, John Woodforde notes that Andrew Jackson was fitted with a complete set of upper and lower dentures. But unlike Washington, he never wore them. He kept public-speaking engagements to a minimum and had no qualms about sitting for official portraits without a tooth in his head.

The only person to be both the son and father of a U.S. president

John Scott Harrison (1804–1878) was the son of William Henry Harrison, ninth president of the United States and the first to die in office. The only one of Harrison's ten children (no other president had as many) to survive his father, he served four years in Congress but otherwise seems to have led a dreary life. His major achievement was the siring of the twenty-third president, Benjamin Harrison.

When John Harrison died, the Cincinnati *Enquirer* sneered, "Most of those who will hear of his death did not know he was living." Neither John nor any member of his family, the paper added, had "given proof of the possession of talents of a high order." As it turned out, Harrison sparked considerably more excitement as a dead man than he ever had when he was alive.

Within hours after Harrison's funeral, grave robbers made off with his coffin, despite its having been buried in an exceptionally deep, brick-lined grave and weighed down with a stone "so heavy that the strength of 16 men was required to move it," according to Joseph Perling in *Presidents' Sons*. A search party found the body the next day, hanging by its neck in an airshaft in the Ohio Medical College.

Harrison's disappearance and return was the scandal of 1878, and the papers had a field day, running endless columns of copy illustrated with ghoulish pictures of the grave robbers and the tools they used to dig up his body. For its part, the *Enquirer* forgot its previous disdain for the dear departed and eulogized him as "an honored citizen whose life of good works had entitled his memory to honor and respect."

Harrison was reinterred in a grave next to his father's.

The only president to get stuck in the White House bathtub

William Howard Taft was unequivocally the nation's most corpulent chief executive, his weight fluctuating between 300 and 350 pounds during his term in office (1909–1913). Once, after getting immovably lodged in the White House bathtub, he ordered a new one installed, large enough for four men.

Taft, who was five feet eleven inches tall, weighed in at a lissome 220 pounds when he graduated from Yale, but his weight quickly ballooned. As governor-general of the Philippines he once cabled Secretary of War Elihu Root, "TOOK LONG HORSEBACK RIDE TODAY. FEELING FINE." Root cabled back, "HOW IS THE HORSE?" At a dinner during a presidential visit to the new Panama Canal, engineers provided him with a dining-room chair carefully reinforced with steel.

Quips and jibes about Taft's girth were common, and he took them with good humor. According to Paul F. Boller, Jr., in *Presidential Anecdotes*, Taft was swimming off Cape Ann, Massachusetts, when two neighbors walked by and said, "We'd better wait. The President is using the ocean." A polite man, Taft, it was said, would never hesitate to rise and give his seat to three people. He often fell asleep at Cabinet meetings and state dinners.

Taft was also **the only former president appointed Chief Justice of the U.S. Supreme Court.** President Warren G. Harding named him to the post in 1921; for Taft, who'd never had much enthusiasm for electoral politics, it was the fulfillment of lifelong ambition.

The only president to study medicine

Born into a wealthy Virginia plantation family in 1773, William Henry Harrison enrolled in the Medical Department of the University of Pennsylvania after graduating from college and studied under the noted physician Benjamin Rush.

However, medical school was his father's idea, and the eighteen-year-old Harrison dropped out in midcourse to join the army, never to return to his studies. In the years that followed, Harrison distinguished himself as a war hero and went on to a career in politics.

According to Harrison's predecessor in office, Martin Van Buren, "He does not seem to realize the vast importance of his elevation. He is as tickled with the presidency as is a young woman with a new bonnet." But Harrison was anything but young: At sixty-eight, he was the oldest man to be elected president until Ronald Reagan.

He caught a chill while taking the oath of office on that raw March day in 1841, and thirty-two days later, he succumbed to pneumonia, the first president to die in office.

The only president turned down for renomination by his own party

The nation's fourteenth president, Franklin Pierce tried hard to broker a peace between pro- and antislavery forces. But in spite of his New England roots, he was seen as soft on slavery and became unpopular in the North. His clumsy efforts to blackmail Spain into selling Cuba to the United States didn't gain him many friends either.

Pierce campaigned vigorously for renomination at the Democratic National Convention in Cincinnati in June 1856. But his party dumped him after the first ballot and nominated James Buchanan on the seventeenth.

The only president to appear unrecognized on nationwide television

Three years into his term as governor of Georgia, Jimmy Carter was not altogether unknown when he turned up as a guest on *What's My Line?* in December 1973.

He did not sign in—that would have been too much of a giveaway—but neither was he billed as a mystery guest, and the four unblindfolded panelists got a good look at him. But his campaign for the presidency was still a good two years off, and few people outside Georgia knew his face. None of the panelists had a clue.

"Does your work involve women?" asked Arlene Francis. "Yes, I would have to say it does," answered the future president.

U.S. presidents who served only one year—give or take—in office:

1. *William Henry Harrison.* Caught pneumonia on Inauguration Day, 1841, and died a month later.

2. *Zachary Taylor.* Inaugurated in March 1849. After consuming heroic quantities of cherries, chilled milk, and raw vegetables during sweltering Fourth of July festivities in Washington the following year, Taylor died of acute indigestion. (Taylor's remains were exhumed in 1991 to determine if he had been poisoned. But the belated postmortem exam revealed no evidence of foul play, and the indigestion diagnosis stands.)

3. *James Garfield.* Took office in March 1881, shot by a thwarted office seeker, Charles Guiteau, on July 2, and died September 19.

4. *David Rice Atchison.* March 4—Inauguration Day—fell on a Sunday in 1849, and president-elect Zachary Taylor refused to take the oath of office. So David Rice Atchison, president pro tem of the Senate and next in the line of succession, was sworn in instead. Immediately upon assuming the presidency, Atchison appointed a number of his cronies to cabinet positions, had a few drinks, and went to sleep for the remainder of his administration. Taylor was sworn in the following day.

The only ambidextrous president

Virtually all biographers of James Garfield describe him as left-handed; some concede he was ambidextrous—and a few note his extraordinary ability to write in Greek with one hand and Latin with the other simultaneously.

In point of fact, Garfield was proficient in both languages and had taught them at Ohio's Hiram Eclectic Institute after graduating from college.

Garfield also spoke fluent German and was **the only president to campaign in German,** delivering several speeches in that language during campaign stops in 1880. His favorite campaign stop of all was his own front porch in Mentor, Ohio, and when a delegation of five hundred visiting German-Americans from Cleveland showed up there that fall, the candidate greeted them with a hearty *"Wilkommen alle!"*

The only national presidential convention—Democratic or Republican—to fail to nominate a candidate

When the Democratic party convened in Charleston, South Carolina, on April 23, 1860, Senator Stephen Douglas of Illinois appeared to have a lock on the presidential nomination.

But hundreds of southern delegates who didn't care for the front-runner's position on slavery mounted a massive stop-Douglas movement. Tempers in the overheated convention hall ran high, and it wasn't long before fights broke out; at least two delegates drew guns. Finally, some two hundred southerners picked up and left.

Party rules required a two-thirds majority—202 votes—to nominate a candidate. But the walkout left only 250 delegates, and even after 57 ballots, they were still hopelessly deadlocked. On May 3, ten days after they had first convened, the Democrats gave up and adjourned. They still didn't have a candidate.

They tried again the following month, and again the southerners walked out in droves. Many went to a nearby convention hall and nominated the U.S. vice-president, Kentuckian John C. Breckinridge, whose pro-slavery views were more to their liking.

In the end, Douglas was the Democrats' standard bearer. Though the Democratic national nominating committee picked Herschel V. Johnson of Georgia as his running mate, Douglas never succeeded in making peace with the southern wing of the party, which stayed with Breckinridge right through Election Day. The split cost him over 848,000 votes—and gave the election to Lincoln.

The only First Lady not married to the president

James Buchanan had been a confirmed bachelor ever since his fiancée took her own life after a lover's quarrel. But when his sister and brother-in-law died, he became guardian of their nine-year-old daughter, Harriet Lane.

He kept her at his side wherever his political career took him—to the American embassies in Great Britain and Russia, and ultimately back to Washington. And when the sixty-five-year-old Buchanan became the nation's fifteenth president in 1857, he installed his niece in the White House as his First Lady.

At twenty-four, Harriet was poised, educated, and beautiful—a gracious and much-admired First Lady who inspired dozens of popular entertainments, such as the song, "Listen to the Mockingbird." Uncle James doted fondly on her, though he never refrained from commenting on her callers or the hours she kept. He even went through her mail, a special source of annoyance to her.

A Pennsylvania Democrat, Buchanan waffled on the slavery issue, antagonizing both the North and the South, and generally having a rotten time of it. By 1860 he was so sick of being president that he refused a second term. On the day his successor, Abraham Lincoln, was to be inaugurated, Buchanan told him, "If you are as happy, my dear sir, on entering this house as I am in leaving it and returning home, you are the happiest man in this country."

With that, he retired to his Lancaster, Pennsylvania, estate, Wheatland, where he died in 1868. Niece Harriet lived till 1903.

The only president targeted for kidnapping

Since 1865, assassins have killed four U.S. presidents and threatened the lives of at least five others—Reagan, Ford, Truman, and both Roosevelts. But only George Washington ever came close to being kidnapped.

It happened in June 1776, during the American Revolution. From a British gunboat in New York Harbor, New York's Colonial governor, William Tryon, directed a plot to sabotage the American war effort. A fierce partisan of King George III, Tryon and his forces intended to blow up strategic bridges and ambush Continental Army soldiers from behind with their own weapons. As the final coup, they would abduct Commander in Chief Washington and hand him over to the British—dead or alive.

It might have worked, but for a waiter in the Sergeant's Arms Tavern who overheard some of the conspirators discussing their plans and tipped off New York

City officials. The next morning, forty of the ringleaders, including New York City mayor David Matthews, were rounded up, and the plot was quashed.

Surprisingly, of all those arrested, only one was tried—Washington's bodyguard, Thomas Hickey. Evidence was presented that he had even gone so far as to poison a dish of peas meant for the general's table. Washington had turned them down, the story went, and they were instead fed to some chickens, who promptly died.

The court found Hickey guilty of mutiny, sedition, and treachery. On June 28 he was hanged in New York City before twenty thousand people.

The only president to weigh under one hundred pounds

Just five feet four inches tall and weighing ninety-eight pounds, James Madison was the puniest president in U.S. history, the Pee Wee Herman of the Federalists. Washington Irving called him "a withered little apple-john," and historian Thomas Francis Moran said he was "a dried-up, wizened little man." When Madison walked down Pennsylvania Avenue with his close friend Thomas Jefferson—a man of slam-dunk proportions—it looked, wrote Moran, "as if they were on their way to a father-and-son banquet."

Throughout his presidency (1809–1817), Madison's diminutiveness and quiet manner belied a superb intellect and a passion for learning. As a student at Princeton—then called the College of New Jersey—he'd crammed all his junior and senior classes into a single year; when he graduated, he tried to enlist in the Continental Army, only to be rejected on grounds of physical frailness.

A clear thinker and a persuasive writer, he never got

over a morbid fear of speaking in public, no matter how small or friendly the audience. His marriage, at forty-three, to socialite Dolly Payne Todd, seventeen years his junior, did little to loosen him up. Had he been president in the 1980s, the press would no doubt have labeled him a nerd.

During the War of 1812, Madison secured a place in history as **the only president ever fired upon by enemy forces while in office.** In fact, Madison briefly assumed charge of an American artillery emplacement returning British fire not far from the White House. When the action got too intense, he climbed back into his carriage and hurried off.

The only runaway slave elected president

Not all slaves were black. Until 1826, many poor white families in the South sold their adolescent children into a sort of bondage by contract known as indentured servitude. In such an arrangement, the master paid the parents a fee and assumed all responsibility for the care and feeding of the youth; he also taught him a trade. Should an indentured servant attempt to escape before he turned twenty-one, he would be hunted down and punished like any runaway slave.

When he was twelve, Andrew Johnson and his brother William were apprenticed in this way to a Raleigh, North Carolina, tailor named James J. Selby. But a few years later, the boys bolted and fled to Carthage, seventy-five miles to the south. Selby ran an ad in the Raleigh *Gazette* offering a ten dollar reward for the two runaways.

Eventually, young Johnson came home to Raleigh to turn himself in, only to learn that Selby no longer had any use for him. Marked a runaway and blacklisted by other employers, the boy picked up his parents and headed west for Tennessee. Only seventeen, he opened a tailor shop in Greeneville, took a sixteen-year-old bride, and entered local politics. He was elected vice-president in 1864 and a year later became president upon the death of Abraham Lincoln.

Like Johnson, Millard Fillmore, our thirteenth president, was also indentured in his youth. But rather than skip town, he stuck out the ordeal until he could afford to purchase his freedom for thirty dollars.

The only president elected to nonconsecutive terms

Grover Cleveland was first elected to the presidency—by a razor-thin margin over Republican James G. Blaine—in 1884. Four years later, in his bid for reelection, he won nearly one hundred thousand more popular votes than his opponent, Benjamin Harrison. But this time he lost the electoral college vote, and on Inauguration Day 1889, he found himself out of a job.

Cleveland staged a comeback in 1892, narrowly edging Harrison in his bid for reelection. With that victory, he became the only president other than Franklin D. Roosevelt to win a popular plurality more than twice. For more than a century, historians have debated—sometimes rather testily—whether Cleveland is properly considered simply the twenty-second president, or the twenty-second and twenty-fourth presidents.

Cleveland entered office a bachelor in 1885 and married during his first term—**the only president ever to be married in the White House.** (A notorious womanizer, he'd fathered an illegitimate child during his tenure as mayor of Buffalo. He was also rumored to be a wife beater.) The Clevelands' first daughter, Ruth, was born in 1891, during the interval between his two terms. It was after her—and not Babe Ruth—that the Baby Ruth candy bar was named.

The only president to have an asteroid named after him

There are approximately thirty thousand asteroids circling the sun between the orbits of Mars and Jupiter, of which only five thousand or so have been named— some for Greek and Roman deities, others for famous scientists, still others for earthly locations. There are asteroids named for Mark Twain, John D. Rockefeller, Anton Chekhov, and Eva Perón. Still others are named Rhoda, Phyllis, Jo-Ann, and Harriet. There is even one named for Mr. Spock. But only one asteroid to date has been named for a U.S. President—Hooveria, celestial namesake of Herbert Hoover.

It was first sighted by Professor Johann Palisa of the University of Vienna in March 1920, nearly a decade before Hoover entered the White House. At the time, Hoover was helping to feed and rebuild war-ravaged Europe as chairman of the Interallied Food Council and director of relief operations in Hungary, Armenia, the Soviet Union, and Palisa's Austria.

An administrator of great competence and compassion, Hoover was considerably better suited to relief work than he would be to the presidency—and he enjoyed a measure of adulation on the continent normally reserved for saints and soccer stars. The *Literary Digest* credited him with "keeping 15 million European children alive." Said astronomer Palisa in dedicating Hooveria, "It is a pity we have only a middle-magnitude asteroid to give to this great man. He is worthy at least of a planet."

The only president with a multiple arrest record

At least two U.S. presidents had police records, although only one was a repeat offender. Galloping back to the White House late one night after dining with a friend, Franklin Pierce (1853–1857) ran down an elderly woman who was crossing the street, injuring her slightly. Police officer Stanley Edelin saw the whole thing and promptly busted the offender—who told him simply, "I am Mr. Pierce." The president was released, thus ending his career in crime.

By comparison to Pierce, Ulysses S. Grant (1869–1877) was a gangland kingpin. In 1866, while commander of the Army of the Potomac, he was stopped for speeding on horseback on two separate occasions, hauled down to the local precinct, and fined five dollars. But there was no slowing him down, not even after he assumed the presidency. Early in his first term, he was speeding his buggy west on M Street in Washington, when Constable William H. West heroically grabbed the bridle and was dragged fifty feet before the rig came to a stop. A former Union soldier, West was stunned to see he had collared the president and apologized profusely. But Grant wouldn't hear of it. "Officer," he said, "do your duty."

Horse and buggy were impounded, but this time Grant was neither arrested nor fined. He did have to walk home, however.

A few years after leaving the White House, Grant was on a fishing trip in Pennsylvania when he realized the season was over and he was in violation of the law. He turned himself in to the justice of the peace, who dismissed the offense. Grant was outraged at the officer's laxity and insisted on paying a fine.

The only president to write a book about another president

Herbert Hoover's *The Ordeal of Woodrow Wilson*, published in 1958, focused on Wilson's thwarted efforts to achieve world peace through the League of Nations in the aftermath of World War I. Hoover wrote from firsthand experience. Long before his own presidency, he was one of Wilson's most trusted advisers, serving on his American War Council, and later, during the Paris peace conference, as a member of its Committee of Economic Advisers. His personal files from that period contained more than one and a half million items.

Ordeal was published to mixed reviews. The *Chicago Tribune* found it "intensely interesting," and *American Historical Review* called it "a work of rare importance." But the Manchester *Guardian* railed at Hoover's "holier-than-thou Americanism," and *The Canadian Historical Review* called it "incredibly naive."

Hoover, of course, was not the only president turned author, nor the most prolific. That distinction belongs to Theodore Roosevelt, who churned out thirty-seven books.

The only president to own a pet alligator

John Quincy Adams kept a pet alligator in the East Room of the White House. Apart from his affection for the animal, contemporaries report that he took deep pleasure in the spectacle of guests fleeing from the room in terror.

The only president to pose as a fashion model

During his Yale Law School days in the late 1930s, Gerald Ford had a girlfriend named Phyllis Brown who worked as a model and talked him into investing one thousand dollars in a modeling agency. For his money, young Ford got more than a stock certificate—he got the chance to pose with Ms. Brown on the slopes of New England in several skiwear ads.

A handsome and athletic six-footer who had turned down offers to play pro football, Ford was a natural for the job. But his modeling career turned out to be short-lived. So did his relationship with Ms. Brown.

The only sterile president

Although he was the father of his country, George Washington left no heirs to carry forth his name. He may, in fact, have been sterile.

While there is certainly no proof that Washington's reproductive powers were impaired in any way, M.J.V. Smith, a urologist at the Medical College of Virginia, noted in 1974 that Washington suffered from several debilitating diseases, including malaria, smallpox, tuberculosis, and amoebic dysentery, as well as a genetic condition called Klinefelter's syndrome, which results in decreased production of reproductive hormone. The collective impact of all these ills, said Smith, could easily have left Washington sterile.

The only president allegedly poisoned by his First Lady

Nearly seventy years after the fact, the exact circumstances of President Warren G. Harding's death are still fuzzy. While most historians say he probably died of natural causes, few completely rule out the possibility that he was done in by his wife.

What we do know is that Harding embarked on a grueling cross-country Voyage of Understanding in the summer of 1923 to meet the people and communicate his policies. Elected in 1920 on a promise to return the country to "normalcy" after World War I, Harding had proven himself a genial but inept chief executive who delegated far too much responsibility to corrupt associates. Two aides already mired in crime—the director of the Veterans Bureau and the chief secretary to the attorney general—had committed suicide that spring. The far more serious Teapot Dome Scandal, which involved the illegal sale of oil leases by several Harding cabinet officers, was about to break. And Harding lived in constant fear that his wife—and the public—would catch on to his extramarital affairs. One tryst with Nan Britton had made him the father of an illegitimate child.

So it was in a state of extreme anxiety and depression that the president left on his journey. In Kansas City he emerged visibly shaken from a surprise visit from Emma Fall, wife of his corrupt secretary of the interior. In Alaska he received a coded message that left him ashen-faced and prompted him to comment on the disloyalty of his associates. When his ship collided with an escort boat in Puget Sound, he remained inside his cabin and muttered, "I hope the boat sinks."

While speaking in Seattle on July 27, Harding appeared disoriented and collapsed later that evening. Surgeon General Charles Sawyer offered that the president was suffering ptomaine poisoning from having eaten tainted crabmeat. Harding was rushed back to San Francisco for treatment. There, his doctors rediagnosed the problem as either pneumonia or heart disease.

He stayed in bed in a suite in the Palace Hotel and appeared to grow stronger. His fever was down, and his pulse was close to normal. On the evening of August 2, he lay propped against his pillows while his wife, Flossie, read to him. When she left the room momentarily, his nurse, Ruth Powderly, came in. She saw him twitch and shiver, and then slump over dead.

The official diagnosis was thrombosis of the brain or heart. But questions remained: Why was Harding's body embalmed even before it left the hotel—and why did Mrs. Harding refuse to allow an autopsy or the casting of a death mask? As for the surgeon general's talk of tainted crabmeat, it turned out the president had never eaten crabmeat on the trip, tainted or otherwise. Rumors circulated that the president had died by his own hand or, worse, his wife's.

Sawyer himself suffered a fatal stroke the following year during a visit from Harding's widow. Could she have poisoned him to keep things quiet? In a 1930 book entitled *The Strange Death of President Harding*, author Gaston Means argued that Mrs. Harding had indeed murdered her husband—either in retribution for his infidelities, or to spare him the humiliation of impeachment.

"My love for Warren has turned to hate," she allegedly told Means, a convicted swindler who claimed to have worked for Mrs. Harding as a private detective. "The President deserves to die. . . . He is not fit to live and he knows it." After his death, she supposedly said, "Warren Harding died in honor. . . . Had he lived 24 hours later, he might have been impeached. . . . I have no regrets. I have fulfilled my destiny." Mrs. Harding, who died six years before Means's book was published, was not around to refute his charges—or to offer a contrasting explanation of her husband's death.

STATESMEN

The only senator ever eaten by his constituents

Victor Biaka-Boda, a distinguished lawyer and former witch doctor who represented the Ivory Coast in the French Senate, returned home just after New Year's Day, 1950, to campaign for reelection. Described by colleagues as "a small, thin, worried-looking man," he set out on a tour of his district and was never heard from again.

On January 28, Biaka-Boda's belongings and a pile of bones were found near the village of Bouaflé. The leftovers were shipped to police labs in Paris for analysis; meanwhile Ivory Coast police questioned tribesmen near Bouaflé, who played dumb. Everyone knew that Biaka-Boda had ended his days in a tureen, but until the facts were in, a successor could not be named and his constituents would have to forgo representation. As *The New York Times* delicately put it, "You cannot have your senator and eat him too."

It took the French overseas ministry another two years before they officially acknowledged that Biaka-Boda had been eaten. Only then could the vacancy be filled.

The only modern head of state to sleep fully clothed

Georges Clemenceau is among France's most revered national heroes. As a journalist in the late 1800s, he spoke out courageously on behalf of Alfred Dreyfus. As premier of France from 1906–1909 and again from 1917–1920, he strengthened ties with Britain and roused his torpid countrymen to victory in World War I.

Nicknamed the Tiger, the fiery Clemenceau often settled political differences through dueling and, during the war, would tour the front under heavy enemy fire. He never conquered his fear of flying, though, and before one flight he urged the pilot to "fly very carefully, very low, and very slow."

Clemenceau's strangest idiosyncrasy was his compulsion for sleeping fully dressed—coat, trousers, vest, and gloves. (His only concessions to normality were to change into an unstarched shirt and to wear slippers rather than shoes.) He slept this way most of his life, and it was only in his dying days, when he was too out of it to protest, that his doctors were able to get him out of his morning coat and into a nightshirt.

The only deceased world leader whose body is a major tourist attraction

When Vladimir Ilyich Ulyanov Lenin died in 1924, the Soviet government agreed that conventional embalming and interment simply wouldn't do. Instead, his almost sacred remains were embalmed according to a—dare we say—revolutionary new method, housed in a transparent tomb, and put on public display in a temporary wooden mausoleum on Moscow's Red Square. (Lenin's brain, however, was not so lovingly preserved. Instead, it was removed whole from his head and julienned into some thirty-one thousand specimens for analysis by Soviet scientists.)

A permanent stone structure was installed in 1930, and it remains the single most popular tourist mecca in the Soviet Union. Lines form early outside the imposing entrance and often stretch for hundreds of yards; the tomb itself is twenty-three steps down in a dimly lit air-conditioned vault. But the wait is worth it: Lenin's body, dead these seven decades, is visible in its casket behind a glass partition. He looks wonderful.

Despite the wholesale trashing of Lenin statues throughout the Soviet Union following the aborted coup of 1991, Lenin's tomb remains intact and open to the public as of this writing. Among those who spoke out against removing Lenin's body was the Soviet minister of culture, Nikolai Gubenko. "The Lenin Mausoleum was a reflection of the historical moment when most of the people loved this man infinitely," he said.

Meanwhile, a quarterly supplement of *Forbes* magazine reported—in jest—that the cash-hungry Soviets had put Lenin's corpse on the auction block, with bids to start at fifteen million dollars. Though *Forbes* editors claimed the article's jocular intent was evident, ABC News took it for fact and reported it that way.

"We were had," said a network official. NBC, however, refused to run a similar story about the spurious sale of Lenin photographs.

"I have no interest in that," said an *NBC Nightly News* producer. "When he comes back to life, give me a call."

The only time Michael Dukakis was mistaken for a heavyweight

From a correction in the Fitchburg-Leominster (Massachusetts) *Sentinel and Enterprise:* "Due to a typing error, Gov. Dukakis was incorrectly identified in the third paragraph as Mike Tyson."

The only British prime minister born in a ladies' cloakroom

Despite the fact that she was nine months pregnant, Jennie Churchill attended a fancy-dress ball at Blenheim Palace, Oxfordshire, on the evening of November 29, 1874, and refused to sit out a single dance. She went into labor on the dance floor while doing a pirouette.

Between contractions Mrs. Churchill stumbled off

the dance floor, followed by servants and her grand-niece, and headed for her bedroom, in a distant corner of the huge palace. She fainted before she got very far.

She was carried into the ladies' cloakroom. "Sprawling, she lay on velvet capes and feather boas, which were deftly drawn from beneath her when the ball ended and the merry guests departed," writes William Manchester in *The Last Lion*. Though it was a long labor, Jennie refused chloroform and delivered her baby—she called him Winston—at 1:30 on the morning of November 30.

Most newspapers of the day reported the birth as premature. It wasn't. The editors were only trying to protect the reputation of Jennie and Sir Randolph Churchill, who had conceived Sir Winston a full nine months earlier—before they were married.

The only U.S. legislator to serve forty years without missing a vote

A month after he settled into office as U.S. congressman from Florida in 1949, Charles E. Bennett got pneumonia and took to his bed. He was absent from a half dozen or so floor votes, the last on June 4, 1951. He returned to Washington soon thereafter and, as of June 1991, hadn't missed a single vote, casting his yeas and nays in 17,400 consecutive legislative actions.

Bennett, who has the tenth-longest term of service of any U.S. congressman ever, walks with a cane, the result of a bout with polio contracted when he served in the army during World War II. But he has driven through blizzards, slipped away early from funerals, and defied doctors to show up in time to cast a vote. Once, after breaking his leg, he left the hospital before the cast had completely set and propelled himself onto the House floor in a wheelchair.

"I'm not a brilliant person," the octogenarian Democrat told *The New York Times*. "But I feel that being there and making the vote is my duty and responsibility. This 40-year thing for me is kind of a big victory."

The only U.S. Cabinet member to work as a TV weatherman

When Henry Kissinger confessed a long-suppressed desire to be a television weather forecaster, Mark McEwen stepped aside from his duties as regular weatherman on *CBS This Morning* and allowed the onetime secretary of state and national security adviser to take over.

Kissinger appeared three times on the early morning show in 1991, and considering his lack of training in telling isobars from isotherms, the kid wasn't bad. He rattled off the temperature readings for such global hot spots as Lebanon (New Hampshire), Palestine (Arkansas), Cairo (Illinois), and Moscow (Idaho), and predicted "eighty-degree temperatures near the Mediterranean Sea."

But Henry the K could never seem to put the pointer where it was supposed to go, and by the time he got to Amman, Jerusalem, and Beirut, he gave up altogether.

"I'm not going to point anymore," he told viewers with diplomatic aplomb. "If you can't figure it out, it's your problem."

The only Republican to run for vice-president after he was dead

Shortly after he took office as vice-president under William Howard Taft in 1908, James Schoolcraft Sherman was diagnosed as having Bright's disease. He still kept up a full vice-presidential schedule (whatever *that* means), but after a particularly exhausting thirty-minute campaign speech on August 31, 1912, he took ill and returned home to Utica, New York, to recover. He died there of uremic poisoning on October 30, six days before Election Day.

Deceased or no, Sherman remained on the ballot and drew 3,484,980 votes—not enough to win, but sufficient to show that in a free country, even a flat EKG is no impediment to public office.

The only person elected to fill the unexpired terms of three different U.S. senators

A liberal Kentucky Republican, John Sherman Cooper (1901–1991) was first elected to the Senate in 1946 to complete the term of Albert "Happy" Chandler, who quit to become commissioner of baseball. Although Cooper lost his bid for reelection two years later, he was elected to fill out the unexpired term of Virgil Chapman in 1952.

In 1954 the voters rejected Cooper in favor of former vice-president Alben W. Barkley. But Barkley died in 1956, and Cooper was elected to fill out his term. He remained in office until he retired in 1973.

The only elected vice-president never to serve

William Rufus King was Franklin Pierce's running mate in 1852. Following the election, he returned home to Dallas County, Alabama, intending to show up in Washington in time to be inaugurated the following March.

He never got the chance. A sickly man, King contracted tuberculosis and sailed to Cuba, where he hoped the sunshine would do him good. Though he was unable to stand unaided, he was sworn in as vice-president by the U.S. consul in Havana on Inauguration Day, 1853. A few weeks later he returned home to Alabama, where he died on April 18, 1853.

The only third-world leader to hold the Pentagon hostage for a planeful of Cokes

Do planes go better with Coke? Evidently so, if Zairian president Mobutu Sese Seko is any authority. After ordering a C-130 military-transport plane from the United States in 1977, he notified the U.S. Defense Department that the deal was off unless the aircraft arrived filled with Coca-Cola.

A Pentagon official told reporters that he didn't "have a clue" as to why strongman Mobutu wanted the Coke, which would have added another sixty thousand dollars to the cost of the plane. *The New York Times* reported that it was "dubious" that the Cokes-for-cash deal would go through.

The only vice-president indicted for murder

Aaron Burr and Alexander Hamilton didn't start out as enemies. They fought together in the American Revolution and later, as successful New York attorneys, they collaborated on cases.

But over the years, as their political views clashed, their differences grew personal and deeply rancorous. When Burr tied Thomas Jefferson in electoral votes for the 1800 presidential election, Hamilton vindictively cast the swing vote in Jefferson's favor; Burr had to settle for vice-president. Four years later, when Burr announced he was prepared to run for governor of New York, Hamilton sabotaged him again, labeling him "a dangerous man"—and worse—in the pages of the Albany *Register*.

With that last outrage, Burr challenged Hamilton to a pistol duel. The two faced each other at dawn in Weehawken, New Jersey, on July 11, 1804. The signal was given, and the vice-president's bullet tore through Hamilton's liver, wounding him mortally. Hamilton's bullet lodged in a tree branch.

Some witnesses said Hamilton never intended to fire—that his gun discharged only when he was shot, and that the vice-president was therefore guilty of murder. The states of New Jersey and New York thought so too, and indicted him the following week.

But Burr vanished from sight, returning later in the year to resume his vice-presidential duties, though he was still under indictment. The public clamored for Burr's neck, and poems like this were common: "Oh Burr, oh Burr, what hast thou done,/Thou hast shooted dead great Hamilton!/You hid among a bunch of thistle/ And shooted him dead with a great hoss pistol!"

While the charges were later dropped, Jefferson dumped him from the ticket in his campaign for reelection, and Burr left Washington for good, his political career and good name destroyed.

The only over-the-counter foot deodorant elected to public office

Reuters reported in the early 1970s that "a controversy is raging because a foot powder named Pulvapies was elected mayor of a town of 4,100."

The coastal village of Picoaza, Ecuador (pop. 4,100), was in the midst of a listless election campaign in the early 1970s when a local foot-deodorant manufacturer came out with the advertising slogan, "Vote for any candidate, but if you want well-being and hygiene, vote for Pulvapies." Then, the day before the election, a leaflet reading, "For Mayor: The Honorable Pulvapies," was widely distributed.

In one of the great embarrassments of modern democracy, the voters of Picoaza elected the foot powder by a clear majority.

Pulvapies also ran well in outlying districts.

The only signer of the Declaration of Independence to recant

Richard Stockton was a wealthy New Jersey lawyer who had visited England in the 1760s, met with King George III, and been favorably impressed. Returning to the Colonies, he advocated conciliation with the king rather than revolution but later reversed his stand and became an ardent champion of independence. He was appointed to the Continental Congress, and in July 1776 he signed the Declaration of Independence.

That November, while inspecting Colonial troops, Stockton was captured by the British and thrown in provost jail in New York City. Interrogated constantly and ill-treated, he finally broke under the pressure and signed a statement recanting his support of independence.

At the urging of the Continental Congress, the British released Stockton. He returned to Princeton, New Jersey, a beaten man, regarded as a traitor by his former friends. His health and spirit destroyed, Stockton died four years later of cancer at the age of 51.

The only U.S. senator to represent three different states

Serving in the U.S. Senate is different from, say, playing minor league baseball or working as a circus clown. Rather than bouncing from venue to venue, you're generally expected to spend your entire career in the same place. It's the rare senator that gets to represent more than one state in his lifetime.

James Shields represented three.

After returning home from combat in the Mexican War, Shields was elected U.S. senator from Illinois in 1849. When he lost his reelection bid six years later, he packed up and moved west, getting himself elected to the Senate from Minnesota when statehood was granted in 1858. His term was up the following year, and he again found himself unemployed.

Shields took a rest from politics and, during the Civil War, served with the Union Army as a brigadier general. In 1866 he took up politics again and settled in Missouri, where he was appointed to serve the last two months of an unexpired term in the Senate in 1879. He died in Iowa later that year during a stop on a lecture tour.

Besides being America's only tristate U.S. senator, Shields had one other claim to fame: He once challenged Abraham Lincoln to a duel.

In the 1820s, as Illinois state auditor, Shields had been the subject of several anonymous diatribes in the Springfield *Journal* ultimately traced to Lincoln's outspoken fiancée, Mary Todd. But as the mores of the day required, Shields directed his challenge at Lincoln. The duel was arranged, only to be canceled at the last minute. The would-be combatants later became fast friends.

The only acknowledged transvestite to serve as an American governor

Edward Hyde, Lord Cornbury, was the Colonial governor of New York and New Jersey from 1702–1708. The ne'er-do-well cousin of England's Queen Anne, he was offered the position by her as an alternative to being thrown in debtor's prison.

Hyde frequently appeared in public elegantly gowned in women's clothes and went so far as to pose for his official portrait in a low-cut evening dress and a lacy kerchief. He raised eyebrows, not to mention doubts about his sanity, by imposing a tax on men for wearing wigs and by charging admission to his private dinners. Once, addressing the Colonial assembly, he rhapsodized at length on the beauty of his wife's ears—he likened them to conch shells—and invited the lawmakers to step up to the rostrum to fondle them.

Hyde's administration was marked by venality, bribe taking, and the worst sort of administrative chaos. His enemies reviled him to Queen Anne as a "peculiar, detestable maggot," pressuring her into removing him from office in 1708 after he'd been caught embezzling. After a brief stint in debtor's prison, he returned to England, where he lived out his remaining years comfortably as the Earl of Clarendon. The debts he had run up back in the Colonies remained unpaid.

The only U.S. citizen to rule a Latin American country

William Walker never could make up his mind what he wanted to be when he grew up. Graduated summa cum laude from the University of Nashville at age fourteen, he tried his hand at medicine, law, newspaper reporting, and even mesmerism before he went west with the gold rush in 1850. That didn't work out either.

At that point young Walker's career goals came into focus: He wanted to rule a country. Rounding up an army of besotted irregulars from the bars of San Francisco, he launched an armed invasion of Baja California in 1853 and declared himself president. "No way, José," said the Mexican authorities as they saw him to the border with orders never to return.

But this crazed adventurer showed up in Nicaragua in 1856, ready again to make his mark on history. In those pre-Canal days, American companies regularly shipped passengers and freight from coast to coast across Nicaragua; the Accessory Transit Company, owned by zillionaire Cornelius Vanderbilt, had a monopoly on the business. With a ragtag army of one hundred men and Vanderbilt's backing, Walker captured the Nicaraguan capital of Granada, deposed the president, and made himself dictator. But he hung on to his U.S. citizenship.

The gringo *jefe* was not loved by the people. He insulted their culture. He brought back slavery. He declared English the official language. He handed vast tracts of Nicaraguan land to his American friends. Weighing barely 120 pounds, he hurled threats and orders in a squeaky voice—and generally got his way. But he went too far when he seized the Accessory Transit Company.

Vanderbilt was not amused. With support from British and American gunships, the financier sent an army across Costa Rica and into Nicaragua that surrounded Granada and, on May 1, 1857, crushed Walker. He was deported to New Orleans, where he was accorded a hero's welcome and became a familiar in half the bars in the French Quarter.

But Walker still considered himself president of Nicaragua in absentia and attempted three more invasions of Central America. None worked, and on his last sortie, he was captured in Honduras and shot by a firing squad there in 1860 while crowds cheered. Even today, parents in Nicaragua get their kids to behave by telling them that if they don't, they'll be eaten by William Walker.

KINGS AND QUEENS (AND A JOKER)

The only English king who could not speak English

When Queen Anne of England died in 1714, George I succeeded to the throne. The great-grandson of King James I, he was fifty-four when he arrived in London from his native Germany to establish the British royal house of Hanover. He reigned for thirteen years, never attempting to improve his English, which was barely at the level of the Katzenjammer Kids.

Instead, the German-speaking monarch made do with his serviceable French, and most official documents requiring his attention were translated into that language. Those that weren't he signed anyway.

George's steadfast German attitudes and mannerisms as well as his refusal to master the language of the country he governed did not endear him to his subjects. "Our customs and laws were all mysteries to him, which he neither tried to understand, nor was capable of understanding," wrote Lady Mary Wortley Montagu. In *The Age of Revolution*, Sir Winston Churchill described the king as "an obstinate and humdrum German martinet with dull brains and coarse tastes."

However, as a Protestant, George enjoyed the grudging support of his subjects, who were thankful that the throne wasn't occupied by a Roman Catholic. An honest if plodding man, he was notorious for letting his ministers run things and usually sat out important cabinet meetings. Chances are, he wouldn't have known what was going on anyway.

The only part of his body that King Louis XIV washed regularly

Chroniclers of his day report that Louis XIV, who reigned over France from 1643–1715, had a morbid fear of water. Small wonder that his elaborate morning rituals, assisted by an army of servants and known as the grand lever, included only the most perfunctory ablutions. In fact, he rarely applied water to any part of his body other than the tip of his nose.

In his aversion to washing, the Sun King was not out of fashion. In his biography of Louis XIV, Prince Michael of Greece writes that "people were terribly dirty at Versailles. Glittering courtiers and women dripping with jewels spat, vomited, urinated, defecated in the corridors and staircases; it was the fashion of the time." Bathing was infrequent; body odor was pervasive. Strangely, the one part of the anatomy that courtiers—and presumably kings—were expected to keep clean was the nose, and it was considered unspeakably bad form to dip a dirty nose into a snuffbox.

The only six-fingered English queen

Understandably self-conscious about the fact that she had six fingers on her left hand, Anne Boleyn, the second wife of King Henry VIII, habitually wore gloves in public. (She was also rumored to have three breasts.) Henry's dalliance with Anne began while he was still married to Catherine of Aragon, who enjoyed humiliating Anne by making her shed her gloves during card games with the king.

In 1533, bored with Catherine and frustrated by her failure to give him a male heir, Henry divorced her and married Anne. By 1536 Anne had given birth to only one child—the future Elizabeth I. His patience worn thin, Henry falsely accused the queen of infidelity and had her beheaded, along with five alleged lovers. One was her brother.

Polydactylism—the presence of extra fingers or toes—is not a turnoff in *all* cultures. To the ancient Chaldeans, a surplus finger or two on the hand of a royal heir was considered a good omen. In the last century, virtually every member of the Foldi family, who belonged to the Hyabite tribe in the Middle East, was endowed with twenty-four digits, thanks to years of inbreeding. Children born with only twenty digits were assumed to be the issue of adultery and slaughtered.

The only evidence that Richard III was really hunchbacked

To hear Shakespeare and other chroniclers tell it, Richard III was as hunchbacked as Quasimodo. But unlike the noblehearted bell ringer, Richard's deformity reflected his true nature. He was evil incarnate—a power-mad usurper and child killer who was born with a full set of teeth and claws and a taste for live frogs. Shakespeare called him "this poisonous bunch-backed toad."

Not true, say the members of the Richard III Society, founded in 1924 to restore the maligned king's reputation. (An American branch was established in 1969.)

They share a unanimous belief that Richard has been given a bum rap by history, and that he really was a docent, if misunderstood, chap.

According to Laura Blanchard, a member of the New Jersey chapter of the society, the reports of Richard's deformities are greatly exaggerated. There is only one portrait showing the monarch with anything remotely resembling a hump, she says. X rays revealed that the hump had been painted on years after the completion of the original painting. "Hump?" she says. "What hump?"

The only king to use an electric chair as a throne

Menelik II (1844–1913) was the George Washington of modern Ethiopia. Crowned in 1889, he expanded the country's boundaries, fought off the Italians at the Battle of Adowa in 1896, and established Ethiopia as a secure and independent state. Most important, he engineered a far-reaching program of modernization that took his empire from the Middle Ages to the twentieth century in less than a decade.

Penal reform was a big item on Menelik's agenda, and following the introduction of the electric chair at New York's Auburn State Prison in 1890, he eagerly ordered three of the devices for use in Ethiopia. But the move proved an embarrassment to the ruler: The electric chairs wouldn't electrocute because the country lacked electricity.

Unwilling to mothball his new purchase, Menelik had one of the chairs installed for use as his throne.

Menelik is also **the only monarch, ancient or modern, known to have died from eating a Bible.** When his health declined late in life, the emperor found that snacking on a few pages torn from the Old Testament would perk him

up. In December 1913, incapacitated from a stroke, he attempted to eat the entire Book of Kings, a page at a time. While the sentiments contained therein were no doubt uplifting, the toxic dyes in the color illustrations disagreed with him. He died in midmeal.

The only known instance of a monarch putting on the dog

Henri III of France (1551–1589) had a full plate as king, what with plotting the St. Bartholomew's Day Massacre, placating the Protestants, and taking part in the War of the Three Henrys. But he always made time for his dogs.

In point of fact, Henri was unarguably the most dog-obsessed head of state who ever lived. Not even Queen Victoria, who owned eighty-three dogs and knew every one by name, came close. Henri had at least two thousand, allowing them free run of the palace and its gardens, and was not above poaching pooches that caught his eye. There were never fewer than one hundred dogs within barking distance.

Henri loved walking with his pups but often had trouble deciding which one to take. To solve that problem, one of his courtiers devised a unique carrier that could accommodate up to ten medium-sized animals or twenty lapdogs and be worn around the neck. The king often wore it on his strolls around the palace, though there is no evidence that he was thus attired when he was assassinated by a crazed monk in 1589.

The only child of Queen Anne to survive infancy

Of the seventeen children to whom Queen Anne gave birth, not one survived her, and sixteen died before they could dress themselves. All are buried, along with their mother and father, Prince George of Denmark, and a number of ancestors, in a single tomb in London's Westminster Abbey.

The last of the Stuart monarchs, Anne succeeded to the throne in 1702 when her sister and brother-in-law, William and Mary, died without any heirs. She married Prince George in 1683. (A dull but well-meaning man, George once prompted Charles II to say, "I have tried him drunk and tried him sober, but there is nothing in him either way.) Their longest-living child, William, duke of Gloucester, died in 1700. He was eleven.

The only bachelor king of England

Edward VIII was a bachelor when he abdicated on December 10, 1936, to marry an American socialite, Mrs. Wallis Simpson—but he'd never been crowned. (Indeed, he was **the only uncrowned English monarch** and **the only one to abdicate voluntarily.**)

And yes, both Edward V and VI never married either, but come on—they were only thirteen and sixteen, respectively, when they died. The fact is, the only English king to reach manhood, be crowned, rule, and die without ever taking a wife was William II (1056–1100), last surviving son of William the Conqueror.

Known as William Rufus because of his ruddy complexion, William was a particularly brutal leader who easily put down uprisings in Scotland and Wales, quelled a rebellion of his barons, and generally took no backtalk from his subjects—or, presumably, his women. He no doubt would have made a lousy catch.

The only monarch literally frightened to death by an eclipse

Louis I (also known as Louis the Pious, and father of Charles the Bald) became Holy Roman Emperor upon the death of his father, Charlemagne, in 814. Most historians adjudge him a good man and a strong leader who banished his father's mistresses, reformed the Church, and did his best to restrain his four power-mad sons. At one point they ousted him from power and threw him in prison for a year.

According to the *Cambridge Medieval History*, Louis took ill and died on an island in the Rhine—most likely of tuberculosis—on May 5, 840, at the age of 62. But a total eclipse of the sun is known to have occurred on that date, and in some accounts the weakened king is said to have lost it completely when the midday skies darkened unaccountably. Frightened beyond words, he went mad and died.

The only modern monarch to die from the bite of a monkey

Alexander became king of Greece at the age of twenty-four in 1917 when his father, King Constantine, was forced by the Allies to abdicate to permit Greece's entry into World War I. Alas, he ruled only for three years. At his summer residence, Tatoi Palace, in October 1920, the king was bitten on his royal nose while attempting to break up a fight between his pet dog and monkey. He died of blood poisoning three weeks later.

Rumors that the monkey had been secretly injected with rabies toxin by the king's enemies were never substantiated.

The only person allowed to wear green in China during the Ming dynasty

Because of its association with emerald and jade, green was deemed a royal color by the Ming emperors (1368–1644), and no one but the reigning emperor was permitted to wear it, on pain of death.

The only English king to be beheaded

Well-mannered and devoted to his family, Charles I was nonetheless an insufferable elitist who believed in the divine right of kings and had only contempt for the House of Commons.

Crowned in 1625, he was doomed from the start. He waged an illegal war against Spain and France, ran up the national debt, jailed his enemies without trial, and totally antagonized parliament. When civil war broke out, Charles fled to Scotland.

The fugitive king was taken prisoner in 1648 and accused of "high treason and other high crimes against the realm of England." He refused to testify on his own behalf, archly insisting that "a king cannot be tried by any superior jurisdiction on earth."

Have it your way, king, the tribunal responded. Charles was tried, convicted and, before a large crowd in London on the morning of January 30, 1649, relieved of his head.

A postscript: When Charles II was restored to the throne in 1660, plans were made to transfer his father's body from Windsor Castle to a more fitting crypt in Westminster Abbey. But somewhere between Windsor and London, the royal remains vanished.

In 1813 workmen at Windsor inadvertently poked a hole in the burial vault known to contain Henry VIII's coffin and also found one marked "Charles I." The lid was pried open, revealing a body and severed head, badly decomposed, but with enough hair and facial tissue to leave no doubt it was Charles. Probing deeper, the royal surgeon, Sir Henry Halford, determined that the head had been lopped off with a sharp blow that sliced through the fourth cervical vertebra.

The remains were placed back in the coffin, which was resealed in the vault. However, Sir Henry kept the vertebra, using it for years as a saltshaker and dinner-table tchotchke. Eventually, his heirs, who found the relic distasteful, gave it to the Prince of Wales, who arranged for it to be returned to its rightful place in the king's spinal column.

The only woman to be queen of both England and France

Eleanor was the daughter of William, duke of Aquitaine and count of Poitiers, a French nobleman whose territorial holdings were said to have been greater than those of the king of France himself. When William died in 1137, fifteen-year-old Eleanor inherited his lands and promptly married the king's son, who succeeded to the throne as Louis VII the very next month. She thus became queen.

Accompanying Louis on the Second Crusade, Eleanor commanded a corps of three hundred women who pulled their weight in the battle against the Saracens and also nursed the wounded. She also spent more time with her uncle, Raymond of Antioch, than the jealous king would have liked, and the couple drifted apart. They annulled their marriage soon after returning to France in 1152.

According to one account, Eleanor made cruel fun of Louis for having come home from the Crusades without his beard and demanded that he grow it back, for she found him ugly without it. When he refused, she dumped him and immediately took up with Henry of Normandy. Upon his coronation as King Henry II of England two years later, Eleanor became queen for the second time. She held on to the job until her death, fifty years later.

The only deposed monarch to collect unemployment insurance

While Siam's King Prajadhipok was vacationing in England in 1935, his enemies took the opportunity to depose him and install his eleven-year-old nephew in his place. Prajadhipok had ruled his kingdom for nine years, an absolute monarch in the old style, with power of life and death over every one of his subjects. He didn't simply rule Siam. He owned it.

Stripped of his throne, Prajadhipok remained in England, retiring with his wife to a baronial estate in Surrey. He had no pension, but never mind: Years before he had cannily taken out unemployment insurance with two European underwriters. He now drew regular monthly checks sufficient to allow him to live the luxurious life of an English country squire.

Educated in Europe, partial to beautiful women and fast horses (and vice versa), Prajadhipok had indulged his pleasures to the tune of three million dollars a year during his reign. In retirement his monthly insurance payments enabled him to live no less lavishly—and with far fewer anxieties—as he told a visiting journalist. He died in England in 1941 at the age of forty-seven.

The only English monarch never to set foot in England

As soon as any national leader dawdles abroad a day too long, his enemies cry absenteeism. But Queen Berengaria reigned over England for eight years without once showing her face on English soil.

She ascended to the throne as the wife of King Richard the Lion Hearted, who agreed to the match mostly to keep his mother happy. As mom saw it, the marriage of her son to the daughter of King Sancho VI of Navarre would give England a valuable political alliance as well as keep Richard's sexual appetites in check.

Berengaria wasn't exactly a knockout, and one chronicler tactfully described her as "more accomplished than beautiful." But Richard could have done worse. The chronicler Ambrose adjudged her "a gentle lady, virtuous and fair, neither false nor double-tongued."

But after their wedding—and Berengaria's coronation—on Cyprus in 1191, the couple didn't see much of each other. Richard was abroad most of the time with the Third Crusade; Berengaria spent most of her life in Italy and France. She died in Le Mans in 1230, outliving her husband by thirty-one years.

Another royal spouse—Sophia Dorothea, wife of King George I—is occasionally referred to as "the English Queen who never lived in England." But she never reigned over England, since she was divorced by George in 1694, long before he left Germany to assume the English throne. She spent the last thirty-two years of her life in a German dungeon.

The only modern European monarch deposed and reinstated within a single day

According to Belgium's Constitution, every bill passed by Parliament must be signed by the king before it can become law. But no king in modern times had ever withheld his imprimatur from any law until 1990, when Baudouin II refused to approve legislation legalizing abortion. As a Roman Catholic, he said, he could not in good conscience sign the bill.

Under a constitutional provision that it can enact legislation on its own if the king is deemed unable to rule, the Belgian parliament removed Baudouin and ratified the law itself. The two-chamber body convened in joint session and voted to restore the king to power—all in the space of a day.

The only English monarch born in a private house with a street address

When the duchess of York became pregnant in 1925, she assumed she would be welcome to spend her *accouchement* in Buckingham Palace, the home of her in-laws, the king and queen. But the best George V could offer was a rustic lodge, and she was in no mood for roughing it. The duchess and her duke were about to rent accommodations in London's Grosvenor Square, when her parents, the earl and countess of Strathmore, invited the couple to stay with them at their Mayfair townhouse at 17 Bruton Street. And that's where the baby, the future Queen Elizabeth II, was born, on April 21, 1926.

Don't go looking for the house on your next visit to England: It was destroyed in 1939 during the blitzkrieg and later replaced with a bank. A plaque, however, marks the spot.

The only European monarch consumed at a dinner

Dr. Francis Trevelyan Buckland, nineteenth-century surgeon, zoologist, and gourmand, never met a food he didn't like—almost. As an Oxford undergraduate he served mouse on toast points to his classmates; later, he helped found the Society for the Acclimatization of Animals, dedicated to stimulating Britons' appetites for such fare as kangaroo and bison. At the annual society dinners he hosted, Buckland served such dishes as trepang sea slug, boiled elephant trunk, and rhinoceros pie.

Not everyone who supped at Buckland's table shared his tastes. A dish of whole roast ostrich grossed out the well-known zoologist Sir Richard Owen, although his wife found it tasty and "very much like coarse turkey." Even Buckland himself confessed an aversion to stewed moles, bluebottles, cockroaches, and broiled porpoise head, which he said tasted like the wick of an oil lamp.

At one memorable dinner, hosted at his London townhouse, Buckland is said to have served the heart of King Louis XIV of France, stolen from his tomb during the French Revolution. It's possible: Among Buckland's collection of relics was a bone from Ben Jonson's foot and a lock of Henry V's hair. "I have eaten many strange things in my lifetime," he confided to his guests. "But never before have I eaten the heart of a King."

The only R-rated comic to work the Kremlin

Shecky Green, move over.

Mikhail Gorbachev's 1990 debut as a stand-up comedian met with rave—if not convincingly sincere—reviews. According to the Associated Press, the Soviet president was chatting with journalists and parliamentarians in the lobby of the Kremlin when he mentioned a joke he had heard about the sagging Russian economy.

"I can't really tell it with ladies present," he said. Then, at the urging of several women in the crowd, he relented.

The story was about François Mitterrand, George Bush, and himself. "They say that Mitterrand has one hundred lovers," said Gorbachev. "One has AIDS, but he doesn't know which one. Bush has one hundred bodyguards. One is a terrorist, but he doesn't know which one." And Gorbachev?

"Gorbachev has one hundred economic advisers. One is smart, but he doesn't know which one."

According to the AP, the leader's joke was "warmly received" by his listeners.

You had to be there.

RELIGION

The only appearance of the expression *Ha, Ha!* in the Bible

As any Bible student will tell you, the Good Book is seriously deficient in chuckles. Ironically, the one and only place where anyone lightens up at all is in Mark 15:29, in his description of Calvary in the hours following the Crucifixion. As the New American Bible translates it: "People going by kept insulting, tossing their heads and saying, 'Ha, ha!' So you were going to destroy the temple and rebuild it in three days! Save yourself now by coming down from that cross!"

The only appearance of Jesus' image in a tortilla

"I was rolling my husband's burrito, and on the last roll I noticed something that looked like a face," Mrs. Eduardo Rubio, of Lake Arthur, New Mexico, told a *Los Angeles Times* reporter in 1979. Looking closer, she beheld the unmistakable image of Jesus Christ, seared into her husband's dinner by the skillet.

The floury icon, dubbed "Jesus in a Tortilla" by Mrs. Rubio, was enshrined in its own room in the Rubios' home, surrounded by flowers and votive candles, and drew flocks of worshipers and curiosity seekers from as far as New York. A local priest, Rev. Joyce Finnigan, blessed the sacred burrito, though he admitted he was "not too impressed with this kind of miracle." Mrs. Rubio insisted it was a sign that "Christ will return to earth."

The only female saint to grow a full mustache and beard

As a child Saint Wilgefortis was converted to Christianity and took a vow of chastity. Nonetheless, her father, the heathen king of Portugal, married her off to the king of Sicily. Wilgefortis prayed fervently for deliverance from the lascivious king, and miraculously, on her wedding day, she sprouted a full black beard and mustache. Her fiancé lost interest. Her father, in a rage, had her crucified.

In England Saint Wilgefortis is known as Saint Uncumber, and in France she is Liberata, the patron saint of women who wish to be rid of beastly husbands. These days, most hagiographers believe she never existed—that medieval clerics mistook a popular representation of Jesus Christ in a gown for a woman and created the Wilgefortis story to go with it.

Still another female saint—Galla, of sixth-century Rome—was urged by physicians to remarry promptly when she was widowed a year after her wedding day. Wait too long, she was warned, and she would grow a beard.

But Galla had had it with marriage. Born into wealth, she remained single the rest of her life, devoting her days to caring for the sick and needy. And she never grew so much as a whisker.

The only saint canonized for laziness

In the year 258, Saint Lawrence was serving as trea-
surer to Pope Sixtus II when Emperor Valerian declared
open season on Christians. The pope himself was an
early victim, but before he was taken away to his death,
he told Lawrence to be ready to follow him in three
days.

In preparation for his martyrdom, Saint Lawrence began distributing the Church's treasures to the poor and
crippled when the Roman prefect demanded that he
hand the goods over to the emperor. Saint Lawrence
rounded up a band of indigent Romans and told the prefect, "These are the Church's treasures."

It wasn't the answer the prefect was looking for. For
his insolence, Lawrence was fried to death on a griddle.

Most friers instinctively turn away from the fire
when one side of the body gets too hot. But Saint Lawrence lay still, telling his tormentors, "Turn me over
now. That side is quite done." While his disciples saw
only courage and fortitude in his defiance, his foes
mocked him for being too lazy to turn, and the expression "as lazy as Lawrence" found its way into the English language. The griddle found its way into the
Church of San Lorenzo, in Rome, where it can still be
viewed.

(In all fairness to Saint Lawrence, he could move
when he wanted to—at least in legend. According to one
tale, two centuries after he died his tomb was reopened
to receive the earthly remains of Saint Stephen. Saint
Lawrence's skeleton considerately slid over to one side
to make room.)

The only book of the Bible that does not mention God

In the Book of Esther, King Ahasuerus of Persia dumps his wife, Vashti, and weds the title character. What he doesn't know is that Esther is Jewish, and when the king's evil prime minister Haman finds out, he plots to kill all the Jews in the kingdom. Esther and her uncle Mordecai courageously lobby the king to save the Jews, and in the end, Haman is hanged on the very gallows he has erected for Mordecai.

The Book of Esther, only 167 verses long, is the basis of the Jewish festival of Purim. Though most biblical scholars consider it a work of fiction, the action is firmly rooted in the real world: Alone among all the books of the Old and New Testaments, it makes no mention of God, prayer, worship, or faith. The story is driven entirely by human willpower.

As books of the Bible go, the Book of Esther is a relatively recent work, probably written between the fifth and first centuries B.C. Its upbeat celebration of courage and moral justice may be the very reason for its inclusion in the Bible.

The only pope to abdicate

Following the death of Pope Nicholas IV in 1292, it took the College of Cardinals over two years to agree on a successor—Peter of Morone, a seventy-nine-year-old hermit living in a cave in the Apennine Mountains.

A delegation from the Vatican informed Peter of his election. Although crowds of well-wishers thronged the streets upon his entrance into Naples, Peter turned out to be a lousy choice. As Pope Celestine V, he was too old, too inexperienced, and too indecisive to lead effectively.

Five months after he was installed, the doddering pontiff decided to call it quits. In one of history's most candid resignation addresses, he said he was leaving "because of my lowliness, my desire for a more perfect life, my great age and infirmities, my inexperience, and ignorance of the world's affairs." He wanted nothing more than to go back to his cave and hairshirt and his diet of water and cabbage leaves.

But it wasn't that simple. After wandering in the woods and mountains for several months, Celestine was taken prisoner by his successor, Boniface VIII, who was worried that his enemies would use the former pontiff against him. Still under house arrest, Celestine died ten months later.

The only three-person church

On the grounds of an old Benedictine monastery in Covington, Kentucky, is a limestone structure not much bigger than a telephone booth. Billed as the tiniest chapel in the world, it was built by Brother Albert Soltis for his personal religious use in 1878 and can accommodate no more than three people at a time.

Officially called Monte Casino, the churchlet is furnished with three small wooden pews—one for each worshiper—a minuscule altar, a few religious miniatures, and a single leaded window. The belfry, towering eight feet above the ground, is too small for a bell.

The only Protestant pope

Clement XIV wasn't *really* Protestant. But he may as well have been, as far as a lot of his critics were concerned. Indeed, he was known to many as "the Protestant pope."

The origin of this epithet lies in his authorship of a

1773 papal bull abolishing the Jesuit order. Founded 239 years earlier, the Jesuits had become far too powerful, in the eyes of many of their critics, who resented and perhaps envied their charisma, influence, and massive egos. Despite nagging from anti-Jesuit forces, Clement waffled, hoping the order could be reformed—or cut down to size by a ban on novices. Finally, France, Spain, Portugal, Austria, Parma, and Naples pressured Clement to get rid of the Jesuits once and for all—which he did.

Given that the Jesuits had devoted themselves to the defense of the papacy against oppression by Protestant kings, many felt Clement's act amounted to treason—and collusion with the Protestants. The prestige of the papacy plummeted and did not rally again until 1814, when Pope Pius XVII gave the Jesuits a second chance.

The only English pope

There is no rule banning Britishers from the papacy, but somehow only one has ever made it to the Vatican's highest office.

Born in Hertfordshire in 1100, Nicholas Breakspear left England as a young man, living as a beggar and later working at a monastery near Avignon, France. His devotion and hard work attracted the attention of Pope Eugene III who appointed him cardinal-bishop of Alba in 1146. Though he made it clear he didn't much want the job, Breakspear was elected Pope Adrian IV in 1154.

Adrian is best-known for his chronic bickering with Frederick Barbarossa, emperor of Prussia, whom he would have excommunicated had he not died before he could get around to it. According to some accounts, Adrian choked to death on a fly that entered his mouth as he drank from a water fountain.

The only American religious reformer eaten by a tree

After he was banished from Massachusetts Bay Colony because of his fierce advocacy of religious tolerance, Roger Williams established a new, less uptight colony in neighboring Rhode Island. By the time he died, in 1683, he was widely adjudged a champion of human rights.

Williams and his wife were buried under a modest headstone on their farm in Providence. Many years later his followers dug up the grave with the intent of reburying the remains in a grander setting.

But the remains were gone. Nary a shred of Mr. and Mrs. Williams—not even a shard of bone—was left in the coffin. Instead, the exhumers found a perfect outline of the two bodies—head, trunk, limbs, and all—formed by the roots of a nearby apple tree. The roots had penetrated the coffin, and then wound their way around the bodies, following the path of least resistance.

Eventually, every last atom of human tissue was absorbed by the roots to nourish the tree and its fruit, leaving only the woody outline. People who had snacked on apples from the tree for years realized with a shock that they had also eaten the remains of one of America's greatest religious reformers.

The only nun elected mayor of a major U.S. city

The city of Dubuque, Iowa (pop. 59,700), elected Carolyn Farrell, a Sister of Charity of the Blessed Virgin Mary, mayor in 1980. Feminist and liberal in her views and an avid golfer, Sister Carolyn remained in office throughout her term in the face of papal warnings that Roman Catholic clergy had no place in politics.

The only woman to witness her lover invested as pope

Alexander VI was certainly not the first noncelibate pope. But according to Marjorie P. K. Weiser and Jean S. Arbeiter, authors of *Womanlist*, he was probably the only one to be sworn in with his mistress in the audience.

Born Rodrigo Borgia in 1431, he met Vanozza dei Catanei during his preclerical days when he was a high-powered lawyer not above bribing officials and poisoning his enemies. He continued his freewheeling ways even while holding high offices in the Holy See and fathered several illegitimate children, many of whom he made cardinals.

Though Alexander openly maintained his relationship with Vanozza in the early years of his papacy, he dumped her when she entered menopause in favor of a seventeen-year-old named Giulia Farnese, who had three children by him. Alexander doted upon them all, but he was especially fond of Giulia's brother, whom he appointed cardinal, and who later became pope himself.

The only pope exhumed, dressed, and tried posthumously for his crimes

Formosus was neither a bad pope nor a bad man, but he had a long list of enemies, of whom his successor, Stephen VI, was the most virulent. Nine months after Formosus' death in 896, Stephen ordered his body dug up, dressed in the papal vestments, and propped in a witness chair, where he was formally charged with perjury and overweening ambition.

Pope Stephen served as prosecutor in the ghoulish

trial; a deacon answered on the defendant's behalf. Finding Formosus guilty, the tribunal invalidated all of his official acts and ordinations and lopped off the three fingers he used for bestowing blessings. His remains were buried in a makeshift grave but later stolen by thugs who dumped them in the Tiber. A hermit fished them out and buried them properly.

As it turned out, Stephen's excesses did not go unpunished. Having subjected Formosus to the most unspeakable desecrations, he made matters worse by requiring that all clerics who had been ordained by him renounce their orders. Meanwhile, partisans of the slain pope, heartened by reports that his mutilated corpse had performed miracles, stormed the Vatican and threw Stephen in jail, where he was murdered.

The only pope to die from eating poisonous mushrooms

A member of the powerful Medici family and a patron of Michelangelo, Raphael, and Cellini, Clement VII (1478–1534) had a fine appreciation of art and beauty; his political sensibility was less finely developed. He grappled ineptly with Henry VIII over the king's divorce and his break with Rome; later, he was captured and held prisoner by the Holy Roman Emperor Charles V.

Restored to the Vatican, Clement died in excruciating gastrointestinal pain at fifty-six after eating a portion of *Amanita phallotides*, a deceptively tasty and attractive mushroom that is considered the world's most toxic fungus. Even today, the dread *Amanita* accounts for as much as 95 percent of all mushroom-related deaths in Europe.

The only pope to father a son who also became pope

Born into an aristocratic family in the Roman Campania, Hormisdas married and fathered a son before he entered the clergy. He was appointed a deacon and papal assistant to Pope Symmachus, whom he succeeded in 514.

Hormisdas has been revered over the years as one of the papacy's great peacemakers. He welcomed the last followers of the antipope Laurentius back to the Church, and he ended the bitter thirty-five-year Acacian Schism that had divided the Constantinople and Rome factions of Catholicism.

Hormisdas died in 523. His son Silverius assumed the papacy in 536, upon the death of Pope Agapetus I. Unlike his father, who was beloved throughout the Church, Silverius had more than his share of enemies. Less than a year after his installation, he was charged with treason and deported. He died of starvation and physical maltreatment on the island of Palmaria, in the Gulf of Gaeta, a few months later.

The only one of the Twelve Apostles to die of natural causes

Being an Apostle of Christ meant hard work, low pay, and, almost invariably, death by beheading, crucifixion, impalement, or some equally nasty means. But somehow, Saint John, the youngest of the Twelve Apostles and the only one to witness the Crucifixion, managed to die in bed.

Not that he led a sheltered life. According to the Roman theologian Tertullian, John was boiled in oil on or-

ders from Emperor Domitian but miraculously emerged without so much as a blister. Afterwards he was exiled to the island of Patmos, where he wrote the Book of Revelation, returning only after Domitian was murdered (by assassins hired by his wife). John died peacefully in Ephesus, in Asia Minor, around A.D. 100, at a very advanced age.

The only church to baptize converts in a hot tub

. . . is located, as if it needed saying, in Southern California.

Actually, the New Song Church has no permanent home as of this writing; Sunday services are held in a junior-high-school gym. The mostly twenty-something congregation describes itself as "the flock that likes to rock."

Baptismal ceremonies take place at Puddingstone Hot Tubs Resort in nearby San Dimas, a Los Angeles suburb. Rev. Sandy Herbold, the associate pastor, does not feel the setting is any less suited to the purpose than a conventional baptismal font.

"The holiness isn't in the place, or in the water," he points out. "It's in the heart of the person."

The only back-to-back popes to die in the saddle

Centuries ago, the Vatican was the place to go if you were looking for a good time. In those days the Holy See was no more a bastion of morality and virtue than Chicago during Prohibition. Popes kept mistresses, fathered children, and generally disported themselves with wild abandon. Two even died in the sack.

The first was John XII. Ordained in 955, he clashed continually with the all-powerful Holy Roman emperor Otto I of Germany, who had him illegally deposed in 963. It was just as well: John was an insatiable gambler, carouser, and lecher who, some say, raped pilgrims within the very walls of St. Peter's Basilica. Within forty-eight hours a crony of Otto's—a middle-management church official with no clerical credentials—was rushed through his orders and ordained as Pope Leo VIII.

To no one's surprise, Leo proved horrendously unqualified for the job and extremely unpopular. At one point the ousted John mustered enough support to excommunicate Leo and reassume the papacy. Then, fearing Otto's rage, he fled to the Roman countryside, where he died of a stroke in the arms of a married woman. He was in his twenties.

As for Leo, being pope did not stop him any more than it stopped John from fooling around. On March 1, 965, less than a year after the death of his predecessor, he too died while committing an adulterous act.

The only female pope

There never was a female pope, actually. But it makes a great yarn, and for several hundred years, it was universally believed there had been.

The story of Pope Joan, as she is popularly known, takes several forms, but the basic details are these: Disguised as a man, a talented young woman works her way up through the Vatican to become a cardinal and, ultimately, pope. She rules wisely and fairly, and no one catches on until she goes into labor and delivers a baby while riding on horseback in a public procession. Her infamy exposed, she is tied to the horse's tail and dragged in disgrace around the city, and finally stoned to death.

The earliest mention of a female pope appeared in the *Universal Chronicle of Metz*, written by Jean de Mailly in the 1240s. He placed her reign just after that of Pope Victor III, who died in 1087. Later, the Dominican monk Martin of Troppau fleshed out the story in his *Chronicle of Popes and Emperors* and set it two centuries earlier. According to Martin, a young Englishwoman, educated in Germany, fell in love with a Benedictine monk whom she accompanied to Athens disguised as a man. When he died, she kept her disguise and went to Rome to study for the priesthood.

Distinguished for her piety and scholarship, she rose quickly within the Vatican and was the obvious choice to succeed Pope Leo IV when he died in 855. As John VIII, she was an able and popular ruler who consecrated King Louis II, ordained fourteen bishops, and built five churches. She successfully concealed her true identity from the world, only to make the fatal mistake of carrying on a torrid affair with a Vatican chamberlain many years her junior. It was he who fathered her child.

It sounds like something out of a supermarket tabloid. But for hundreds of years, everyone—even respected writers like Petrarch and Boccaccio—bought it. Pope John, a.k.a. Joan, Joanna, Agnes, Gilberta, and Jutta, was included among the busts of popes in the cathedral of Siena. And one feminist writer, Mario Equicola, even cited Joan's papacy as a demonstration of God's support of women's rights.

But by the 1600s, the story of Pope Joan was greeted with increasing skepticism. When Emmanuel Royadis wrote an 1886 biography, *Papissa Joanna*, treating her as a historical personage, he was excommunicated by the Roman Catholic Church.

No one gives much credence to the story of Pope Joan anymore. Yet there is a street near the Colosseum that papal processions have always made a point of avoiding. People used to say it was because Joan's cover was blown there and that the place is considered tainted. Now, of course, they know better. But popes still stay away.

SCIENCE AND TECHNOLOGY

The only words spoken by Sir Isaac Newton as a member of Parliament

Sir Isaac Newton (1642–1727) is widely regarded as the greatest scientific genius of all time—a mathematician, physicist, and theoretician whose three laws of motion explained why apples fall from trees and how the planets move. He invented calculus, discovered that white light consists of every color of the spectrum, explained how tides work, and built the first reflecting telescope.

It is also believed that he died a virgin, and that his lifelong celibacy caused him chronic insomnia.

Along with his scientific undertakings, Sir Isaac immersed himself in politics and public service. He served as director of the Royal Mint and was elected twice as Cambridge University's representative to the House of Commons—in 1689 and 1701.

He was far less active a lawmaker than he was a theoretician. Although he appeared to have a good grasp of most of the issues under debate, he was known to be painfully shy and rose to speak only once in his entire career. That was to announce that a draft was causing him discomfort and that he would like the window closed. He resumed his seat and never spoke as a law-maker again.

The only bone in the body not connected to another

The hyoid is a U-shaped bone located at the base of the tongue between the mandible and the voice box. The only bone not jointed to another, its function is to support the tongue and its muscles.

The only sperm bank to solicit—and get—deposits from Nobel Prize winners

There were no free toasters or fruitwood salad bowls for opening an account with Graham's Repository for Germinal Choice. What you did get was the chance to have William Shockley's baby.

Shockley won the 1956 Nobel Prize in physics for helping to develop the transistor. Later, he won notoriety for his public pronouncements on the genetic inferiority of nonwhites. In 1980, it was revealed, he was one of several high-IQ sperm donors to the repository, a venture of California millionaire Robert Graham.

Women who wanted to produce superintelligent offspring could apply to the repository for a small container of frozen sperm that would be sent to them, postpaid. (Insemination, fertilization, and all the rest were up to them.) Though recipients were not told whose sperm they were receiving, each shipment was annotated with descriptive blurbs such as "a very famous scientist," or "a mover and shaker."

Why would a Nobel laureate like William Shockley participate in such a, well, seedy venture? Possibly because it offered an opportunity to improve on his own genetic track record, as he noted in an interview with *Playboy*. "In terms of my own capacities," he said, "my children represent a very significant regression." His kids included a Stanford Ph.D. with so-so grades and a college dropout.

"My first wife—their mother—had not as high an academic achievement standing as I have," he explained.

The only potentially moonless month

Because the lunar cycle is approximately twenty-nine and a half days long, every month of the year except February is guaranteed to have at least one full moon. To be sure, even moonless Februaries are a rarity, occurring once in about every twenty or thirty years. In 1866 February had no full moon, while January and March each had two. Astronomers say that arrangement won't reoccur for another two and a half million years.

The only element named after a state

At least three elements are named for countries (germanium, francium, and indium), four for mythological figures (tantalum, neptunium, titanium, and uranium), and six for scientists (einsteinium, fermium, curium, rutherfordium, nobelium, and lawrencium). But the only state to give its name to an element is California.

A synthetic radioactive metal, californium was thus named because it was first produced in 1951 by four scientists at the University of California at Berkeley: Glenn T. Seaborg, Albert Ghiorso, Kenneth Street, and Stanley Thompson. (Seaborg holds the distinction of rating the longest entry in *Who's Who in America*—one hundred lines.)

Californium is principally used as a source of neutrons for the radiographic marking of pipelines and mine shafts. At one thousand dollars per microgram it is the world's most expensive substance.

The only metal that is a liquid at room temperature

The freezing point of mercury (a.k.a. quicksilver) is −38°F, which means that unless you hang out a lot in Fairbanks, you've probably never seen it in solid form. In fact, prior to 1759, when mercury was first frozen in a laboratory, scientists did not even consider it a metal.

But liquid doesn't mean lightweight. Mercury is twice as heavy as iron and 33 percent heavier than lead; a cupful weighs over seven pounds (not counting the cup). The combination of density and fluidity makes mercury ideal for barometers, since you need but thirty inches of the stuff to measure atmospheric pressure. If water were used, a four-story-high column would be required.

Until a century ago, English hat makers commonly used mercury in the treatment of wool. Prolonged inhalation of mercury fumes can scramble the brain and cause hyperexcitability and bizarre personality changes. The madness of the Mad Hatter in *Alice's Adventures in Wonderland* was based on the result of just such exposure.

The only planet whose craters are named exclusively for women

A month after it slipped into orbit around Venus in May 1989, the *Magellan* spacecraft began beaming back the first views of the planet's cloud-shrouded surface, including views of about one hundred hitherto unseen craters. Given that Venus is the only planet with a female name, the National Aeronautics and Space Administration proposed naming the craters after famous women, such as Pearl Buck; Lillian Hellman; Rachel Carson; Margaret Mead; Clare Boothe Luce; Mary, Queen of Scots; and Gertrude "A planet is a planet is a planet" Stein.

The names won't become official, however, until they are approved at the next meeting of the International Astronomical Union, in 1994. By then, another four thousand Venusian craters, volcanic vents, ridges, and mountains are expected to be photographed, and NASA is open to suggestions for names from the general public.

To be eligible to have a Venusian land form named in her honor, a woman must have been dead at least three years and proven "in some way notable or worthy of the honor." Military and political figures of the last two hundred years are ineligible; so are prominent figures "in any of the six main living religions," as well as women with "specific national significance."

The only temperature at which Fahrenheit and Celsius thermometers read the same

Anyone who has listened to a weather report on the radio or looked at one of those time-temperature signs on suburban banks knows that where Celsius and Fahrenheit are concerned, never the twain shall meet.

Well, hardly ever. On the Fahrenheit scale, the freezing and boiling points of water are 32 ° and 212 ° respectively; on the Celsius scale, the analagous reference points are 0 ° and 100 °. Since one Fahrenheit degree equals five-ninths of a Celsius degree, Fahrenheit can be converted into Celsius using this formula: $C° = \frac{5}{9} \times (F° - 32)$. Alternatively, Celsius can be converted into

Fahrenheit according to this formula: $F° = (\%_5 \times C°) +$ 32. The only point at which both scales show identical readings is $-40°$.

The only asteroid sold at auction

The Austrian astronomer Johann Palisa (1848–1925) discovered so many minor celestial bodies that he evidently grew tired of naming them. When he discovered asteroid 250, he auctioned off the christening rights. The buyer was Baron Albert von Rothschild, who paid £50 for the privilege of dubbing the asteroid Bettina, after his wife.

The only planet that rotates from east to west

The next time you visit Venus, if you plan to get up early and watch the sun rise, make sure to look west, not east. While the eight other planets all rotate in tandem from east to west, Venus spins the other way. (Actually, if you were on Venus, you wouldn't see the sun regardless of where you looked, even though it is only sixty-seven million miles away, since the planet is enveloped in a thick blanket of poisonous gas. Sort of like Elizabeth, New Jersey.)

Venus's east-to-west orientation isn't its only rotational quirk. One complete spin takes 243 Earth days. But it takes only 225 for the planet to complete an orbit around the sun. In other words, a Venusian day is longer than a Venusian year.

It was only recently that astronomers were able to observe and measure Venus's rotation period with any accuracy, because its opaque atmosphere rotates at its own, much faster pace and hides all underlying land forms and surface markings. That atmosphere, which reflects most of the sun's light and heat, is what illuminates Venus and makes it the brightest nonlunar object in the night sky.

The only guaranteed way to spot aliens in our midst

Dr. Hugo Kornhelm of Switzerland has perfected a first-of-its-kind camera that can photograph and identify extraterrestrials masquerading as earthlings.

The camera, says the good doctor, senses and records the otherwise invisible green halos around the heads of the aliens. In one recent trial, he took his camera to a Swiss shopping mall, where he photographed a crowd of two hundred people. The telltale halos showed up on seventy-six of them.

The only cells in the human body that don't regenerate

Take care of those brain cells. They're the only ones you'll ever have.

Other cells in the body—blood, skin, muscle, etc.—are replaced when they die. Brain cells are not.

And die they do. A person is born with approximately thirty billion brain cells, some of which begin sloughing off almost immediately. Even so, brain growth continues until around age twenty—but only because the remaining cells get bigger. By early adulthood, the average person—even the average rocket scientist—is playing with far, far less than a full deck of cells, and by age sixty, the daily casualty rate can easily top one hundred thousand.

By and large, it's not a problem. In fact, many scientists believe that human intelligence actually expands and improves with age. Even when massive amounts of brain tissue are destroyed by illness or injury, the surviving parts of the brain have a remarkable capacity to compensate for the loss. In one 1966 case, surgeons removed fully one half of the brain of a forty-seven-year-old Soviet man. Far from living out his remaining days in vegetative reverie, the man learned to sing, recognize colors, and relearn reading, writing, and arithmetic within a few months.

The only guaranteed way to prevent false alarms

Lawrence Hartshorn was sitting in a phone booth reading a newspaper report about the growing cost of false alarms, which account for as much as 25 percent of all fire alarms turned in. Suddenly, the idea hit him: Why not install fire alarms in a specially designed booth that would lock the caller in until the fire trucks arrived?

Though the idea has yet to catch on, a prototype of Hartshorn's anti–false-alarm booth was placed near a high school in North Providence, Rhode Island. The tall red cylinder, looking somewhat like a mammoth lipstick, bore the words "Fire Alarm. Enter Only in Emergency." The alarm could not be activated until the user locked the door behind him; it would then remain locked for five minutes—or until police or firefighters arrived to open it from outside.

And did Hartshorn's brainchild eliminate the menace of false alarms in North Providence? "I think it's working out real well," reported Mayor Salvatore Mancini. "Kids were pulling the alarm when they got out of school, and to get out of tests. We stopped that." However, no legitimate alarms had been turned in at the time, either.

The only guarantee against premature burial

Mexican inventor Roberto Monsivais bills his patented Life Detector system as "the only way in the world to avoid being embalmed or buried alive."

While the files of the United States Trademark and Patent Office abound with antiburial devices, all depend on timely intervention from outside; Monsivais' is unique in that the rescue mechanism is built in. Attachable to any standard casket, it incorporates equipment used to monitor vital signs in hospital patients. If the deceased revives, an alarm goes off and an emergency oxygen supply is activated until rescuers can open the coffin.

The Life Detector was unveiled at the 1982 International Inventors Expo in New York City. There is no indication yet that it has gone into commercial production. However, the risk it addresses is a very real one—at least to some people.

In England some years ago, the Society for the Prevention of People Being Buried Alive commissioned several devices to avert premature interment—or to help the prematurely interred become disinterred. The simplest was a coffin fitted with an electric buzzer, which a tenant could sound to summon help.

Hans Christian Andersen was known to be phobic about being buried alive and went to great lengths to make sure it never happened. A card in his pocket warned anyone who might find him unconscious not to conclude he was dead before having him examined by a physician. While sleeping, he often left a note near his bed saying, "I only seem dead."

The only solar-powered vehicle ticketed for speeding

Swiss designer René Jeanneret is certainly not the first person to build a drivable solar-powered car. But he is the first to get ticketed for driving one too fast. In 1990 he was stopped by highway police outside Bienne, about a mile from the French border, doing eighty-eight kilometers per hour in an eighty-kilometer-per-hour zone.

The only sporting event called on account of solar eclipse

India and England were scheduled to go at it during the jubilee test cricket match in India on February 16, 1980, when the officials announced a postponement. The reason: A total eclipse of the sun would occur that afternoon, and the authorities were concerned that many of the fifty thousand-plus spectators would risk retinal damage and blindness looking at the sun.

In point of fact, much of India ground to a halt that day in deference to the eclipse: No marriages were arranged, weddings were postponed, stores were closed, and pregnant women were urged to stay indoors. Normal life resumed—and with it, the jubilee test—the following day.

The only artillery patent ever awarded to a Hollywood screen siren

In the summer of 1940, the actress Hedy Lamarr met composer George Antheil at a Hollywood dinner party and asked him how she might go about enlarging her breasts. Antheil, an endocrinology buff, was reputed to be well informed about such matters and recommended pituitary-hormone injections. The conversation proceeded logically to torpedoes.

Lamarr told Antheil that she felt uneasy living a sybaritic existence in Hollywood while Hitler was ravaging Europe. She had learned something about the design and manufacture of heavy armaments during her marriage to Fritz Mandel, owner of Austria's largest munitions works, and now "she was seriously thinking of quitting MGM and going to Washington, D.C., to offer her services to the newly established Inventors' Council," Antheil wrote in his 1945 autobiography, *Bad Boy of Music*.

The composer had a better idea: Stick with the movies, but let him help her develop her weapons ideas. Working closely together on the project, they were jointly awarded patent No. 2,292,387 for a first-of-its-kind, radio-controlled torpedo-guidance system, on October 1, 1941.

The Lamarr-Antheil invention was deemed so vital to the national defense that government officials kept details about it secret, *The New York Times* reported. Colonel L. B. Lent, chief engineer of the Inventors' Council, put it in the "red-hot" category.

According to the patent application, the device "relates broadly to secret communications systems involving the use of carrier waves of different frequencies, and is especially useful in the remote control of dirigible craft, such as torpedoes. . . ." It was used effectively by the United States in the naval war against Germany, and Lamarr was later enshrined as a war hero when Antheil dedicated his concert overture, "Heroes of Today," to her.

LANGUAGE AND LITERATURE

The only epic poem about gum and tooth disease

Dr. Solyman Brown was more than just another tooth puller. In the 1830s he spent as much time as he could spare from his busy New York City dental practice preaching the new gospel of oral hygiene to the rank-mouthed millions. He founded important dental journals, lectured before medical students, and wrote the epic *Dentologia: A Poem on the Diseases of the Teeth.* Published in 1840, it was thoughtfully annotated with a list of three hundred qualified dentists throughout the United States. Herewith, the tale of Urilla's sorry plight, excerpted from Canto the Third:

Urilla is fair in form and grace;
Her glance is modesty, her motion grace.
Her smile, a moonbeam on the garden bower,
Her blush, a rainbow on the summer shower. . . .

When first I saw her eyes' celestial blue,
Her cheeks' vermillion, and the carmine hue
That melted on her lips:—her auburn hair
That floated playful on the yielding air. . . .
I whispered to my heart:—we'll fondly seek

The means, the hour, to hear this angel speak. . . .

'Twas said,—'twas done—the fit occasion came,
As if to quench the kindling flame
Of love and admiration:—for she spoke,
And, lo, the heavenly spell forever broke!
For when her parted lips disclosed to view
Those ruined molars, veiled in blackest hue,
Where love had thought to feast the ravish'd sight
On orient gems reflecting snowy light,
Hope disappointed, silently retired,
Disgust triumphant came, and love expired!

Let every fair one shun Urilla's fate,
And wake to action, ere it be too late:
Let each successive day unfailing bring
The brush, the dentifrice, and the spring,
The cleansing flood:—the labor will be small,
And blooming health will soon reward it all. . . .

The only seminal twentieth-century literary figure to have a sex-gland implantation

William Butler Yeats suffered from impotence in his late sixties, and as if that weren't enough of a cross to bear, he also felt creatively blocked. Then the poet read a brochure hailing the success of Dr. Erwin Steinach, of Vienna, in pepping up flaccid libidos using sex-gland transplants.

Despite the reservations of his personal physician, Yeats went to London in 1934 to undergo the procedure, which was more like a modern-day vasectomy than a bona fide gland transplant. Steinach claimed it would stimulate testosterone production and restore the poet's virility.

It did not. However, Yeats did start writing again and

even dallied in several extramarital affairs, although none could be consummated. When a physician friend asked why he'd had the surgery, Yeats was less than forthright.

"I used to fall asleep after lunch," he said.

The only word formally voted into the English language

Until the 1950s the words *imbecile, idiot,* and *moron* were technical terms as well as insults, constituting a sort of pecking order among the mentally deficient. At the low end was *idiot,* designating an adult with the intelligence of a three- or four-year-old child. Next up the ladder was *imbecile,* or an adult with the intelligence of a seven- or eight-year-old. The highest level of subnormality was *moron.*

The word *moron* didn't exist in English before 1910, when Dr. Henry H. Goddard proposed it to the American Association for the Study of the Feeble Minded as an elegant way to refer to an adult with an IQ of between 50 and 69 and with the mental powers of an eight- to twelve-year-old. *Moron,* he explained, derived from the Greek word *moros,* which means "foolish." More recently, it had been used as the name of a dull-witted character in Molière's *La Princesse d'Elide.*

At its annual convention, the association voted on Goddard's proposal. It passed, and *moron* immediately became part of the English language.

The only item of headwear named for a poem

Tam o' Shanter, a.k.a. Tom of Shanter, was the drunken hero of a narrative poem of the same name written by Robert Burns in 1791. Fleeing for his life from some put-upon witches, Tam held fast "his gude blue bonnet." About a century later, the tam-o'-shanter hat was introduced in England—a sort of floppy woolen cap that became the rage among factory girls and later, among hard-drinking ploughmen.

The only author named Mark Twain *not* to wear white linen suits and write a book about a boy and a slave traveling down the Mississippi on a raft

Samuel Langhorne Clemens was the *second* author to write under the name Mark Twain.

The first was Isaiah Sellers, a venerable Mississippi riverboat pilot who used the phrase *mark twain*, meaning "two fathoms deep," to sign a series of stories he contributed to the New Orleans *Picayune*.

When Clemens, a cub reporter for the rival New Orleans *True Delta*, unmercifully parodied Sellers's pompous style, the older man was so mortified that he never wrote for publication again.

It's possible that the young Clemens may have assumed the pen name as a way of making amends. In any event, he atoned further in *Life on the Mississippi*, wherein he acclaimed Sellers "the patriarch of the craft" of steamboat piloting.

The only dermatological reaction to sudden literary acclaim

When novelist Harper Lee was informed by her agent, Maurice Crain, that she had just been awarded the 1961 Pulitzer Prize in fiction for *To Kill a Mockingbird*, she did not utter a word but immediately broke out in hives.

The only human calculator to achieve worldwide success as a mystery writer

"I was a prodigy," Rex Stout (1886–1975) once admitted to an interviewer—more in regret than pride. The boy who grew up to create the character of Nero Wolfe began to read at eighteen months, and by the age of three he had gone through the Bible twice, from cover to cover. When he was four, his sister May once caught him making marginal notations in Gibbon's *Decline and Fall of the Roman Empire*. For entertainment the boy often read the dictionary, and at eleven he was crowned spelling champion of Kansas, Nebraska, and Illinois.

Equally adept at figures, young Stout went on a tour of Kansas schools with John McDonald, editor of *Western School Journal*, and reluctantly gave a series of mind-boggling demonstrations. McDonald would blindfold the boy, then write down a long series of six-digit numbers on a blackboard. When the blindfold was removed, Rex would add the columns at lightning speed and shout out the answer within five seconds. He was never wrong.

Almost invulnerable: mythical figures who could be mortally wounded in only one part of their body:

1. *Achilles*, Greek warrior and hero of *The Iliad*. His mother dipped him in the river Styx as a child to render him invulnerable. But she neglected to dunk his heel, which was fatally pierced by an arrow in battle.

2. *Orlando*, hero of Ariosto's Renaissance epic, *Orlando Furioso*. He could be killed only by the prick of a large pin in the sole of his foot.

3. *Ferraù*, evil giant of *Orlando Furioso*. Thirty-six feet tall and as strong as forty men, he was fine as long as no one bothered his navel. Orlando stabbed him there fatally.

4. *Megissogwon*, a.k.a. "the Great Pearl-Feather." An evil magician, he slew Nokomis, grandmother of Hiawatha in the Longfellow poem. A woodpecker told Hiawatha that Megissogwon was invincible but for a single tuft of hair. Hiawatha shot three arrows at the spot, and that was that.

5. *Orillo*, the robber-magician of *Orlando Furioso*. He had the power to regenerate any part of his body that was lopped off, except for a single hair on his head.

6. *Siegfried*, warrior hero of the *Nibelungenlied*. He was sometimes called Siegfried the Horny because he washed himself in the blood of a dragon he slew, causing a protective shell of horn to grow over his body. But he didn't notice a linden leaf that had settled on a spot between his shoulder blades, keeping them dry. He was shot with an arrow there by the treacherous Hagan while taking a water break during a hunting trip.

The only rejection slip Gertrude Stein ever received that was worthy of her talents

Even after phrases like "Rose is a rose is a rose" and "Pigeons in the grass alas" had made her famous, Gertrude Stein (1874–1946) still encountered difficulty in placing her works with major publishers.

Once she cabled Modern Age Books with a proposal that they bring out an inexpensive edition of her collected poems, only to have editor A. J. Firfield write back:

> I am only one, only one, only one. Only one being, one at the same time. Not two, not three, only one. Only one life to live, only sixty minutes in one hour. Only one pair of eyes. Only one brain. Only one being. Being only one, having only one pair of eyes, having only one time, having only one life, I cannot read your MS. three or four times. Not even one time. Only one look, only one look is enough. Hardly one copy would sell here. Hardly one. Hardly one.

The only attempt to compile a biographical directory of every graduate of Harvard

In a frenzy of school spirit, Harvard chief librarian John Langdon Sibley began compiling a biographical reference that would include a sketch of every person to attend the university from its founding in 1636 up to the present. He never quite finished the task.

When Sibley died in 1885 after twenty-five years of painstaking research, he had gotten only as far as the class of 1689. But he bequeathed $161,169 to the Massachusetts Historical Society to carry on the Sisyphean task.

The work continues even today. But Harvard keeps turning out new graduates at a rate of three thousand a year and the biographers keep falling farther and farther behind. Of the 200,000-plus men and women to have earned Harvard degrees, about 190,000 lack biographies.

The only typographical error ever to appear on the cover of *Time*

No publication, however obsessive its proofreaders, is totally immune to typographical errors. But a typo on the cover of a national newsmagazine?

It happened on the March 21, 1983, issue of *Time*. A cover blurb referred to a featured story on Henry Kissinger's "New Plan for Arms Control"—except that the word *Control* came out as *Contol*.

As it turned out, few, if any, of the flawed copies made it to the newsstands because a pressroom employee spotted the error in time—but only after 200,000 issues had been printed. *Time* spent over one hundred thousand dollars to correct the mistake.

The only person who ever committed six errors in one sentence

That's how e. e. cummings eulogized Warren G. Harding upon the president's death in 1923. Although he'd been a newspaper publisher and editor in Marion, Ohio, before he entered politics, Harding's grasp of the English language was shaky at best. He ran for president on a "return to normalcy" campaign, blithely unaware that no such word as *normalcy* existed. Later, he said, "Progression is not proclamation nor palaver. It is not pretense nor play on prejudice. It is not personal pronouns, nor perennial pronouncement. It is not the perturbation of a people passion-wrought, nor a promise proposed."

Cummings was not alone in his views. Of Harding's oratory—which he wrote himself—H. L. Mencken said, "It reminds me of a string of wet sponges; it reminds me of tattered washing on the line; it reminds me of stale bean soup, of college yells, of dogs barking idiotically through endless nights."

The only novel by e. e. cummings

While serving as a volunteer ambulance driver in France during World War I, poet e. e. cummings was interned in a concentration camp as the result of an administrative error. That experience inspired cummings's only novel, *The Enormous Room.*

To render the book fit for publication, the author's father, a Harvard English professor turned pastor, painstakingly edited out the obscenities and sold it to publisher Horace Liveright. Editing, typesetting, and publication all proceeded without assistance from the author, who was in Europe. The absence proved unfortunate: The book came out riddled with flubs in spelling, grammar, punctuation, and typography, and horrifying gaps in pagination.

But far costlier than this rampant sloppiness was the single occurrence of the word *shit,* which had escaped the elder Cummings's scrutiny and appeared correctly spelled and used just as the author had intended. Fearing prosecution, Liveright ordered one of his secretaries to go through the entire press run, book by book, and ink out the expletive.

As it turned out, sales were sluggish. Feeling he'd been had, Liveright developed a bitter dislike for the book, and rather than allowing the unsold copies to be remaindered, he had them sold as wastepaper. The publisher later had reason to regret his pique: In the late 1920s, *The Enormous Room* enjoyed a revival and went through several reprints.

The only direction Dickens faced when he wrote

In his twenties and already an established author, Charles Dickens became obsessed with mesmerism, a popular pseudoscience named for its originator, Austrian physician Franz Mesmer.

At the heart of Mesmer's theories was the notion that the universe was bathed in an invisible "mesmeric fluid," and that by aligning yourself with the earth's magnetic poles—through hypnotism, magnets, giant batteries, or body position—you could achieve physical and spiritual well-being, tap into your unconscious dreams and impulses, and write better novels. Beginning in 1838, Dickens arranged the writing desk in his study to face north and took pains to face in that direction whenever he worked away from home. He slept facing north, too.

The only language you can play on a kazoo

There are no native speakers of Solresol; like the better-know Esperanto, it's an artificial language, designed to dissolve international communication barriers and units mankind. Invented by a French music teacher, Jean-François Sudre, in 1827, Solresol is written in musical notation, and its words are constructed entirely from notes of the diatonic scale—do, re, mi, fa, so and ti. Depending on which syllable is accented, a single word can serve as a noun, adjective, verb, and adverb.

Solresol's complex grammar and vocabulary were not easy to master, yet the language achieved a surprising degree of popularity in nineteenth-century Europe. Victor Hugo, John James Audubon, and Napoleon III were among its devotees, and formal instruction in the language was offered at Oxford, the Sorbonne, and the University of Padua. Chief among its appeals was that it could be hummed, whistled, sung, or played on a kazoo.

The only novel written by Benito Mussolini

Years before he became dictator of Italy, Mussolini served his political apprenticeship as a young polemicist helping the Italian Socialist cause by penning anticapitalist and anticlerical screeds for several newspapers and radical journals. But his sole effort at fiction was *Claudia Patricella; or, The Cardinal's Mistress*, an anticlerical historical novel.

It was first published in 1909 as a weekly serial in *L'Avventire*, a socialist newspaper. Set in the seventeenth century, it is the story of Madruzzo, the debauched cardinal of Trentino, and his wicked paramour, Claudia Patricella. Claudia, it turns out, is the daughter of the cardinal's closest friend, and both she and her father are highly unpopular with the local peasantry, who would like nothing better than to see them banished. The cardinal, for his part, would just as soon give up the clerical life and get married, but the Vatican won't hear of it.

Though Mussolini originally intended to kill off Claudia early in the story, he kept her alive at the insistence of his editor, who felt it was her very depravity that drew readers, much as Joan Collins's exquisite witchiness kept *Dynasty* near the top of the charts for years. Mussolini openly regarded *The Cardinal's Mistress* as trash, and while it was translated into several languages, it did not appear in book form in Italy until after his death in 1945.

The only English word whose pronunciation remains unchanged when the last four letters are dropped

It's *queue*. And *queuing* is the only word in the language with five consecutive vowels.

The only seven-letter word that contains all five vowels

The word is *sequoia*, referring, of course, to the giant trees of California. The sequoia is named after the Cherokee Indian scholar, Sequoya, who created a Cherokee alphabet—the first written alphabet for any Indian language.

The only American novel written without use of the letter *e*

A musician by trade, Ernest Wright was intrigued by the idea of constructing a "lipogram"—a book totally lacking in a specific letter. To be sure, he wasn't the first; the Greek poet Lasus tried it around 500 B.C., and Tryphiodorus' retelling of the *Odyssey* ran to twenty-six volumes, the first totally devoid of the letter *a*, the second devoid of *b*, and so on.

The Spanish dramatist Lope de Vega (1562–1635), who wrote over two thousand plays, also produced five lipogrammatic novels, each missing a different vowel. But the most heroic lipogrammatist of all was the eighteenth-century German poet Gottlob Burmann, whose clinical lettraphobia found expression in 130 poems minus the letter r, as well as a refusal to speak the letter at any time. This ruled out uttering his own name—which Burmann is said to have disliked anyway.

To fashion his lipogram—a fifty-thousand-word novel entitled *Gadsby*—Wright first removed the E key from his typewriter. The book was published in Great Britain in 1939, where it sold about fifty copies. Its e-lessness notwithstanding, the prose is surprisingly smooth and straightforward, as one may gather from the following passage: "Gadsby was walking back from a visit down in Branton Hills' manufacturing district on a Saturday night. A busy day's traffic had had its noisy run; and with not many folks in sight, His Honor got along without having to stop to grasp a hand, or talk; for a Mayor out of City Hall is a shining mark for any politician. . . ."

BANKS, BRIDGES, AND OTHER WORKS OF MAN

The only bank built entirely out of bricks sent through the mail

In Utah in 1916, railway-freight costs were $2.50 a pound, and the town fathers of Vernal were resigned to paying that amount to ship in bricks from nearby Salt Lake City to build the Bank of Vernal. Then a local businessman discovered that the same bricks could be sent by parcel post for a mere $1.05 a pound.

There were no laws against sending bricks through the mail, but there were some stipulations to deal with. According to postal regulations, no package could weigh more than fifty pounds, nor could more than five hundred pounds be mailed to the same address. No problem: Bricks were bound up in parcels of seven and mailed daily to Vernal residents at their homes. According to the *WPA Guide to Utah*, "the Salt Lake City, Price and Vernal post offices were flooded with bricks."

Meanwhile, local merchants figured that if the postal system worked for bricks, why not heavy machinery, farming implements, and wagon parts? Farmers started mailing their crops to market; one shipment of corn filled 10 four-ton trucks. Mail trucks filled to capacity plied between Vernal and neighboring towns—without carrying a

single letter. Later, postal regulations were tightened, making such freewheeling use of the mails impractical.

Today, Vernal (pop. 7,500) remains one of northeastern Utah's largest communities. And it's still served by the Parcel Post Bank, at 3 Main Street.

The only Y-shaped bridge

When Moses Dillon applied to the Ohio legislature for permission to build a bridge at the confluence of the Muskingum and Licking rivers in 1812, he made it clear that a conventional span wasn't what he had in mind. Since the rivers divided the town into three parts, he proposed a bridge shaped like a Y. The lawmakers said, "Why not?"

Dillon's bridge was completed two years later and rebuilt with steel and concrete in 1900. Named simply the Y Bridge, it remains the only span in the United States with a built-in fork.

The Y Bridge isn't Zanesville's only attraction. U.S. 40, which runs through Zanesville, was originally called the National Road and follows the path of what was the only major overland route between the East Coast and the western frontier in the early 1800s.

(There are also a few Z-shaped bridges in the Midwest. Some people believe they were built as a memorial to Ebenezer Zane, for whom Zanesville is named. More likely, they were built that way to make them stronger and more stable.)

The only aluminum bridge

The fact that most major bridges are made of steel doesn't mean there aren't better materials to work from. Consider aluminum: Strong, lightweight, abundant, and noncorroding, it would appear to be ideally suited to the purpose.

But for the most part aluminum is far too expensive to build bridges with, and that's why only a single aluminum bridge of any magnitude (apart from a handful of mousy little minispans) has ever been constructed—the Arvida Bridge, which spans the Saguenay River in Quebec, Ontario, in the heart of Canada's aluminum industry.

Constructed in 1950 by the Dominion Bridge Company, this 290-foot arch bridge weighs two hundred tons—about half of what a comparable steel span would weigh. And unlike steel bridges, it never rusts, so it's much easier to maintain and never needs repainting.

The only bridge built out of eggs

Located behind Lima's presidential palace is the Roman-style Puente de Piedra, or "Bridge of Stone," built in 1610 from mortar mixed with the whites of hundreds of thousands of eggs.

Local engineers believed that eggs would fortify the stone. They couldn't have done better with steel girders: Although Lima has been rocked by numerous earthquakes over the past three centuries, including a 1746 killer that pretty much leveled the city, the Puente de Piedra has survived intact.

The only bridge named after a skin condition

In Peru there is a railroad crossing that spans a deep six-hundred-foot-wide chasm along the route from Lima to La Oroya. Although building the bridge was a dangerous undertaking, there were surprisingly few accidents among the construction workers, most of them former sailors who were used to working at dizzying heights.

However, many succumbed to bubonic plague, which broke out during construction, and in their memory the bridge was officially named Puente de las Verrugas, or "Bridge of Boils."

The only canal to connect two oceans

Five hundred feet across and fifty miles long, the Panama Canal is neither the widest ship canal in the world nor the longest. But in many ways it's the most remarkable.

For one thing, it is the only canal in the world to link

two oceans. Prior to its completion, naval and commercial vessels plying the waters of North and Central America had no way of getting from New York to California other than by rounding Cape Horn at the tip of South America. The canal provided them with an unbelievable shortcut; it saved them more than seven thousand miles.

It was also the most ambitious engineering and construction job ever undertaken. Before the canal could be built, a vast jungle had to be tamed, 232 million cubic yards of dirt and rock had to be dug, and nearly 5 million cubic yards of concrete had to be poured. More than forty-three thousand men took part in the ten-year effort, and many died of yellow fever and other tropical diseases by the time the canal opened for business in 1914.

The canal slices across the Isthmus of Panama on a bias, so that vessels actually move east as they pass from the Atlantic to the Pacific. It takes about eight hours to go through, and ships are charged according to their tonnage, with a supertanker paying well into five figures. One of the smallest tolls ever collected was seventy-one cents—from Robert F. Legge, a U.S. naval physician who swam through the canal in 1958. He saw only two other living creatures during the twenty-two-hour journey—an iguana and a boa constrictor—and was welcomed by a large throng of well-wishers when he stepped ashore at Balboa.

The only fifty-foot-tall barber's pole

As a prank, friends of barber James Boatfield stole his mailbox several years ago and replaced it with a fifty-foot-tall candy-striped barber's pole. Boatfield took it in good humor and left the pole standing. You can still see it in front of his house on Walker Road in Alexander, New York.

The only apartment building sentenced to beheading

From time to time, builders play Icarus and put up skyscrapers higher than local zoning codes allow. When the law catches up with them, the buildings are usually allowed to stand as is, and the builder is either hit with massive fines or made to atone for his sins by providing low-cost housing or some other amenity at his own expense.

But when a builder in New York put a thirty-one-story apartment building in the wrong place in 1986, local residents protested, and the city ordered him to lop off the top twelve stories.

The builder, Lawrence Ginsberg, insisted he never had any intention of breaking the law, and that he was misled by an error on a city map. "We built what the law appeared to allow, no more, no less," he said. The protesters insisted that he knew all along what he was doing.

Buildings far taller than thirty-one stories are razed all the time; the trick here was in amputating only the top twelve stories while leaving the lower nineteen intact—a surgical procedure as delicate as separating Siamese twins or cutting out a pound of flesh without spilling a drop of blood. No one involved with the case could cite a precedent for so draconian a measure—or a building-code violation so flagrant. As of this writing, the operation had not commenced, and no one knew if Ginsberg could pull it off, so to speak. Meanwhile, he continued protesting his innocence; the protesters continued shouting, "Off with its head!"

The only chicken coop listed in the National Register of Historic Places

It's not much as national shrines go—a smallish clapboard shack nailed together in 1923 by Mrs. Wilmer Steele on the family chicken farm in Georgetown, Delaware. But Mrs. Steele went on to become the mother of the American broiler industry, and the coop has been listed on the National Register since 1974 as "First Broiler House." Restored to its original condition by the Delmarva Poultry Industry Association, it is protected by federal regulations from being razed to make way for a new superhighway or a shopping mall.

The only man-made structure on earth visible from outer space

Astronauts who have orbited the earth report that it's not hard to pick out the Great Wall of China from 180 miles up, if you know where to look. It shows up as a hair-thin line meandering across China.

To be sure, the Great Wall didn't start out as a great wall but as a series of unconnected walls and fortresses dotting the Chinese landscape, dating back to the fourth century B.C. It wasn't until several centuries later that the dots were connected and the wall took its ultimate form. Today, much of it is in serious disrepair.

The most massive structure ever built, the Great Wall extends some fifteen hundred miles from the Gulf of Chihli deep into central Asia. You'd *expect* to be able to see it from a distance.

The only nonexistent dam listed and described in *The Encyclopaedia Britannica*

Until 1988, the *Britannica* included a detailed description of the Salem Church Dam—194 feet high, 8,850 feet long, and located near Fredericksburg, Virginia, on the Rappahannock River. Unbeknownst to the *Britannica*'s editors, the Salem Church Dam exists in name only—it was designed by the Army Corps of Engineers in 1944 but never built.

All mention of the dam has been expunged from subsequent editions of the *Britannica*.

The only structure that becomes stronger as it gets bigger

When his four-year-old daughter died in 1922 from the combined effects of influenza, polio, and spinal meningitis, architect R. Buckminster Fuller (1895–1983) blamed the environment and embarked on a lifelong quest for a way to control it better.

The closest he came was the geodesic dome, which he designed in the 1950s. Unlike conventional domes, Fuller's requires no foundation or supports and can be set directly on the ground. Constructed from a latticework of interconnected triangular or polygonal planes, it embodies a unique way of distributing stress and supporting weight. In fact, the geodesic dome's stability and strength increase logarithmically with its size. To put it more simply, the bigger it gets, the stronger it gets. Only wrestlers and corporations can make the same claim.

Geodesic domes are relatively cheap and easy to build, transport, and dismantle, and provide maximum interior space for the minimum surface area. And, since adding size adds strength, there's no practical limit on how big they can be.

Fuller's dream was to create perfect living environments by building domes over entire cities and even unlivable areas like the Sahara and the Antarctic. It never happened, but the form has been used with great success in the construction of concert halls, factory buildings, weather stations, exhibition halls, and greenhouses. The biggest to date is the Union Tank Car Company in Baton Rouge, Louisiana—384 feet wide by 116 feet high. And a few years ago, builders in East St. Louis, Illinois, were talking about enclosing an entire shopping mall in a half-mile-wide dome.

As for the *smallest* geodesic domes, in 1985 researchers at Rice University, in Houston, Texas, discovered a new kind of molecule consisting of sixty atoms of carbon that was shaped exactly like a geodesic dome. They called it buckminsterfullerene, though it is more commonly known as bucky ball.

No one has yet found a use for the new structure—but wait. Scientists say that because of its unique properties, bucky ball could serve variously as the world's most slippery lubricant, a molecule-sized ball bearing, or even a high-temperature superconductor.

The only brassiere museum

Over the years, Italian fashion designer Samuele Mazza's keen interest in woman's inner being has led him to collect more than fifteen hundred brassieres of all nations. They include models made of wood, glass, stone, bulletproof metal, and pasta. As of this writing, Mazza was transferring his holdings to a new museum in Florence.

The only mousetrap museum

Procter Security Fencing Ltd. markets and manufactures mousetraps. It also exhibits them. In 1989 the company established the Museum of the Mousetrap, located at its main factory in Bedwas, Mid Glamorgan, Wales.

The museum's holdings include some two hundred different varieties of antirodent matériel, including a trap from 3000 B.C., several seventeenth- and eighteenth-century British models, and a guillotine-shaped affair from France. "My interest in mousetraps is hereditary," explains marketing director Jeremy Procter, "as my company has been making the 'Little Nipper' mousetrap to the same design since 1897."

The only one of the Seven Wonders of the World still standing

The Greeks listed seven wonders of the ancient world—the Colossus of Rhodes, the Pharos (Lighthouse) at Alexandria, the Mausoleum at Halicarnassus, the Statue of Zeus by Phidias at Olympia, the Temple of Artemis at Ephesus, the Hanging Gardens of Babylon, and the Pyramids of Giza in Egypt. You can still see a few artifacts from the Mausoleum on display at the British Museum. But the Mausoleum itself, and all but one of the other wonders are, like nickel beer and the Washington Senators, dead and gone.

Not the Pyramids, though. When last we looked, they were still there on the west bank of the Nile, a short tour-bus ride from Cairo and, because of the shifting of the earth's crust, two-and-a-half miles south of their original site. About eighty remain, of which the biggest and best-known is the Great Pyramid of Khufu.

According to Herodotus it took 100,000 men 20 years to build this architectural marvel, which occupies more acreage than New York's Lincoln Center. Some two-and-a-half-million tons of stone were used—not including a marble exterior, long since obliterated by erosion and theft.

It's hard to account for the Pyramids' survival, alone among the Seven Wonders. Most likely its sheer mass has been a bulwark against erosion and other ravages. Not so the Sphinx, which has lost part of its beard to erosion and air pollution, and its nose to vandals.

The only skyscraper without a steel framework

First-year architectural students know you can't raise a building very high unless it's reinforced with a steel skeleton; otherwise it will collapse under its own weight.

But architects Daniel Burnham and John Root broke that rule in 1891 when they designed the Monadnock Building, near the intersection of Jackson Boulevard and Dearborn Avenue in Chicago. The all-masonry skyscraper towers sixteen stories above the street, as sturdy as a fortress.

Not an ounce of steel was used in the Monadnock's construction. The secret of its stability seems to be in the foundation walls, which are six feet thick; in addition, the building is slightly tapered toward the top, giving it a graceful sweep and greater stability.

The only postage stamp to determine the location of a canal

When the Panama Canal was still in the planning stages, its French and U.S. backers wavered between putting it in Nicaragua and Panama. Then, in 1900, a series of Nicaraguan postage stamps showed Mount Momotombo, a long-dead volcano, spewing fire and ash.

One ardent lobbyist for Panama, a French engineer named Philippe Bunau-Varilla, circulated the stamps throughout the U.S. Senate, proof positive that so untamed and volcano-ridden a country was no place to put a canal. Though the lawmakers were leaning toward Nicaragua, principally because the existence of Lake Nicaragua would have simplified construction and reduced costs, they bought the volcano story and promptly eliminated Nicaragua from further consideration. Four years later, they voted to build the canal in Panama.

The only monument to an insect pest

In downtown Enterprise, Alabama, at the corner of College and Main, a statue of a robe-clad female figure stands atop an ornate pedestal. The statue is surrounded by a fountain and a wrought-iron fence. Her arms are raised heavenward; in them she holds a giant bug.

It is, in fact, the Mexican boll weevil, or *Anthonomus grandis*, that she proffers to the gods. A commemorative plaque reads, "In profound appreciation of the boll weevil and what it has done as the herald of prosperity, this monument was erected by the citizens of Enterprise, Coffee County, Alabama."

As a rule, cotton growers have been more inclined to gas boll weevils than dedicate monuments to them ever since the insect first showed up in the United States in 1892. Today, crop destruction and eradication efforts cost U.S. cotton growers over two million dollars a year. But in 1915, after a catastrophic infestation destroyed twelve thousand bales of cotton in southeast Alabama—a third of the annual harvest—and wrecked future crops for years, farmers first realized a truth that had always eluded them: The path to prosperity lies in diversification.

So farmers who had relied solely on cotton for generations now raised peanuts, potatoes, sugarcane, corn, hay, and livestock. Coffee County became more prosperous than it ever had during cotton's reign. In 1917 the county harvested more than one million bushels of peanuts. It's a record that still stands.

None of the county's good fortune would have been

possible without the good offices of the Mexican boll weevil, and in 1918 the county erected its monument. The chamber of commerce claims that it is "the only monument in the world glorifying a pest."

The only sculpture Michelangelo ever signed

As a mature artist, Michelangelo evidently thought it was neither appropriate nor necessary to sign his work. But he had no qualms about billboarding himself on the *Pietà*, which he created c. 1499 when he was in his midtwenties. The sculpture is the most widely viewed work of art in St. Peter's Basilica in Rome. A ribbon on Mary's chest clearly shows the artist's signature.

The *Holy Family*, a painting of Mary, Joseph, and Jesus, is also unique among Michelangelo's work. Commissioned by Doni Strozzi upon his marriage to Maddalena Strozzi around 1503, the work is also known as the *Doni Madonna* and may well be **the only painting the artist ever did on an easel,** according to Irving Stone. Virtually all his other work was painted directly on ceilings and walls.

The only classical marble statue with eyelashes

In 1503 a life-size marble figure of Ariadne—the Cretan princess who saved Theseus' neck, only to be dumped by him on the island of Naxos—was unearthed in Italy. Dating back to ancient Rome, the statue was of Ariadne sleeping fitfully on a rock.

The discovery caused quite a stir in the Roman art world—not because of its extraordinary beauty but because the napping Ariadne had eyelashes. No one, before or since, has ever seen an eyelashed statue from the classical world. Later, the statue was donated to the Vatican.

The only museum devoted entirely to the potato

The world grows three hundred million tons of potatoes annually, but until 1979 there had never been a museum devoted to the lowly *Solanum tuberosum.*

Tom and Meredith Hughes fixed all that in 1979, when they established the Potato Museum in the basement of their rented Washington, D.C., townhouse at 704 North Carolina Avenue S.E., about a fifteen-minute walk from the Capitol.

Alas, the museum, which honored what Meredith Hughes calls "the perfect food," is no more: It closed in 1990 when the Hugheses' landlady reclaimed their townhouse. They have since appealed, without success, for financial backing from such organizations as H. J. Heinz and the National Potato Promotion Board.

It's a shame the museum had to close its doors. In its time, it had more than two thousand items on exhibit, such as Mister Potato Heads, a pack of Spud cigarettes, a reproduction of Van Gogh's "The Potato Eaters," a four-thousand-year-old Peruvian potato, early American potato-farming implements, jars of preserved potato bugs, a potato dating back to the Great Potato Famine of 1845–1849 in Ireland, pre-Columbian drinking vessels in the shape of potatoes, postage stamps and comic books with potato themes, etc., etc. The museum's reference library contained at least two thirds of the material ever published about potatoes. The Hugheses also published *Peelings,* a monthly newsletter read by about three hundred ardent potatophiles.

Those who've been there say the Potato Museum was

a refreshing change of pace from better-known D.C. tourist meccas like the National Gallery and the National Air and Space Museum—homier and more informal. "It's just mind-boggling that a corporate sponsor hasn't come forward," says Merle Jensen, a University of Arizona professor and one of the erstwhile museum's trustees.

Singular museums:

1. *Buford Pusser Museum.* Adamsville, Tennessee. Buford Pusser was the small-town sheriff popularized in the *Walking Tall* movies. You can see his size 13D shoes, a map showing where he was born, lived, and died in a car crash, and other Pusserana. Buy a souvenir ax handle in the gift shop and whack a few bad guys, Pusser-style.
2. *Philips Mushroom Museum.* Kennett Square, Pennsylvania. Watch an eighteen-minute video on mushroom farming, or see a dynamite diorama about shiitakes, the upscale fungus from Japan.
3. *American Mechanical Fan Museum.* Dallas, Texas. Most popular exhibit: the illuminated funeral fan, used to shoo flies—and the odor of putrefaction—from the deceased.
4. *Nut Museum.* Old Lyme, Connecticut. See it for the bride and groom carved out of a walnut, or the eight-foot-long nutcracker. Admission: Three dollars and a nut.

---

5. *Thermometer Museum.* Sacramento, California. Two hundred years of temperature-taking devices. Not so hot.

6. *American Angora Goat Breeders Association Museum.* Rocksprings, Texas. "Not a whole lot here," says museum spokesperson Patty Shanklin. "We have some papers, photos, and one old stuffed goat." Only if you're in the neighborhood.

AMERICA THE BEAUTIFUL

The only state without houseflies

The lowly *Musca domestica*, spreader of filth and breeder of disease, is found in virtually every country of the world. But it cannot survive or breed in cold climates and has thus never been able to establish a real presence in Alaska. Even house flies inadvertently imported via food shipments have died without reproducing. However, if you're planning a visit to the forty-ninth state, pack a swatter or two anyway: Hardier pests, such as stable flies and bottle flies, which don't require tropical warmth to survive, are common throughout Alaska.

The only U.S. city that spells its name with an exclamation point

No one ever claimed that the southern Ohio city of Hamilton (pop. 65,000) was *totally* lacking in appeal. It was the birthplace of William Dean Howells, after all. It is the home of the College Football Hall of Fame. And it is the nation's major manufacturing center for coated paper, food mixes, and safes.

But crime, corruption and general urban decay had

taken their toll on Hamilton when the city council decided a bit of creative punctuation was all the town
needed to perk things up. In 1986, by a vote of 5–1, they
changed Hamilton to Hamilton!.

That's Hamilton!, as in Hamilton! is my kind of
town, or When in Hamilton!, do as the Hamiltonians do.
Official guidelines require that the exclamation point *not*
be used with a question mark, lest an innocent query
(Where is Hamilton?) become an intended jibe (Where is
Hamilton!?).

The exclamation point became the focus of a one-hun-
dred-thousand-dollar public-relations campaign aimed at
boosting civic pride and persuading businesses looking to
relocate that Hamilton! has it all. But not everyone got the
point—or liked it.

In a Hamilton *Journal-News* opinion poll, 48 out of
68 respondents said the ! was a crock of #@$?. Long-
time resident Ed Brown said it was like grafting a shiny
new Cadillac hood ornament onto a tired old Volkswagen. Ornament or no, "It's still a tired old Volkswagen,"
he said, "and it still stalls at every light." And *American
Demographics* found Hamilton!, no less than Hamilton,
to be among Ohio's most unlivable cities.

The only virgin in the United States with a post office

The Times Atlas of the World lists no fewer than a
dozen U.S. place-names incorporating the word *virgin*
and several others outside the boundaries of the United
States, such as Virginiatown, Ontario; Virginia, New
Zealand; and Virginópolis, Brazil. Some are named for
the Virgin Mary, others for the Virgin Queen (Elizabeth
I), and still others for various and sundry religious mar-
tyrs. Las Virgenes Creek, California, is named after the

Ursulines—an army of eleven thousand Christians who were supposedly slaughtered by the Huns while on a pilgrimage to Rome.

But the only town anywhere in the world with the name *Virgin* is a small farming community tucked away in a canyon pocket in Washington County, Utah. (It was originally called Pocketville.) J. N. Hook, author of *All Those Wonderful Names*, calls it "the only Virgin in the United States that has a Post Office."

The only American place-name with seven consecutive vowels

Seventeenth-century maps showed an area in what is now the American Midwest called Ouaouiaton, named for a local Native American tribe. The name, eventually shortened to Ouaouia, was later applied to a river, a territory, and a state. Its modern form: Iowa.

Hawaii, predictably, is the only U.S. state where you'll find place-names incorporating the same letter three times in a row. Consider Ka'a'awa (a stream on Oahu), Pu'-u'uao (a peninsula on Molokai), and P'u'ua'u (a town on Oahu).

The only town named after a radio show

The people of Hot Springs, New Mexico, weren't especially wedded to the name *Hot Springs*. So, in 1950, when Ralph Edwards, host of the radio game show, *Truth or Consequences*, announced on the air, "I wish that some town in the United States liked and respected our show so much that it would like to change its name to Truth or Consequences," they voted to rename the town by a vote of 4 to 1.

In response, Edwards made good on his offer to air the show's tenth-anniversary broadcast from Truth or Consequences, or T or C, as locals know it. Over the years the name has survived several campaigns to change it back, and current host Bob Barker still shows up every May for the annual Ralph Edwards Fiesta and Sheriff's Posse Race.

The only state flag designed by a child

In 1927, long before Alaska achieved statehood, the Alaska branch of the American Legion sponsored a contest to find a design for a new territorial flag. The competition was open to schoolchildren; the winner was thirteen-year-old Benny Benson, a seventh grader at the territorial school in Seward. His entry: the Big Dipper and the North Star on a field of blue.

The design was officially adopted in May 1927, and the territorial government appropriated one thousand dollars to send young Benny to Washington to present the new flag to President Coolidge. The trip never worked out, however, and the money was set aside for the boy's education instead. Benny grew up to be a fisherman; his flag flies over the Alaska statehouse in Nome to this day.

The only state whose population density is less than one person per square mile

Averaging 0.89 people per square mile, Alaska is the most sparsely populated state in the nation. Ironically, its 570,833 square miles make it the *largest* in terms of area. Texas is a distant second with 262,017.

The only point from which you can see all six New England states

Rising only 3,166 feet above sea level and barely 2,000 feet over the surrounding countryside, Mount Monadnock is barely a pimple on the face of New England. But there are no other mountains nearby to block the view from its peak, and on a clear day, you can see seventy-five to one hundred miles in every direction.

Located near Dublin, New Hampshire, about ten miles north of the Massachusetts line, Mount Monadnock was a favorite haunt of Ralph Waldo Emerson. He called it "an airy citadel" and claimed he could see all the way south to New York's Catskill Mountains. That's probably an exaggeration, but you *can* see parts of all six New England states, including the Boston skyline, the Green Mountains of Vermont, and the Rhode Island shore. Not even New Hampshire's more celebrated Mount Washington, nearly twice as high, offers such a breathtaking view.

The only six-foot-square national park

Newspaperman Gene Fowler (1890–1960) is best remembered for biographies of such luminaries as John Barrymore, Jimmy Durante, and Jimmy Walker, as well as several novels and screenplays, and more than his share of quotable quips. "Success," he once said, "is a toy balloon among children armed with sharp pins."

Fowler is also the only person to single-handedly design and build a national park.

According to David Wallechinsky, Irving Wallace, and Amy Wallace, authors of *Significa*, Fowler con-

structed a six-foot-square rock garden for his wife Agnes
in the backyard of their Los Angeles home. When the
project was completed, he installed a sign reading st.
AGNES NATIONAL PARK.

It was supposed to be a joke, but the Fowlers' neigh-
bor, actor Thomas Mitchell, noticed the sign and men-
tioned it to his nephew, Secretary of Labor James P.
Mitchell, who in turn mentioned it to Secretary of the
Interior Fred A. Seaton. On their next trip out to the
West Coast, the two Eisenhower Cabinet members vis-
ited Gene and Agnes and officially dedicated St. Agnes
National Park.

The only U.S. town continuously inhabited since the *eleventh* century

When an earthquake sent them in search of a new
home, Indians from New Mexico's Enchanted Mesa established a pueblo community atop a nearby sandstone
mesa and called it Acoma, meaning "close to heaven."
That was in 1075—four centuries before Columbus—and
incredibly, the village still stands and people still live
there. Often called Sky City, Acoma is the oldest continuously occupied town in the United States.

Located about sixty-five miles west of Albuquerque,
Acoma sits on top of a seventy-five-hundred-foot-high
mesa, a well-defended fortress that was originally acces-
sible only by burro, or by climbing steep ladder trails.
These days, improved access routes allow even paunchy
tourists to reach the top without risking cardiac arrest.

Over the centuries, two additional settlements have
arisen further down the mesa, and that's where most
present-day Acomans live, tending farms, running businesses, and commuting to jobs in neighboring towns.
But a small cadre of residents lives atop the mesa year-

round, in Acoma proper, to keep the seventeenth-century flagstone and adobe church and other buildings in good repair. All Acomans make the climb to the top every September 2 for the Feast of Saint Stephen, Acoma's patron saint.

The only 110-mile-long bowling alley

About fifteen miles south of Fargo, North Dakota, just off Interstate 29, you can get on North Dakota Route 46 and drive 110 miles without once bothering your steering wheel. It's the longest stretch of road without a curve anywhere in the United States, and probably in the world.

The only mile-long city block

There aren't too many unique things about Charleston, West Virginia, but one of them is the 1500 block of Virginia Street. Residents proclaim it the longest unbroken city block in America. You can drive about a mile along this pleasant, tree-shaded thoroughfare without stopping at a single traffic signal or intersection.

The only city in the United States where Bastille Day is a public holiday

Kaplan, Louisiana, is an unpreposessing little town about 130 miles west of New Orleans. But on or around every July 14, the place shucks off its southern gentility and holds a two-day celebration of Bastille Day, a reminder of the town's French heritage.

There are outdoor fairs, street dancing, and the kind

of merriment most people associate with Mardi Gras, though on a smaller scale. But a Frenchman parachuting into Kaplan's annual *fais dodo* might be somewhat bewildered by the frenetic goings-on: Traditional French music is rarely heard, and the sound is distinctly New Orleans Cajun.

The only state with a carpetbagging official state flower

No peonies grow in Indiana—not naturally, anyway. But that didn't stop Governor Harold H. Handley from signing a 1957 bill making the peony the official state flower.

The fragrant but alien perennial was chosen to replace the homegrown zinnia as Indiana's state flower—though not without opposition. A large minority of lawmakers favored the dogwood blossom, which *is* native to Indiana; the idea of honoring a flower that only grows out of state struck them as absurd. But they were handily outvoted by the peonists. Some say a well-connected commercial peony grower may have influenced them.

The only hyperallergenic state flower

There are some 125 species of goldenrod, or *Solidago*—a bright yellow perennial that brings color to the countryside and the agonies of hell to millions of hayfever sufferers. Goldenrod grows just about everywhere in the continental United States, but for some perverse reason the Nebraska state legislature designated it the official state flower in 1895, and Kentucky followed suit in 1926. Neither state has yet taken the next logical step and made sneezing the official state sport.

Airborne goldenrod pollen inflicts its worst tortures from late summer, when the plant blooms, until the first frost. Marilyn Sande-Friedman, a New York City psychoanalyst whose husband Richard is from Nebraska, swears that on family visits to Omaha, her hay fever begins to act up before the plane is on the ground.

"I see those vast fields of yellow from the window," she says, "and my eyes and nose start to run."

The only desert in New England

About a mile and a half south of Freeport, Maine, is a three-hundred-acre expanse of sand dunes known as the Desert of Maine. At least that's what the guidebooks call it. And despite the absence of cacti, camels, and other traditional desert furnishings, it really does look like a desert. Even experts say it exhibits many of the characteristics of the Gobi and Sahara.

The place wasn't always so un-Maine-like. In the early 1800s, it was the site of a well-maintained potato farm owned by the Tuttle family. But over the years the Tuttles' cattle ate all the grass cover, leaving the topsoil prey to Maine's harsh winters. Sand blew in from the coast, and eventually, what had once been thriving, arable farmland became a desert.

Shifting sand dunes, some as high as seventy-five feet, have buried or destroyed most of the original buildings and trees. Only the barn remains, now used as a museum, where one can view "the world's largest sand painting." The local chamber of commerce bills the desert as "Maine's most famous natural phenomenon." It's probably the only desert in the world with its own gift shop.

The only municipality to outlaw visiting-team touchdowns

There's a lot of talk in sports about the home-field advantage. At the University of Arizona, that advantage has been legislated and institutionalized.

An ordinance duly passed by the city council of Tucson reads in part, "It shall be unlawful for any visiting football team or player to carry, convey, tote, kick, throw, pass or otherwise transport or propel any inflated pigskin across the University of Arizona goal line or score a safety within the confines of the City of Tucson, County of Pima, State of Arizona." Violators who dare trespass on the Arizona Wildcats' end zone face a three-hundred-dollar fine and a three-month jail sentence, if convicted.

The only Henniker in the world

"The only Henniker on earth"—that's how Henniker, New Hampshire, bills itself on postcards and T-shirts and in travel brochures. The quiet New England village dates back to Colonial times and was named for John Henniker, a wealthy English merchant.

The only state with a unicameral legislature

The bicameral legislature has been a fixture of the U.S. political landscape since Colonial times. Just as Congress has two houses, so does the legislature of every state in the Union—Nebraska excepted.

Nebraska went unicameral following a popular referendum in 1934. Proponents of the daring experiment argued that bills would get out of committee and onto the floor faster, and that the state would be spared the bickering and blame laying that inevitably arise between the houses of bicameral legislatures. With fewer lawmakers on the payroll, they added, the state could save money while raising salaries, thereby attracting a better class of person to the job.

By and large, the system has worked well, though there was one drawback no one counted on: Nebraska's striking four-hundred-foot-high capitol building, completed in 1932, was designed with a bicameral legislature in mind. When the state went unicameral two years later, it found itself in the embarrassing position of having an extra chamber on its hands, and no one to put in it.

The only east-west mountain range in the continental United States

The Uinta Mountains, which extend from northeastern Utah into southwestern Wyoming, lie at right angles to every other mountain range in the lower forty-eight. Formed around three hundred million years ago during the Carboniferous Period, the Uintas are an extension of the more conventionally aligned Rocky Mountain chain. They include Gilbert Peak (13,422 feet), Mount Emmons (13,428 feet), and King's Peak—the highest point in Utah (13,528 feet).

The only state whose state sport is jousting

Jousting was popular throughout most of the South in Colonial times. Though interest in the sport waned in many places, it held firm in Maryland, where a major tournament is held every October, drawing competitors from Virginia, the Carolinas, and even Louisiana. In 1962 Governor J. Millard Tawes signed a bill making jousting the state sport.

Unlike earlier forms of the sport, the object of jousting Maryland-style is to place the lance through a small metal ring—not an opponent's eye socket. Participants typically forgo armor in favor of modern-day riding attire.

The only one of the original thirteen American Colonies still governed by its original constitution

After the Colonies declared independence, the Massachusetts General Court drafted a state constitution. But the voters rejected it because it lacked a declaration of human rights and because it wasn't the work of an officially sanctioned constitutional convention.

So, in 1779 a proper convention met and drafted a new constitution. This time, the authors were careful to incorporate a detailed and compelling declaration of human rights; they also included provisions for an executive, judicial, and legislative branch, with each keeping the others honest through a system of checks and balances. In fact, the document was so well thought out that it later served as a model for the United States Constitution. By the time it was ratified by the voters in 1780, all the other states had constitutions in place. But only Massachusetts' remains in force—the oldest governing constitution of any sort in the world.

The only state whose laws are based on the Napoleonic Code and not English common law

English common law, with its emphasis on the binding power of custom and legal precedent, is the basis of the legal system in every state but Louisiana. There, the Napoleonic Code prevails.

Before it was purchased by the United States in 1803,

Louisiana had been colonized by France, Spain, and France again. So it's hardly a surprise that its laws were modeled after the edicts of French kings, the Royal Schedules of Spain and, above all, the Napoleonic Code—all of which were in turn derived from ancient Roman law. In fact, until 1898, all Louisiana state laws were published in English and French.

Louisiana is also the only state to have adopted the crawfish as its official state crustacean, and petrified palm wood as the state fossil.

The only state with a round border

Look at a map of the United States. Among the fifty states, you won't find one with a border that can be described as round—with the exception of Delaware. Its northern boundary is a geometrically perfect arc of a circle whose radius extends from the courthouse spire in New Castle, twelve miles to the south.

In the mid-1600s, Lord Baltimore, the founder of Maryland, and William Penn, the founder of the Pennsylvania Colony, squared off in a prolonged and agonizing boundary dispute. But it wasn't until 1732, long after their death, that any real progress was made toward settling the conflict. It was agreed to set the boundary between Delaware—Penn's turf—and Maryland with a north-south line bisecting the Chesapeake Peninsula, and then twelve miles past New Castle, which would then become the center of a circle. A draftsman's compass was used to measure and draw the arc.

But drawing precise lines was difficult, and the Penns and the Baltimores continued to quibble. It wasn't until 1769 that King George III approved the treaty and fixed the boundaries permanently.

The only state whose borders are entirely formed by nature

The obvious answer is Hawaii, since it's the only state surrounded entirely by water, consisting as it does of 8 major islands and 124 islets, all of them volcanic in origin. There isn't another state whose boundaries are not at least partly the work of surveyors, cartographers, and treaty makers.

On a 1989 visit to the Aloha State, Vice-President Dan Quayle was moved to observe, "Hawaii has always been a very pivotal role in the Pacific. It is in the Pacific. It is a part of the United States that is an island that's right here."

The only state bordered by only one other state

The only other state Maine touches is New Hampshire. Its other borders are shared with Canada. (The two chummiest states, geographically speaking, are Missouri and Tennessee: each touches eight other states.)

The only state where executions are carried out by firing squad

Utah law allows prisoners sentenced to death to choose between lethal injection and execution by firing squad. One who chose the latter was Gary Gilmore, whose execution on January 17, 1977, made headlines throughout the world and inspired a best-seller, Norman Mailer's The Executioner's Song.

Gilmore was the first person to be executed in the United States in ten years. Rather than standing at attention in front of a bullet-pocked wall in the manner of military-style executions, Gilmore was strapped into a chair; behind him was an embankment of sandbags and mattresses. From thirty feet away, five marksmen aimed at a paper target pinned over Gilmore's heart. Four had real bullets in their rifles; the fifth had blanks. All the bullets hit their mark, and Gilmore died within two minutes.

The only diamond-producing area in the United States

In 1906 a Murfreesboro, Arkansas, dirt farmer named John Huddleston couldn't figure out why no crops would grow on certain parts of his land. Poking around in the soil for a clue, he discovered two small crystals that he showed to a jeweler. They were diamonds.

A smallish diamond rush ensued, and Huddleston sold his farm to a mining company for thirty-eight thousand dollars. The land, which lay atop an ancient volcanic pipe, yielded diamonds for several years, though most were used for industrial purposes rather than jewelry. Exceptions include the 40.23-carat Uncle Sam diamond, and the 15.33-carat Star of Arkansas.

Eventually, the mine closed down, but the thirty-five-acre area was reopened to tourists in 1972 as Crater of Diamonds State Park. Since then, tourists have carted home nearly four thousand carats of diamonds. "Bring any find you suspect to be a diamond to the park office for a free weight and certification," reads a notice posted at the park entrance. "Anything you find is yours, no matter the value."

Digging tools can be rented at the gift shop, and lucky visitors have found amethyst, garnet, jasper, agate, and opal as well as diamonds. The park bills itself as "the world's only diamond site open to the public."

The only part of Manhattan on the United States mainland

Many Americans living west of the Hudson River are thankful that dirty, decadent Manhattan is an *island*, safely quarantined by water from the rest of the continent. What they don't know—and neither do many New Yorkers—is that a piece of New York City's most populous borough actually sits on the U.S. mainland.

It's called Marble Hill, a quiet fifty-two-acre neighborhood that's geographically part of the Bronx and joined to Manhattan Island by a bridge over the Harlem River. Until 1895 Marble Hill was physically one with Manhattan and separated from the Bronx by a shallow stream called Spuyten Duyvil Creek. With the digging of the Harlem Ship Canal that year—a 400' × 15' channel blasted out of solid rock—Marble Hill was severed from the rest of Manhattan; later the creek was filled in, welding the neighborhood forever to the U.S. mainland.

In 1693 a wealthy Dutch landowner named Frederick Philipse built one of the first toll bridges in the New World over the old creek and charged farmers as much as fifteen pounds a year to bring their produce into the city. The farmers cried foul, and one activist, John Palmer, rallied support for a second, free bridge until Philipse used his clout to get him drafted into the French and Indian Wars.

Palmer paid a mercenary to fight in his place and resumed his campaign for a free bridge. Philipse had him conscripted again, and Palmer hired a second mercenary. Drafted a third time, he again bought his way out and this time got the Free Farmers' Bridge completed.

Better, Palmer lived to see Philipse's bridge seized and turned into a free crossing by the new United States government following independence.

The only state without a wildlife refuge

There are over 380 publicly funded wildlife refuges in the United States, covering more than 30 million square miles, and home to some 220 species of mammal, 600 different birds, and a mind-boggling variety of amphibians, fish, trees, flowers, and plants. Every state in the Union has at least one refuge—with the exception of West Virginia.

The only state to attempt to make slandering a brisket a legally actionable offense

Food critics, breathe easy. A Colorado legislative initiative aimed at making it hot for people who snicker at Snickers, or give the raspberry to raspberries, has been defeated.

A bill passed in 1991 by the state legislature but vetoed by Governor Roy Romer would have allowed producers, marketers, and distributors of food to sue people who publicly defame their products.

The legislation was the brainchild of Colorado state representative Steve Acquafresca, an apple grower who said he was reacting to "a general trend in this country to unfairly and inaccurately disparage perishable food products." Reports that apples had been sprayed with Alar, a toxic preservative, had stung growers to the core, he said. And President George Bush's virulent antibroccolism seriously hurt sales of the vegetable.

The law would have permitted "any producer of perishable agricultural food products who suffers damages as a result of another's disparagement . . . to bring an action for damages." But not everyone in the food business was happy about it. One grocer told reporters that he occasionally griped to suppliers about the size and quality of their produce. "Am I safe?" he asked. "Could they come after me for saying these things?"

The only state that has never seen sub-zero weather

The mercury fell to 14°F at Haleakala National Park on the island of Maui, on January 2, 1961. It's the lowest temperature ever recorded anywhere in the Hawaiian islands. Even sunny Florida has weathered sub-zero temperatures.

Hawaii is also one of only two states where the thermometer has never risen above 100°. The other is Alaska.

The only Great Lake located entirely within the United States

Lake Michigan is bordered by Wisconsin, Illinois, Indiana, and Michigan. The shorelines of the other Great Lakes are all partly Canadian.

The only true desert in the United States

This may come as a surprise to anyone who has ever taken a midday stroll through California's Death Valley or the Mojave Desert, but they aren't deserts at all—strictly speaking. True, they look, feel, and behave the way deserts are supposed to; but the National Climate Center defines desert as a hot, arid tract *with less than eight inches of annual rainfall.* Applying those criteria, only the seventy-thousand-square-mile Sonoran desert, which occupies most of southwest Arizona, qualifies. It averages between three and seven inches of rainfall a year. The Mojave and Death Valley get more.

Death Valley may not qualify as a true desert, but it is unique. It is **the only place in the United States where nighttime temperatures often remain above 100°F.**

The only U.S. state that was once a kingdom

Discovered by Captain James Cook, who called them the Sandwich Islands, the Hawaiian islands were proclaimed a kingdom in 1810 under the warrior chief Kamehameha I, who had succeeded in uniting several lesser kingdoms under his rule. Western traders and missionaries soon arrived and began gnawing away at the kingdom's rich cultural underpinnings.

Though France and Britain, both looking to expand their empires, drooled over the subtropical paradise, Hawaii held fast to its independence through most of the nineteenth century.

In 1893 American sugar interests orchestrated a coup in the kingdom. The government was toppled and Queen Liliuokalani placed under house arrest for eight months in Iolani Palace in downtown Honolulu—**the only royal palace ever built on U.S. soil.**

Liliuokalani was the last of Hawaii's eight monarchs and its only queen; she was succeeded in 1894 by the first president of the republic of Hawaii, pineapple baron Sanford Dole, who lobbied Washington to annex the islands. Hawaii became a U.S. territory in 1900 and joined the union as the fiftieth state in 1959.

The only nonrectangular state flag

Forty-nine of the fifty states are content to be represented by rectangular flags; Ohio's is tapered, with a forked, or swallow-tailed, end. According to *Your State Flag*, by John Robert Gebhart, the fork points symbolize Ohio's hills and valleys; the broad red and blue horizontal stripes evoke the state's roads and waterways. The design was adopted in 1902.

The official state beverage of Ohio is tomato juice.

The only state with two constitutions

From the moment it was called to order on July 13, 1857, Minnesota's first constitutional convention was wracked by bitter personal and political differences between the Democratic and Republican delegations. Things got off on the wrong foot when the leaders of both parties seized the podium simultaneously, each refusing to yield to the other. After a day of bickering, the two parties retreated to separate halls, where they held their own conventions and drafted their own constitutions.

Not surprisingly, the two documents differed wildly, so a committee of five Democrats and five Republicans was formed to weld them into a single constitution. It was hard work and the sessions were stormy; once, former Democratic governor Willis Gorman answered a critic by smashing his cane over his head.

At summer's end, when the committee finally produced a document acceptable to both parties, many delegates on each side balked at signing it unless members of the opposing party were barred from doing so. The solution: Two constitutions were prepared by scribes—one on white paper, for the Republicans to sign, the other on blue paper, for the Democrats. Today, both are in the hands of the Minnesota Archives Commission.

Although the two handwritten documents were supposed to be identical, about three hundred discrepancies, mostly involving spelling, punctuation, and grammar, crept in. They were never resolved, and Minnesota remains the only state governed under the authority of two different constitutions.

The only place where you can simultaneously be in four states and two Indian reservations

Thirty-eight miles southwest of Cortez, Colorado, a large stone slab set into the ground and surrounded by a low wooden rail marks the point where Utah, Arizona, New Mexico, and Colorado—as well as the Ute Mountain and Navajo Indian reservations—meet.

Although 5 national parks and 18 national monuments are located within a 150-mile radius of the Four Corners Monument, there is little of interest to see at Four Corners itself. But never mind—on a typical summer day, the spot draws at least two thousand visitors. Most come for no other reason than to wait their turn to stand in the center of the slab and to be photographed straddling the borders of four states.

Few visitors linger more than ten minutes at Four Corners. One exception was World War II correspondent Ernie Pyle, who once paid a long, reflective visit to Four Corners in prewar times and wrote a memorable column about it the next day.

The only single-tree national forest in the United States

In 1958 several members of the 748th Aircraft Control and Warning Squadron of Kotzebue Air Force Base, Alaska, took a few days off to go fishing in warmer climes. They came back with a black spruce seedling that they planted in the tundra to see if it would survive. There was no reason to think it would—in Kotzebue, the permafrost is forty feet thick and the Arctic Circle is just a short cab ride away. Trees don't grow easily there.

This one did, however. Tended lovingly by base personnel and honorary forest rangers recruited from nearby villages, the lone spruce is still there, enclosed by a white picket fence and marked with a sign reading KOTZEBUE NATIONAL FOREST. Tours of northwestern Alaska invariably include a stop at the tree, which today stands more than thirteen feet high.

The only point in the United States from which you can walk across the international date line

Little Diomede, Alaska, is a dot-sized island in the Bering Strait, just off the tip of the Seward Peninsula, and about one and a half miles from the international date line. When much of the strait freezes in winter, it's possible to walk from Little Diomede across the date line and into the future. Keep going and you'll hit Big Diomede, two miles farther west.

Big Diomede looks pretty much like Little Diomede—remote, icebound, sparsely settled. The big difference is that it's in Siberia. In fact, the icy midwinter link between Big and Little Diomede constitutes **the only footpath connecting the United States and the Soviet Union.**

The only state whose name is pure gibberish

The name *Idaho* was first made popular in 1860 by mine owners who thought it would make an appropriate name for the Pikes Peak mining country. It was, they claimed, the Kiowa Apache word for "Comanche"—the dominant tribe in the area. Congress was set to put its imprimatur on the name when it was discovered that *Idaho* meant nothing in Apache or any other language. It was a hoax. The area was instead christened Colorado at the last minute.

But Idaho would not die. That same year, the name began cropping up in the Pacific Northwest. Now it was said to derive from the Shoshonean *ee-dah-how,* meaning "Behold the sun coming down on the mountains." Others claimed it meant "gem of the mountains," and still others, "salmon eaters," a term by which the Shoshone themselves were known.

In any event, a county in Washington Territory was officially named Idaho. An area rich in silver became known as the Idaho mines. In 1863, one of the senators who had blocked the use of the name two years earlier, now supported it wholeheartedly. Congress, strangely unwilling to accept that the word was a fake, went along and dubbed the territory Idaho.

The only major city named by tossing a coin

In 1843 William Overton was canoeing up the Columbia River in western Oregon, in search of a piece of land to farm, when he happened upon a densely wooded tract at the mouth of the Willamette River. In exchange for a twenty-five-cent loan to pay the filing fee, he ceded half his six-hundred-forty-acre claim to another settler, Amos L. Lovejoy; later, Overton backed out entirely, bartering his share to Francis W. Pettygrove for one hundred dollars' worth of food and supplies.

The following year, Lovejoy and Pettygrove began surveying their holdings, clearing the land, laying out streets, and building the first houses. Pettygrove, who had lived in Maine, wanted to call the new settlement Portland, after Maine's capital; Lovejoy, who hailed from Massachusetts, favored Boston. They tossed a coin and Pettygrove won. Portland it was.

Twenty-four states with only one area code:

1. Alabama (205)
2. Alaska (907)
3. Arizona (602)
4. Arkansas (501)
5. Connecticut (203)
6. Delaware (302)
7. Hawaii (808)
8. Idaho (208)
9. Maine (207)
10. Maryland (301)
11. Mississippi (601)
12. Montana (406)
13. Nevada (702)
14. New Hampshire (603)
15. New Mexico (505)
16. North Dakota (701)
17. Oregon (503)
18. Rhode Island (401)
19. South Carolina (803)
20. South Dakota (605)
21. Utah (801)
22. Vermont (802)
23. West Virginia (304)
24. Wyoming (307)

WIDE, WIDE WORLD

The only country in the world small enough to have a street address

Ministates like Monaco and the Vatican may be smaller than the average shopping mall, but they are vast empires compared to the Sovereign Military Order of Malta, or SMOM. A walled piazza about half the size of a football field, SMOM is tucked away on a side street in central Rome at 68 Via Condotti. It's next door to a menswear shop, and a three-minute walk from the American Express office.

SMOM originated in Jerusalem in 1048 as the Knights Hospitaler, an order of monks who cared for sick pilgrims and, later, for Christian soldiers wounded in the First Crusade. Eventually, the Hospitalers developed into a formidable military power in their own right. They relocated to Cyprus in 1291, and to Rhodes in 1309, and took over the Mediterranean island of Malta in 1530. By then, they were a naval presence to reckon with, although Napoleon succeeded in ousting them in 1798. The order has occupied its present address since 1834.

Despite its sovereign status, SMOM is not exactly a superpower these days. Its population is well below one hundred and its air force consists of fifty planes (most in disrepair). Ruled by a grand master, SMOM has delegates to several countries and issues license plates, money, passports, and postage stamps.

As in the beginning, SMOM's principal export is good works: It tends hospitals, clinics, and leprosariums throughout the world. In the 1960s and 1970s, unarmed SMOM medical teams treated wounded children in Vietnam.

The only guided tour of a municipal sewer system

If liquid- and solid-waste disposal is your cup of tea, put the Eiffel Tower and the Louvre on your B list next time you visit Paris and, instead, make a guided tour of the Paris sewers, or *les égouts*, your first order of business.

Built by Baron Georges-Eugène Haussmann in the 1800s, the Paris sewers are among the finest and most extensive in Europe. Indeed, the vast maze of pipes, sumps, and subterranean tunnels make up one of the great achievements of civil engineering.

The system consists of four main 18′ × 15′ tunnels, plus countless branches. Street signs and building numbers are posted, corresponding to above-ground locations. Tour guides are fond of pointing out the underside of Paris's most elegant restaurants.

Tours, offered every Monday and Wednesday and the last Saturday of each month, from 2:00–5:00 P.M., depart from the Pont de l'Alma on the Left Bank. (Alma-Marceau is the nearest Metro station). The tour lasts about an hour and costs eight francs. There is a museum and gift shop but no snack bar.

The *Michelin Green Guide to Paris* gives the tour no stars out of a possible four.

The only middle-eastern country without a desert

Lebanon has most of the earmarks of a middle-eastern nation—a large Muslim population, a Mediterranean climate, and a lot of olive trees. What it doesn't have is a desert.

Lebanon's chief geographical features include several mountain ranges, a narrow coastal plain, and a central highland known as the Bika Valley. But if you're looking for a desert, the nearest one is in Syria.

The only present-day gynecocracy

Most countries these days are governed by humorless men in business suits. But in Norway it's the women who run things—as ably (or ineptly) as their male counterparts do anywhere else.

The dominant figure in Norwegian politics is Prime Minister Gro Harlem Brundtland, a Harvard-educated physician elected in 1986. Half her cabinet members are also women, as are the leaders of both opposition parties, the mayor of Oslo (who was elected over a female candidate in 1991), and nearly half the members of the Storting, the Norwegian parliament.

Norway has long been light-years ahead of Britain, the United States, and other industrialized countries in granting equal rights to women. But in 1983 feminism got an extra boost there when Dr. Brundtland's Labor party ruled that at least 40 percent of its candidates henceforth had to be women. The other major parties soon followed Labor's lead.

Not surprisingly, Norway's political agenda has leaned sharply toward such issues as sexual equality and child care in recent years. Political observer Bernt Aardal notes another development. The country's female leaders, he says, "all call each other by their first names. The men would never have been so informal."

The only Hindu kingdom

There aren't many countries left where the real power resides in the hands of a monarch. Nepal is one, and the only kingdom ruled by a Hindu monarch.

Nearly 90 percent of the population of this tiny land-locked Himalayan nation is Hindu. Over the past few decades, Nepal has made a few concessions to democratic processes—a new constitution was ratified in 1962, and the government now includes a national assembly, the Panchayat, and a council of ministers. But the constitution still vests absolute authority in King Birenda Bir Bikram Shah Dev, political parties are illegal, and members of the assembly and the cabinet have only advisory powers.

The only place from which you can see the Atlantic and Pacific oceans simultaneously

If you have the stamina to scale Mount Irazú in Costa Rica (it's 11,200 feet above sea level), as well as the nerve (it's an active volcano), you'll be treated to the world's only simultaneous view of the Atlantic and Pacific oceans. The mountain rises from the town of Cartago, about fourteen miles southeast of the Costa Rican capital, San José.

The only city in the world with coin-operated oxygen dispensers

Anyone who has wheezed through an afternoon in smog-choked, mile-high Mexico City and found relief in publicly dispensed oxygen may very well ask, "Why didn't they think of this before?" In 1991 the city installed twenty-five *casetas de oxigeno* (oxygen booths) throughout the downtown area. Two dollars buys you a minute's worth of O_2.

If no other city offers its pedestrians similar amenities, it's only because no other city is plagued with such filthy air. Many if not most of the three million cars that drive through Mexico City each day lack any sort of emission-control device; together with nearby oil refineries and factories, they belch twelve hundred tons of pollution into the air daily.

Nor does the altitude help matters—at seventy-five hundred feet, a pedestrian gets about one third less oxygen in every lungful than he would at sea level. The city's number-one killer is respiratory diseases.

The *casetas* may improve matters, but as *The Economist* noted, "If they are anything like the city's telephone booths, they will not work for very long either."

The only single-color national flag

Between 1972 and 1977 Libya was content to fly the same flag as Egypt. It was red, white, and black—the pan-Arab colors—denoting Tripoli's strong ties to the Cairo government.

Those ties came undone in November 1977 when Egyptian president Anwar Sadat visited Israel for peace talks with Israeli president Menachem Begin. To protest Egypt's treachery, Libya quit the Federation of Arab Republics and redid its flag entirely in green, a sacred color to Muslims. Libyan strongman Muammar Qaddafi insisted the new color scheme was only temporary, but it remains unchanged as of this writing.

The only foreign capital named after a U.S. president

Liberia was founded in 1822 as a project of the American Colonization Society, whose objective was to repatriate freed American slaves in West Africa. Their main settlement was named Monrovia, after President James Monroe, who was an active member of the society; it later became Liberia's capital. Today, many Monrovians are descendants of American blacks, and much of the local architecture has a distinctly antebellum-South look.

The only country in the world where the major cause of injuries is trees

In Papua New Guinea these days, headhunters aren't anywhere near the danger they're purported to be. Neither are venomous snakes, scorpions, or quicksand. The real killer there is trees.

A four-year study conducted by the *British Medical Journal* revealed that 41 percent of admissions to Provincial Hospital, in Milne Bay Province, were for injuries resulting from falling trees, falls from trees, falling coconuts, and tripping over fallen branches.

The only country in Southeast Asia never colonized by a European power

Except for Thailand, every nation in Southeast Asia has been ruled at one time or another by a European power—not that the colonialists haven't lusted after Thailand too.

Portugal was the first of the Western powers to pay attention to Siam—it wasn't called Thailand until 1939—sending traders and missionaries there beginning in 1511. In 1767 Siam was conquered by neighboring Burma, which maintained control for fifteen years before an uprising led by King Rama I put them to rout.

By the nineteenth century Siam had established loose rule over lands in what are now Cambodia, Malaysia, and Laos. These were annexed by France and Great Britain, who then threatened to gobble up the remainder of Siam until an 1896 treaty established Thailand's present boundaries beyond question. At the time, and for many years to come, Thailand was the only sovereign southeastern Asian nation from New Guinea west to Pakistan.

The only continent that has no glaciers

One tenth of the earth's land area is covered by glaciers. Other than Australia, every continent has at least one.

The only nonrectangular national flag

Shaped like a sideways W, the Nepalese flag looks less like a national icon than the kind of souvenir pennants handed out at supermarket openings. The lower part depicts the sun, originally the symbol of Nepal's royal house; the upper part shows the moon, representing the Rana dynasty, which ruled this tiny Himalayan kingdom from 1846–1951.

The only mountain taller than Everest

Measured in the conventional way—from sea level—Mount Everest, at 29,028 feet, is the world's tallest peak. Chimborazo, in the Ecuadorean Andes, is about eighty-five hundred feet lower.

But in 1975 a Smithsonian Institution geophysicist,

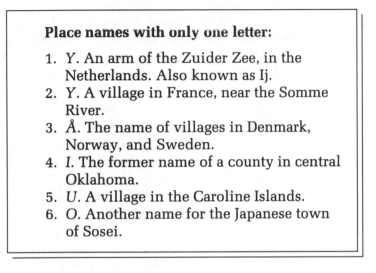

Place names with only one letter:

1. Y. An arm of the Zuider Zee, in the Netherlands. Also known as Ij.
2. Y. A village in France, near the Somme River.
3. Å. The name of villages in Denmark, Norway, and Sweden.
4. I. The former name of a county in central Oklahoma.
5. U. A village in the Caroline Islands.
6. O. Another name for the Japanese town of Sosei.

E. Michael Gaposchkin, pointed out that Chimborazo sits smack atop a prominent equatorial bulge; Everest, meanwhile, is situated on a comparatively flat part of the globe. Measured from the center of the earth, therefore, Chimborazo is 7,058 feet taller than Everest.

The only major city heated entirely by natural hot springs

Since early times, Iceland's vast network of underground geothermal springs have been used for bathing, washing, and even baptism—early converts to Christianity were said to prefer it to baptism by ice water. Today, the same springs are used to heat most of the country's schools, homes, hospitals, greenhouses, and public baths. The nation's capital, Reykjavík, (pop. 95,799), is totally reliant on geothermal heating.

Heating by gas, electricity, wood, and oil is all but

unknown in Reykjavík. Instead, spring water, heated naturally almost to boiling, is pumped from outside the city through two 10-mile-long pipes directly into the city's kitchen taps and heating elements. Losing fewer than 2°F along the way, the water is used to heat homes to a toasty 70°–75° year-round. But there's a catch: Kitchens and bathrooms often smell of sulfur.

Even outdoor pools are heated geothermally, allowing Reykjavíkians to swim comfortably in the dead of winter. But don't be fooled by the "Ice" in Iceland. Though the country is hardly tropical in climate—its northern border abuts the Arctic Circle—Iceland is warmed by the Gulf Stream, and even in midwinter, temperatures rarely fall below freezing. Reykjavík's name is likewise a misnomer: It means "smoky bay," but a less smoggy or smoky city you're not apt to find. It takes its name from the smoke that rises from the hot springs; the city is virtually pollution-free.

The only country in South America whose native language is English

Although French, Spanish, and Dutch settlers established colonies in the territory known as Guiana, it was Great Britain that finally declared sovereignty in 1815. Located on the north coast of South America, east of Venezuela, Guiana became a British Crown colony in 1928 and achieved independence—and a new spelling of its name—in 1966. The country achieved a different kind of prominence in 1978, when nine hundred members of the Jonestown cult committed suicide there.

Today, Guyana's population consists largely of East Indians, Africans, and indigenous Indians; British-born inhabitants are a tiny minority. Yet English is overwhelmingly the language of choice in most schools, and in government and commercial affairs. Most shop signs, newspapers, and TV shows are in English; the national anthem is "Dear Land of Guyana." And the look of Georgetown, the capital, is more English than South American.

The only place outside the United States where alligators are found

All those stories you've heard of missionaries and hunters winding up as fast-food for alligators in the Amazon are a "croc." Outside the southeastern United States, the only place in the world where alligators occur naturally is the Yangtze-Kiang river basin in eastern China.

Although American alligators (*Alligator mississippiensis*) are still found in abundance, their much smaller Chinese cousins (*Alligator sinensis*) are rapidly becoming extinct. As for the fierce-looking lizards who patrol the waters of South America, they are either crocodiles or caimans. While all three are members of the order Crocodilia, alligators have broader heads, blunter snouts, and more conventional dental work. When an alligator shuts its mouth, the teeth stay inside; when a crocodile clams up, its fourth tooth on either side of the lower jaw remains visible outside the mouth.

The only Islamic country in Europe

Officially, the People's Socialist Republic of Albania is an atheist state: One of the few outposts of hard-line Stalinism left in the world, Albania has banned churches, mosques, and religious observations since 1967. In actuality, however, 70 percent of all Albanians belong to the Sunni or Bektashi sects of Islam. Most others are Eastern Orthodox or Roman Catholic.

A small, mountainous country north of Greece on the Balkan Peninsula, Albania, then ancient Illyria, went Christian after the fall of Rome, but was converted to Islam after being conquered by the Turks in 1478. The country remained an Ottoman province until it proclaimed independence in 1912. But at the grass-roots level, at least, its Islamic heritage survives.

The only country ever relocated from one continent to another

Annexed by Colombia in 1821, Panama remained a province of that South American country until 1903, when it declared its independence. To be sure, the idea of secession wasn't altogether Panama's: U.S. president Theodore Roosevelt wanted to build a canal across the Panamanian isthmus and knew the only way that would happen would be if Panama were free of Colombian rule.

In concert with Philippe Bunau-Varilla, a French engineer and businessman who stood to gain handsomely from the construction of the Canal, Roosevelt instigated a revolt—and accorded the rebels diplomatic recognition ninety minutes after they seized power. Meanwhile, Bunau-Varilla wrote a declaration of independence and constitution for the new regime in Room 1162 of New York's Waldorf-Astoria Hotel; back home in Highland Falls, New York, his wife stitched the first Panamanian flag.

The United States sent warships to protect the new government against counterattack. Construction crews and dredging equipment soon arrived. And the cartographers declared that Panama, which had always been part of South America, was henceforth part of Central America—the southernmost section of North America.

The only country with an orchestra bigger than its army

The tiny principality of Monaco, about half the size of New York City's Central Park, has a standing army of eighty-two at last count. There are eighty-five musicians in the Monte Carlo National Orchestra.

The only road in London where traffic is required to keep to the right

Savoy Court is a short street leading to the Savoy Theatre and Savoy Hotel, both built in the Strand in the 1880s. To facilitate arrivals and departures at the theater, Parliament enacted a law many years ago requiring vehicles on Savoy Court to drive on the right. It may well be the only road in all Great Britain with that quirky rule.

The only place in the world that can truly be described as nowhere

. . . is the point where the equator and prime meridian intersect, or latitude 0°0′; longitude 0°0′. Since that nonpoint happens to be in the Gulf of Guinea, off the west coast of Africa, the elevation above sea level is equally nonexistent.

The nearest point on dry land is Dixcove, Ghana—latitude 5°31′ N; longitude 0°12′ W. Cartographers have dubbed it "the land nearest nowhere." Those who've been there say the description is apt: According to Alex Newton, author of *West Africa: A Survival Kit*, Dixcove has no drinkable water, millions of mosquitoes, and little else to recommend it. For some reason, however, it is popular among European residents as a weekend beach resort.

SPORTS

The only woman to strike out Babe Ruth

On their way north from spring training in 1931, the New York Yankees stopped off in Tennessee to play a preseason exhibition game against the minor league Chattanooga Lookouts. Pitcher Clyde Barfoot started for Chattanooga, but after getting shelled by the Yankees in the first inning, he was relieved by rookie lefthander Virne Beatrice "Jackie" Mitchell.

Seventeen years old, Ms. Mitchell didn't have much speed, but she had flummoxed a batter or two with her breaking stuff. "I had a drop pitch," she later said, "and when I was throwing it right, you couldn't touch it."

Ruth was the first batter she faced. After missing the corner with her first pitch, she fooled the Babe on the next two. He took the fourth pitch for a ball, then got called out on strikes. He hurled his bat in rage; the crowd went crazy. "It wasn't a show," said Ms. Mitchell years later. "He was really mad."

Lou Gehrig was next up, and incredibly, Mitchell fanned him too—on three straight pitches. Then Tony Lazzeri walked, and Ms. Mitchell was pulled for a reliever. Despite her talent, she never made it to the majors—probably because of Commissioner Kenesaw

Landis's opposition. It didn't matter to Ms. Mitchell. All she wanted, she told reporters, "was to stay in baseball long enough to get money to buy a roadster."

The only three-sided baseball game in major league history

Interest in baseball was not exactly running at a fever pitch in 1944. The nation's attention was more intensely fixed on places like Bastogne and Dieppe than Crosley Field and the Polo Grounds. Besides, most of the good players were away on military duty, leaving the likes of Pete Gray, one-armed outfielder for the St. Louis Browns, and fifteen-year-old Joe Nuxhall of the Reds, the youngest player in major league history, to help maintain ballpark attendance at minimal levels.

To stir interest in baseball and raise money for war bonds, the New York Yankees, New York Giants, and Brooklyn Dodgers locked horns June 26 before a capacity crowd at New York's Polo Grounds in major league baseball's only three-way matchup. Paul Althaus Smith, a Columbia University mathematics professor, worked out a system that had two teams on the field at any given time, with the third team sitting out every third inning.

While the Giants watched from the dugout, the Dodgers jumped on the Yankees for a run in the first inning. They scored two more runs in the second inning and another two in the eighth. The Yankees did all their scoring—a single run—in the eighth, courtesy of a pair of errors by Giant shortstop Buddy Kerr. Final score: Dodgers 5, Yankees 1, Giants 0.

The only one-armed major league player in modern baseball

Pete Gray lost his right arm in a car accident at age six but remained determined to make baseball his career. In 1942, his first year as a professional, he played for the Three Rivers Club in Quebec, leading the Canadian-American League with a .381 batting average. He batted .299 for Memphis the following year, and .333 in 1944, when he also stole 63 bases.

In 1945 Gray played center field for the St. Louis Browns. His batting average slipped to .218 in the majors, but he hit 6 doubles and 2 triples in 61 games. Playing a cautious defense, he would field a ball with his gloved hand, then tuck the glove under the stump of his right shoulder, grab the ball with his left hand, and throw it to the infield, all in one fluid motion.

After the 1945 season, Gray went on a barnstorming tour, often playing opposite Jess Alexander, a Negro Leagues center fielder with one arm. But he never played big league ball again and finished up his professional career with Dallas in 1949.

The only major league pitcher to start for both the American and National leagues in the All-Star game and to post victories for each league

Vida Blue was the phenomenal twenty-two-year-old rookie lefthander for the Oakland Athletics who started for the American League in the 1971 All-Star game. In three innings on the mound, he gave up only two hits and three runs while striking out three, and was the pitcher of record as the American League won 6–4.

Blue's performance fell off in subsequent years, but in 1978 he was on his way at midseason to an impressive 18–10 record for the San Francisco Giants and was named the National League starter in the All-Star game. Although he didn't figure in the Nationals' 7–3 win, he achieved the distinction of becoming the only pitcher ever to start an All-Star game for each league.

Again, as a Giant, Blue pitched an inning of no-hit ball in the 1981 All-Star game. It was enough to give him the win and a place in the books as the All-Star game's only two-league winner.

Blue's career ended with a sad postscript: Following his 1981 All-Star triumph, his pitching deteriorated, and he was traded to the Kansas City Royals. In the early 1980s he served a prison term for cocaine use and was suspended from baseball for a year. He later made a brief comeback with the Athletics but retired abruptly after failing a urine test to detect cocaine use.

The only pitcher to win a World Series game without having won a game during the regular season

Virgil Trucks was a superb pitcher who compiled a 177–135 record over seventeen years, mostly with the Detroit Tigers. In fact, he tossed two no-hitters for the last-place Tigers in 1952, winning only three other games all season.

Trucks missed most of the 1945 season because he'd been in the navy. Discharged after V-J day, he returned in time to pitch five innings of three-hit ball against the St. Louis Browns on the last day of the season and help the Tigers clinch the pennant. He was not credited with the win, however, and he ended the season with an 0–0 record.

That October, the so-so Tigers faced the lackluster

Cubs in a World Series so barren of promise that Chicago sportswriter Warren Brown predicted, "I believe neither team will win a single game." The Tigers triumphed in seven; the winless Trucks went the distance in the second game, beating the Cubs 4–1.

The only baseball player to catch a baseball dropped from a hovering blimp

It happened on July 3, 1939, at the Golden Gate Exposition in San Francisco. The San Francisco Seals, of the Pacific Coast League, were on hand, and manager Lefty O'Doul thought the crowd might get a kick out of seeing one of his stars try to catch a ball dropped from the Goodyear blimp, circling above the fairgrounds at fifteen-hundred feet.

He had only one taker—catcher Joe "Mule" Sprinz, who stood below while O'Doul released a baseball from the airship. It was wild and fell into the stands. He dropped another, and it hit the ground. The third was right on the money.

"I saw it all the way," Sprinz later said. "But it looked about the size of an aspirin tablet."

Gaining speed at thirty-two feet per second squared, the ball slammed into Sprinz's upraised catcher's mitt with the force of a howitzer shell, driving his gloved hand into his face. He suffered lacerations of the mouth and nose and a fractured jaw and lost five teeth. But he remained conscious and fielded the ball cleanly.

It was probably the most daring, if not the greatest, fielding play in baseball history. But why did he do it?

"All the other players refused and walked off the field," Sprinz said. "But I said to myself, 'God hates a coward.'"

A sturdy .300 hitter with the Seals, Sprinz would

later prove less impressive in the majors. In two years with the Cleveland Indians and one with the Cardinals, he got into 21 games and batted .170.

Less heroic than Sprinz's achievement, but worthy of mention nonetheless, is Washington Senator catcher Gabby Street's clean handling of a ball released in 1908 from the observation deck of the Washington Monument, 555 feet up. And a former minor league outfielder named Leonard Burton fielded a ball dropped from an airplane flying at the same height at a Birmingham, Alabama, picnic sponsored by the Stockham Valve Company in 1946.

During spring training in 1915, manager Wilbert Robinson, of the hapless Brooklyn Dodgers, agreed to catch a ball dropped from an aircraft as part of a publicity stunt at Daytona Beach, Florida. But someone replaced the baseball with a grapefruit, which plunked Robinson on the head, shattering on impact.

Never a model of grace under pressure, and blinded temporarily by the stinging juice, Robinson assumed the juice was blood and the jagged shards of rind were pieces of his skull, and began screaming that he was dead. Though he accused Casey Stengel of the prank, it turned out to be the work of the pilot, famed aviator Ruth Law.

"They were supposed to deliver a ball to me at the hotel, but when it got time to take off, no one had showed up from the ball club," she said years later in an interview. "I asked around, and one of my mechanics asked, 'How about a grapefruit?' He had one along in his lunchbox. I took it and when I got over the ballpark I let it go, never figuring it would come even close. When I heard it had hit the manager, I stayed away from the park for the rest of the spring."

0 for 1: baseball players whose entire career consisted of only a single at bat—or less:

1. *Walter Alston.* St. Louis Cardinals, 1936. Later achieved greater diamond fame as longtime manager of the Brooklyn and Los Angeles Dodgers.
2. *Lefty Atkinson.* Washington Senators, 1927. Reached first on an error and later scored. Never heard from again.
3. *Red Barbary.* Washington Senators, 1943. A wartime rookie.
4. *Honey Barnes.* New York Yankees, 1926. Drew a walk in his only plate appearance. Credited with *no* official at bats.
5. *John Corriden.* Brooklyn Dodgers, 1946. Drew a walk, later scored. Afterward vanished from sight.
6. *Moonlight Graham.* New York Giants, 1905. Never made it to the plate, but Burt Lancaster played him in the film *Field of Dreams.*
7. *Carl McNabb.* Detroit Tigers, 1945. His team went on to beat the Cubs in the World Series—without him.
8. *Bob Meinke.* Cincinnati Reds, 1910. Actually played in two games, but made it to the plate only once. A real baseball dynasty: His father, Frank, had a lifetime .163 batting average with the Detroit Wolverines in 1884 and 1885.

9. *Gene Patton*. Boston Braves, 1944.
   Never batted, but in his own small way,
   helped pace Boston to a sixth-place
   finish.
10. *Tom Richardson*. St. Louis Browns,
    1917. A rookie at thirty-four, made a
    single pinch-hit appearance, then sank
    without a trace.

The only telegraph operator listed in the players' roster of *The Baseball Encyclopedia*

In every edition since it was first published in 1969, the respected *Baseball Encyclopedia* accorded Lou Proctor a one-line entry. His lifetime stats: one game played (in 1912, with the St. Louis Browns), no official at bats, hits, strikeouts, stolen bases, or fielding plays. In his only plate appearance he walked.

But in 1988 the editors of the encyclopedia discovered they'd gone for Proctor's scroogie: He was actually a press-box telegraph operator who'd inserted his name into a box score. He never appeared in a game.

Proctor was ejected from subsequent editions.

The only professional pitcher to give up more than fifty runs in a nine-inning game

A star pitcher for the Texarkana Texas Leaguers, C. B. DeWitt was on the mound on June 15, 1902, as his team squared off against Corsicana. He was still on the mound nine innings later after having yielded fifty-one runs, including eight home runs to one batter, surely the most generous pitching performance on record.

Final score: 51–3.

The only fly ball to violate the axiom that whatever goes up must come down

During a 1984 game at the Metrodome, home of the Minnesota Twins, Dave Kingman of the Oakland Athletics hit a fly ball into the fiberglass-fabric netting of the dome, 180 feet up, where it stuck. With no specific rule to guide them, the umpires gave Kingman a ground-rule double. It didn't help the Athletics' cause, however; they lost 3–1.

The ball, later retrieved by stadium groundsmen, is on display at the National Baseball Museum in Cooperstown, New York.

The only baseball game called on account of rain in a domed stadium

Torrential rains drenched Houston, Texas, in June 1976. Flooding near the Astrodome, home of the Houston Astros, was so bad that it was inaccessible by foot or car, and a game with the Pirates had to be postponed.

Though umpires, ground crew, and fans couldn't get near the place, about twenty players and ballpark employees couldn't get *out*, and wound up eating dinner on tables set up on the field. "It's not exactly a rainout," said an Astros spokesman. "It's a rain-in."

The only modern baseball player to steal six bases in a game twice

Until Otis Nixon managed the feat in 1991, Eddie Collins was the only player to have stolen six bases in a single game. More remarkably he did it twice, within the space of a week and a half, in September 1912.

Over the course of a twenty-five-year major league career—another record—Collins distinguished himself as one of the game's greatest players—a .333 lifetime hitter who led the American League four times in stolen bases (though not in 1912) and three consecutive times in runs scored. One of the few innocent players on the 1919 Chicago Black Sox, he was inducted into the Baseball Hall of Fame in 1939.

The only Brooklyn Dodger to play in every World Series game against the New York Yankees

The Bombers and the Bums met forty-four times during their seven Subway Series between 1941 and 1956, and shortstop Harold "Pee Wee" Reese never missed a game. He was there when Mickey Owen dropped the third strike in 1941, when Al Gionfriddo stole a home run from Joe DiMaggio in 1947, and when Don Larsen pitched his perfect game in 1956. As a World Series competitor, Reese batted .272, hit 2 homers, and drove in 16 runs.

Though the Dodgers often gave the Yankees a run for their money, they managed to win only once—in 1955. As the Los Angeles Dodgers, their record against the Yankees is considerably better.

The only major league team with three 40-home-run hitters

The Atlanta Braves didn't win the National League pennant in 1973 or even the division title. In fact, they barely finished in the league, winding up in fifth place with an anemic 76–85 record.

Yet, remarkably, the Braves turned in so forgettable a showing while hammering out a near record 208 home runs, of which 124 were hit by three starters: Davey Johnson, future manager of the New York Mets, hit 43 (one of baseball's most baffling flukes: in no other season did he hit more than 18). Darrell Evans hit 41. And Hank Aaron, who would go on to break Babe Ruth's career home run record the following year, hit 40.

The only midget to play major league baseball

The St. Louis Browns were thirty-six games out of first place on August 19, 1951, when they came to bat in the first inning of a Sunday game against the visiting Detroit Tigers.

Though Browns' owner Bill Veeck made no mention of a midget in the starting lineup, 3'7", sixty-five-pound Eddie Gaedel, wearing number 1/8, was sent to pinch-hit for the posted lead-off batter, Frank Saucier.

Crouching, Gaedel offered the pitcher a one-and-a-half-inch-high strike zone. However, he stood tall at the plate, assuming what Veeck later described as "a fair approximation of Joe DiMaggio's classic style." He walked on four pitches and trotted down to first, where he was replaced by a pinch runner.

Though baseball commissioner Ford Frick banned Gaedel, and all other midgets, from further baseball play, Gaedel showed up several more times on the diamond. In a 1960 stunt arranged by Veeck, then the owner of the Chicago White Sox, Gaedel and three other midgets, dressed in Martian garb, were lowered from a helicopter onto the infield. There they pronounced the White Sox' diminutive Luis Aparicio and Nellie Fox honorary Martians and pledged eternal support in their struggle against all earthlings.

Another player to put on your short list is Frank Shannon, a 5'3" infielder who played thirty-two games

for the old Washington Senators and the Louisville Colo-
nels in the 1890s. He's the shortest nonmidget ever to
see action in the major leagues.

The only physical therapist ejected from a major league game

Pat Screnar, the Los Angeles Dodgers' physical thera-
pist, was tossed out of a 1983 home game by umpire Bill
Williams for disputing a strike call too vociferously.

The only home run Babe Ruth hit in the minors

In all fairness, Ruth didn't get much of a chance to
hit during his brief stint in the minors. He was primarily
a pitcher who batted only 121 times in 46 games with
the Baltimore Orioles and the Providence Grays, of the
International League.

Ruth had spent part of 1914 with the Red Sox but
was sent down to Providence late in the season. In Toronto, on September 15, 1914, the nineteen-year-old
Ruth homered off Ellis Johnson along the way to
pitching a 9–0 one-hitter. As The New York Times noted
"the only time in the minors that Ruth hit a ball out of
the park, he also hit it out of the United States."

The only bird ever struck and killed in midflight by a batted ball

Leading off the third inning in a 1987 game against the
Mets in New York, the Atlanta Braves' Dion James hit a
routine fly ball that fatally beaned a dove in midflight and
dropped for a double amid a shower of feathers.

Mets shortstop Rafael Santana retrieved the stricken

bird and gave it to the ballgirl, who seemed relieved to hand it off to Ozzie Virgil, a Braves utility catcher. He put the bird in a box and brought it out to the bullpen. "I saw the whole thing," he said. "Imagine. A dove. A bird of peace."

Both the Elias Sports Bureau and the Audubon Society confirmed that no other bird had ever been fatally struck in midflight by a batted ball in the majors.

Fatal *throws* are another story. Four years earlier, for example, Yankee star Dave Winfield was arrested for killing a seagull with a between-innings warm-up throw in Toronto. The outfielder was released after posting a five-hundred-dollar bond and promising to appear for a trial during the Yankees' next visit to Toronto. The charge—cruelty to animals—was later dropped.

At Boston's Fenway Park in 1945, a hard peg from the arm of Philadelphia Athletics outfielder Hal Peck skulled a pigeon in midflight and caromed over to second baseman Skip Newhouser, who tagged out the runner. Credit the pigeon with an assist.

The only player to get a hit for two different teams in two different cities on the same day

When he awoke on the morning of August 4, 1982, Joel Youngblood was an outfielder for the New York Mets. He started in right field that day against the Chicago Cubs at Wrigley Field and singled in the third inning, but was immediately lifted from the game and told to pack because he'd just been traded to the Montreal Expos.

Youngblood caught a flight to Philadelphia and took a taxi from the airport to Veterans Stadium, where the Expos were playing a night game with the Phillies. Suiting up in the Montreal clubhouse, he went in to play right field in the sixth inning. In his one time at bat, he singled again.

The only Baseball Hall of Famer memorialized on another player's plaque for a failure

One of the finest second basemen of all time, Tony Lazzeri played on the great Yankee teams of the 1920s and 1930s, batting .292 lifetime and collecting 178 home runs. But he always labored in the shadow of Ruth, Gehrig, and DiMaggio, and it is his misfortune to be best remembered for striking out with the bases loaded in the seventh inning of the deciding game of the 1926 World Series against the St. Louis Cardinals.

It was an aging, over-the-hill Grover Cleveland Alexander, just called in from the bullpen, who fanned Lazzeri; that unforgettable David-and-Goliath showdown was recounted on Alexander's Hall of Fame plaque, installed in 1938: "He won 1926 World Championship for Cardinals by striking out Lazzeri with bases full in final crisis at Yankee Stadium."

"Funny thing," Lazzeri once told a reporter, "but nobody seems to remember much about my ballplaying except that strikeout. There isn't a night goes by what some guy leans across the bar or comes up behind me at a table and brings up the old question."

It wasn't until 1990—forty-five years after he died in a fall at the age of forty-two—that Lazzeri was elected to the Hall and given his own plaque. It made no mention of the strikeout.

The only major league pitcher to toss consecutive no-hitters

The date was June 15, 1938. The place was Brooklyn's Ebbets Field. The Dodgers, in their first night home game ever, were facing the Cincinnati Reds and pitcher Johnny Vander Meer.

In his last appearance, Vander Meer had no-hit the

Boston Braves, winning 3–0, and it looked now as if he might repeat the feat. He got through the first eight innings without yielding a hit to the Dodgers, but he opened the ninth by throwing three straight wild pitches to the leadoff batter before getting him to ground out. After walking the bases full, Vander Meer retired another Brooklyn batter, then got Leo Durocher out on an easy fly ball to center field. That gave him his second straight no-hitter and a place in history.

Less well known than Vander Meer's two no-hitters is how close Howard Ehmke of the Boston Red Sox had come to beating him to the punch fifteen years earlier.

Four days after Ehmke no-hit the Philadelphia Athletics in 1923, he started against the Yankees in New York. The Yankees' first batter, Whitey Witt, hit a grounder to the third baseman, who bobbled the ball long enough for Witt to reach first. Both teams and all fifteen thousand fans assumed the play was scored an error.

Ehmke retired the next twenty-seven batters in a row to earn the victory and his second no-hitter—until it was discovered that the official scorer, sportswriter Fred Lieb, had called the first-inning grounder a hit. His colleagues, Ehmke's teammates, and even the home-plate umpire prevailed on him to reconsider, but Lieb stood firm, and Ehmke had to content himself with a one-hitter.

The only major league baseball manager fired in spring training

An unwritten rule among baseball owners requires that you give a manager at least a few weeks of regular-season play to embarrass himself before yanking him for a replacement. But Phil Cavarretta was fired as manager of the Chicago Cubs in spring training.

The year was 1954. Cavarretta, who was nearing the end of an outstanding twenty-one-year playing career, had been player-manager of the Cubs since 1951. Under him, the hapless Chicagoans had compiled a 169–213 record, finishing in seventh place in 1953, though Cavarretta was hardly to blame. During a meeting with team owner Phil Wrigley at the Cubs' training camp in Mesa, Arizona, Cavarretta confided that the team could use some extra help in the catching department. The infield, outfield, and pitching staff might also benefit from new blood.

Cavarretta wasn't telling Wrigley anything he didn't know. But the owner accused his manager of having "a defeatist attitude." And with that, he fired him.

"I'd never had a defeatist attitude in my life," Cavarretta told a newspaper reporter years later, at seventy-four. "Mr. Wrigley was wrong."

The only six-inning eight-hour professional baseball game

The longest baseball game on record was played between San Luista and the Piedras Negras Internationals at Eagle Pass, Texas, on July 4, 1926. Details remain sketchy, but the game began at ten o'clock that morning and was called on account of darkness at six in the evening after six innings. The score was 129–119, in San Luista's favor.

Pitchers for both teams walked ninety-seven batters, and Mirales, the Internationals' shortstop, made twenty-four errors in the third inning.

The only father and son to play on the same major league baseball team

Outfielder Ken Griffey broke into the majors with the Cincinnati Reds in 1973, and he was still playing in 1989 when his son, Ken junior, was signed by the Seattle Mariners. Late the following season, forty-year-old Griffey père was traded to the Mariners. At that point, he and his son, an outfielder like his dad, became the first father-son combo ever to play on the same team at the same time.

The only baseball game called on account of flying LPs

White Sox owner Bill Veeck lured fans out to Chicago's Comiskey Park for a 1979 doubleheader against the Tigers with a unique promotion: Bring a disco LP to the ballpark and get in for ninety-nine cents. Veeck's plan was to burn the records in a spectacular outfield bonfire between games—his way of joyously proclaiming the death of disco music.

But things didn't work out as planned. Before the first game was over, seven thousand crazed fans started scaling the LPs like Frisbees at the field and at each other. By the time the second game was about to begin, there were still hordes of fans on the playing field, frolicking among jagged shards of vinyl and basking in the glow of a huge toxic bonfire. On order of the umpires, the flames were doused, and the White Sox forfeited the second game.

The only baseball game delayed on account of teakettle

White Sox shortstop Luke Appling was fielding a routine grounder in a home game back in the 1940s when his spikes struck something metallic embedded in the infield dirt. Time out was called, and groundsmen unearthed a weathered blue and white teakettle—a reminder that Comiskey Park had been built on the site of a former garbage dump.

The only National League team with a losing record against every other team in the league

Since joining the league in 1969, the San Diego Padres have finished the season with a record of .500 or above eight times and even won a pennant. But as of this writing there isn't a single team against which they have a winning record.

The only American League team with a losing record against each of its rivals is the Seattle Mariners. But unlike the Padres, the Mariners have finished above .500 only once and never come close to winning a pennant.

The only Steinbrenner worth rooting for

Steinbrenner—Gene, not George—was a second-string infielder for the Philadelphia Phillies in 1912. In a major league career that spanned all of three games, he got two hits in nine at bats and then vanished without a trace.

The only baseball player busted on a street named after him

Years before he was packed off to federal prison on charges of tax evasion, Cincinnati Reds great Pete Rose was ticketed for parking illegally on a street near the Cincinnati ballpark. The name of the street: Pete Rose Way.

The only two-inch touchdown pass

The Dallas Cowboys were within inches of the Washington Redskins' goal line on October 9, 1960, when quarterback Eddie LeBaron took the snap and turned to hand off to the fullback—or so the Redskins expected. Instead, he faked out the defense and twenty-one thousand fans by fading back and tossing a short pass to tight end Dick Bielski, who stepped across the goal for an officially recorded two-inch gain.

The micropass didn't do the Cowboys much good, though. They lost 26–14 for their third straight defeat.

The only 210-yard touchdown run

Playing for Lehigh College in a 1918 contest, Raymond "Snooks" Dowd scooped up a fumble within crawling distance of the opposing team's goal line and then inexplicably ran one hundred yards *away* from the goal. He was deep in his own end zone before realizing the error of his ways, but unlike Minnesota's Jim Marshall (see **The only wrong-way run in pro football history,** page 192) he escaped without mishap. Without slowing down, Dowd made a U-turn around the goalposts and ran *back* the length of the field to the proper goal line, thus achieving history's only 210-yard touchdown.

The only wrong-way run in pro football history

As a starting lineman with the Minnesota Vikings, Jim Marshall didn't have much opportunity to handle the ball. So when he scooped up a fumble in a game against the San Francisco 49ers on October 25, 1964, he hugged it to his chest and jubilantly headed for the goal line.

Unfortunately, it was the wrong goal line. Unable to hear his teammates' screams over the roar of the crowd, Marshall galloped sixty-six yards to the Minnesota end zone, where he was tackled for a two-point safety. San Francisco's Bruce Bosley gave the addled Marshall an appreciative bear hug; Minnesota coach Norm Van Brocklin later said, "I may not live long enough to collect my pension."

In any event, the blunder caused no harm: Minnesota won 27–22. As for Marshall, he was deluged with fan mail and built a nice little off-season career recounting his misguided run at banquets and conventions. Among those who wrote to commiserate with him was Roy Riegels, who had pulled the same boner in the 1929 Rose Bowl.

The only football team that still regularly uses the single-wing offense

Once a staple of college and professional football playbooks, the single-wing formation has long since gone the way of the dropkick and the leather helmet. Its distinguishing feature is a backfield that includes a wingback, fullback, and tailback, any of whom receives the snap from the center; the quarterback merely calls the signals.

While modified single wings still appear from time to time, the only team to use it consistently, and in its classic form, is the Dennison eleven, of Granville, Ohio. Coach Keith Piper introduced the single wing to Dennison in 1962 and used it on and off over the next sixteen years, bringing it back for good in 1978. Call Piper old-fashioned, but Dennison has posted a thoroughly modern 93–52–7 record using the single-wing offense.

The only nonprofit, publicly held professional football team

The Green Bay Packers joined the National Football League in 1922 with the financial backing of the Acme Packing Company. (Hence the name.) When the team faced bankruptcy the following year, a group of five local merchants, led by newspaper publisher A. B. Turnbull, rallied to the rescue. They took the Packers public and sold one thousand shares of stock to area residents for five dollars each. The team has been owned and operated by its fans ever since.

It hasn't always been a going concern. In 1934 a fan toppled out of the bleachers at the Packers' old playing grounds and was awarded five thousand in damages, sending the team into receivership. Again, a team of business leaders came through, pumping fifteen thousand dollars in needed cash into the dying team and staving off bankruptcy.

Today, the 4,627 shares of Green Bay Packers stock are owned by 1,856 shareholders who receive no dividends on their initial investment nor any profits. Although the team operates healthily in the black, all earnings are either donated to charity or reinvested in the corporation, which is governed by a forty-five-member board of directors and a seven-member executive committee. No one receives a salary.

Should the Packers ever go out of business, all assets will be divided between the local American Legion branch and the community chest. But that prospect is unlikely: Though the Packers have not appeared in the Super Bowl since 1968, they have won more championships—eleven—than any other team in NFL history.

The only football player to punt the length of the field

With his team forced back to its own one-yard line, New York Jets' rookie Steve O'Neal got off a ninety-eight-yard punt against the Denver Broncos in September 1969. The ball, which Neal booted from well within the end zone, wound up on the Broncos' one, the longest kick ever in the history of professional football.

Said one sportswriter on the scene, "It went further—literally—than a lot of home runs I've seen."

The only two-time winner of the Heisman Trophy

All-American halfback for Ohio State in the early 1970s, Archie Griffin helped pace OSU to a four-year 40–5–1 record and scored at least one hundred yards in thirty-one straight games—an NCAA record.

Only 5'8", Griffin received the Heisman Trophy as College Football Player of the Year in 1974 and again, incredibly, in 1975. He later went on to play eight seasons with the Cincinnati Bengals.

The only coach to pilot two teams to the Super Bowl

A former NFL defensive back, Don Shula is best known for skippering the Miami Dolphins to the Super Bowl in 1972, 1973, 1974, 1983, and 1985. But he was also at the helm when the Baltimore Colts went to the 1968 Super Bowl (in January 1969). They lost to the New York Jets, 16–7.

The only team to play in a Super Bowl and not score a touchdown

In Super Bowl VI, in 1972, former Yugoslavian soccer star Garo Yepremian kicked a second-quarter field goal for Miami. But that was all the scoring the Dolphins did as they lost to the Dallas Cowboys 24–3.

No team has ever been shut out in the Super Bowl.

The only major college president to coach the school football team

After Susquehanna University lost the first seven games of the 1965 football season, coach Jim Garrett quit in frustration and took his staff with him. Unable to coax him back or find a replacement, university president Gustave Weber decided he had no choice but to coach the squad himself.

He wasn't exactly overqualified for the job. The fifty-seven-year-old academic and Lutheran minister had been a nine-letter man at Wagner College, in Staten Island, New York, but that was nearly forty years before. And his coaching experience was limited to a brief stint at the high-school junior-varsity level.

No one expected the freshman coach to work miracles when his players took the field against Geneva College the following Saturday. But by using some unconventional pass and run strategies, Weber made Geneva work hard for its 29–28 victory; Susquehanna hadn't totaled twenty-eight points all season up till then. After a 41–28 loss to Tufts the following week, Weber found a real coach to replace him and went back to just running the college.

"If I had known that I would receive so much publicity, I wouldn't have taken the job," he said afterwards. "I could do something really important in the field of education, and nobody would pay attention."

The only person enshrined in both the Baseball and Pro Football halls of fame

One of the most formidable offensive *and* defensive linemen of his day, the 6'5", 240-pound Cal Hubbard began his NFL career with the Giants in 1927. At his own request, he was traded to Green Bay two years later and helped the Packers win three straight league championships. He was voted NFL All-Pro six times.

After retiring from active play, Hubbard coached college football for a few years and then went on to become one of the most skilled and respected umpires in the history of major league baseball, working from 1936–1961 in the American League. When an eye was injured in a hunting accident, he gave up calling balls and strikes and became a supervisor of major league umpires.

He was inducted into the Baseball Hall of Fame at Cooperstown, New York, in 1976, and the Pro Football Hall of Fame in Canton, Ohio, in 1963.

The only person enshrined in both the Basketball and College Football halls of fame

No other person has had a fraction of the impact on American sports that Amos Alonzo Stagg (1862–1965) had. Graduated from Yale in 1888, he turned down an offer to pitch for the New York Giants and signed on as an instructor at the YMCA training school in Springfield, Massachusetts. There he helped Dr. James Naismith develop the sport of basketball and took part in the first game ever played.

At the University of Chicago from 1892–1932, Stagg introduced basketball, coached four undefeated varsity football teams, helped organize the first American baseball tour of Japan, and invented the football huddle, the lateral pass, the T formation, the place kick, and the tackling dummy as well as pioneering the use of numbered uniforms and inventing the indoor baseball batting cage and overflow troughs for pools.

After leaving Chicago, Stagg went on to coach football at the College of the Pacific from 1933–1946 and was named Coach of the Year in 1943 at age eighty-one. He retired at ninety-eight from his post as punting and kicking coach at California's Stockton Junior College. His seventy-one-year coaching career is the longest in football history.

Inducted into the College Football Hall of Fame in 1958 and the Basketball Hall of Fame in 1959, Stagg died in 1965. He was 103.

The only back-to-back NCAA basketball final played by the same two teams

In the 1961 NCAA final, coach Edwin Jucker's University of Cincinnati Bearcats beat the defending champion Ohio State Buckeyes in overtime, 70–65. A year later the same two teams met a second time in the final, with Cincinnati winning again, 71–59.

The only other rematch in NCAA history occurred in 1953, when coach Branch McCracken's Indiana beat Phog Allen's Kansas 69–68. The same two schools and coaches had locked horns in 1940, with Indiana winning 60–42.

The only all-southpaw starting lineup in the history of the National Basketball Association

Having won the American Basketball Association championship the year before, the New York Nets fizzled in 1976–1977, their first season in the NBA, compiling a 22–60 record and finishing dead last in their division. It's hard to say whether their cause was helped or hindered by the fact that they played part of the season with an all-lefty starting five—Tim Basset and Al Skinner, forwards; Bubbles Hawkins, guard; and Kim Hughes, center. Hughes's .275 free-throw percentage—he sank 19 out of 69—is the lowest in NBA history.

**The only professional basketball coach to win more
than a thousand games**

Over the course of a long coaching career—sixteen
seasons with the Boston Celtics, as well as earlier
stints with the old Washington Capitols and the Tri-
Cities Blackhawks—Red Auerbach amassed a record of
1,037–548. No one else ever broke into four figures in
the victory column—or lit up so many victory cigars.

Basketball's counterpart of baseball's Connie Mack
and football's George Halas, Auerbach built the great
Celtics dynasty of the 1950s, dominating the game more
than any player and piloting his charges to eight straight
NBA championships between 1958 and 1966. That, too,
is a record that may never be threatened.

"In terms of influence on the professional game, Auerbach was without peer," says sports historian Zander
Hollander. "He not only molded the Celtics into the
NBA's dominant franchise, he was the league's dominant personality."

**The only NCAA basketball championship game to go
into triple overtime**

The University of North Carolina Tarheels finished
the 1957 regular season with a 25–0 record and then
went on to tackle Kansas in the NCAA final. It was a
nerve-racking contest, with several players and both
coaches getting into fights. At the end of the fourth period, the score was locked at 48–48, and it took three
overtimes before the Tarheels pulled out a 54–53 victory. The hero: Joe Quigg, who sank two foul shots in

the final six seconds to put North Carolina ahead by a point, and who then blocked a pass to Jayhawk Wilt Chamberlain to secure the win.

The only time all college basketball games were divided into quarters instead of halves

For as long as anyone can remember, professional basketball games have been divided into four quarters and college games into two halves. The National Collegiate Athletic Association takes its lead from Dr. James Naismith, who invented basketball in 1891.

In 1938 the NCAA allowed opposing teams to decide before a game whether to play a two-half or four-quarter game. (They had to agree; one team couldn't play halves while the other played quarters.) The experiment was dropped after one season.

Then, for one three-season period—1951–1954—the NCAA mandated that *all* its games be divided into four 10-minute quarters instead of two 20-minute halves. The Naismith system was restored at the beginning of the 1954–1955 season, and that's the way it has been ever since.

The only tennis player beaten in both the men's and women's singles of the U.S. Open

Richard Raskind made his premiere appearance at the U.S. Open in 1960, losing to Australia's Neal Fraser 6–0, 6–1, and 6–1 in the first round.

The player's second outing in the Open came in 1977, a year after he underwent a sex-change operation. As Renee Richards, she was beaten 6–1, 6–4 in the first round by Virginia Wade. Richards advanced as far as the third round of the U.S. Open in 1979, getting trounced by Chris Evert 6–2, 6–1. But she made it to the finals of the women's doubles that year, playing alongside Betty-ann Stuart. The two lost to Martina Navratilova and Betty Stove.

Richards later retired from the tennis circuit to devote herself full-time to her practice as an eye surgeon in New York City.

The only tennis player to compete at Wimbledon as a citizen of four different countries

Jaroslav Drobny showed up at Wimbledon as a Czech in 1938. Then Hitler rearranged the map of eastern Europe by annexing the Sudetenland, and when Drobny appeared at the tennis classic the following year, it was under the flag of Bohemia-Moravia.

After the war, Drobny regained his Czech citizenship and played at Wimbledon from 1946–1949. He was also a member of the Czech Olympic hockey team in 1948. But he was disturbed by the rise of communism in his native country, and in 1949 he switched his citizenship to Egypt.

Drobny played at Wimbledon as an Egyptian from 1950–1956, winning the men's singles title in 1954, as well as the 1951–1952 French Open. In 1960 he moved to England and became a naturalized subject of the queen, playing several more years with a British passport before retiring to open a sporting-goods store in London.

The only woman to knock out John L. Sullivan

Hessie Donahue was the wife of a Worcester, Massachusetts, boxing-school owner named Charles Converse who hired out sparring partners for Sullivan. In 1892 the heavyweight champion toured vaudeville, sparring on stage with Converse's men and even with Mrs. Donahue, clad in gloves, tights, blouse, skirt, and bloomers. No real punches were thrown, of course, until the Boston Strong Boy momentarily forgot where he was during one performance and let Mrs. Donahue have one full in the face. Stunned, she walloped him a blow to the ear that laid him out cold for a full minute.

The freak knockout drove the audience wild, and Sullivan and Mrs. Donahue repeated it in all their ensuing vaudeville performances. Typically, they'd go at it for three rounds, and at the end of the third, she'd floor him with her haymaker and be pronounced the new champ. It wasn't until September of 1892, when Gentleman Jim Corbett knocked him out in a twenty-one-round marathon in New Orleans, that Sullivan was ever defeated in the ring by a man.

The only world heavyweight champion never to lose a fight

From the time he turned professional in 1947 until his retirement in 1956, Rocky Marciano fought forty-nine bouts and won them all—forty-three by knockouts.

Ironically, Marciano's first love was not boxing but baseball. A pretty good catcher, he once tried out for the Chicago Cubs, who turned him down because he couldn't make the throw to second with any accuracy. He took up boxing in the army during World War II.

At New York's Madison Square Garden on September 23, 1952, Marciano knocked out Jersey Joe Walcott in the thirteenth round for the world heavyweight title. Over the next three and a half years, he defended his title against a succession of challengers. He retired from the ring undefeated on April 27, 1956, vowing never to attempt a comeback. He never did.

Marciano died in the crash of a single-engine plane near Des Moines, Iowa in 1969. He was 46.

The only grandfather to win a world boxing title

The Hawaiian-born fighter Dado Marino defeated Terry Allen for the world flyweight championship in 1950 and held it for two years. The 34-year-old, 112-pound grandfather suffered a few bruises and a cut over his left eye in his 15-round-decision win.

(Marino, however, was not the *oldest* titleholder. That honor belongs to Archie Moore, who became light-heavyweight champion of the world in 1952 and retained his title until 1960, when he was in his late forties.)

The only boxer to hold three undisputed world titles simultaneously

The wiry but indomitable Hammerin' Hank Armstrong (a.k.a. Homicide Hank) defeated Petey Sarron for the world's featherweight title on October 29, 1937. The following May, he beat Barney Ross in fifteen rounds for the welterweight title. Three months later, he defeated Lou Ambers for the lightweight title. He remained the uncontested three-way champ until that December, when his weight ballooned to 127, and he was forced to relinquish his featherweight crown.

The only boxer to lose and regain the same world title four times

The great Sugar Ray Robinson won his first middleweight title in 1951 against Jake La Motta, "the Raging Bull," but lost it that same year to British challenger Randy Turpin—from whom he won it back two months later. On March 25, 1958, Sugar Ray outpunched champion Carmen Basilio in Chicago for a fifteen-round split decision—and his fifth world middleweight title.

The only boxing title holder to weigh under one hundred pounds

World flyweight champion Jimmy Wilde, of Great Britain, weighed in at ninety-six pounds when he knocked out challenger Frank DiMelfi, the "Young Zulu Kid," in the eleventh round of a title bout in London on December 16, 1916. DiMelfi, too, came in under his usual fighting weight, but minimauler Wilde remains the only double-digit champ in any weight class in boxing history.

The only brothers to hold world boxing titles simultaneously

In Sicily, on February 9, 1983, Don Curry scored a first-round knockout over Roger Stafford to become world welterweight champion. The following May 18, his brother Bruce won the world's lightweight title with a twelve-round decision against LeRoy Haley.

Mrs. Curry's boys reigned together until Bruce was hammered into ground round by challenger Billy Costello in a Beaumont, Texas, title bout the following January; brother Don remained welterweight champ till 1985.

The only boxer to get married on the day of a title fight

World bantamweight champion Pete Herman successfully defended his title against Frankie Burns in New Orleans on November 5, 1917. It wasn't much of a scrap as championship bouts go—few solid punches were thrown during the twenty-round marathon, with Herman outfoxing his challenger and winning on points. Presumably, the champ was saving himself for his new bride, whom he had married that morning.

Down—and out: fifteen championship boxing bouts that went only one round:

1. April 7, 1914: Al McCoy (U.S.) beat middleweight champion George Chip (U.S.) in forty-five seconds.
2. May 11, 1922: Light-heavyweight champion Georges Carpentier (France) beat Kid Lewis (Great Britain).
3. March 2, 1929: Emile Pladner (France) beat flyweight champion Frankie Genaro (U.S.) in fifty-eight seconds.
4. June 22, 1938: Heavyweight champion Joe Louis (U.S.) beat Max Schmeling (Germany) in the first of Louis's record 5 first-round title wins.
5. December 11, 1939: Middleweight champion Al Hostak (U.S.) beat Eric Seelig (Germany) to become the only man ever to win two boxing title fights in under two minutes of the first round.
6. May 15, 1953: Heavyweight champion Rocky Marciano (U.S.) beat Jersey Joe Walcott (U.S.).
7. September 25, 1962: Sonny Liston (U.S.) beat heavyweight champion Floyd Patterson (U.S.).
8. July 22, 1963: Heavyweight champion Sonny Liston (U.S.) beat Floyd Patterson (U.S.)—the only man ever to lose two title bouts in the first round.
9. May 25, 1965: Heavyweight champion Muhammad Ali (U.S.) beat Sonny Liston (U.S.).

10. June 3, 1971: Featherweight champion Kuniaki Shibata (Japan) beat Raul Cruz (Mexico).
11. October 17, 1973: Ben Villaflor (Philippines) beat world junior-lightweight champion Kuniaki Shibata (Japan).
12. October 15, 1976: Lightweight champion Roberto Duran (Panama) beat Alvaro Rojas (Mexico).
13. May 8, 1982: Ray Mancini (U.S.) beat lightweight champion Arturo Frias (U.S.)
14. December 26, 1986: Light-heavyweight champion Bobby Czyz (U.S.) beat David Sears (U.S.).
15. August 30, 1987: Welterweight champion Lloyd Honeyghan (Jamaica) beat Eduardo Tunon (Panama) in forty-five seconds.

The only person ever to refuse an Olympic gold medal

A Canadian, George Lyons, was the gold-medal winner in golf—yes, golf—at the 1904 Olympic Games in St. Louis. (He had attracted as much interest by walking up to the awards stand on his hands as he had with his prowess on the golf course.) When he arrived in London four years later to defend his title, he discovered there was no one to defend it against: The other entrants in the golf event had squabbled among themselves and withdrawn, leaving Lyons the winner by default.

Offered the gold medal on that basis, Lyons turned it down and went home. And as David Randall notes in

Great Sporting Eccentrics, "since golf has featured in no further games, he is still, therefore, the reigning Olympic golf champion."

The only person to win a gold medal in the same event in four consecutive Olympic Games

Al Oerter of the United States was no one's pick to win the discus competition in the 1956 Olympics in Melbourne. Only twenty, he was going up against such formidable hurlers as teammate Fortune Gordien and Italy's Adolfo Consolini. But he outdistanced the competition on all three throws and won his first gold medal.

Despite an automobile accident that nearly killed him the following year, Oerter qualified for the 1960 Olympics in Rome and won a second gold medal with a performance that included a throw of 194'2"—his best ever.

In the Tokyo games of 1964, Oerter set an Olympic distance record with a first throw of 198'8" on the way to earning an unprecedented third straight gold medal; he eclipsed that mark on his third try, with a throw of 200'1". Chances are the discus would have gone into orbit around Pluto had Oerter not been in excruciating pain from torn cartilage in his ribs.

Oerter made his final Olympic appearance in 1968 in Mexico City. The smart money was on his teammate, Jay Silvester, world record holder and five years younger; Oerter was, at best, the sentimental favorite. But again Oerter overcame the odds, with three 210-plus-foot throws, to win his fourth straight gold medal. Only nine other Olympic track and field competitors have won even back-to-back golds.

The only Olympic competitor to publicly throw away his gold medal

Eighteen-year-old Soviet rowing champion Vyacheslav Ivanov was so ecstatic over his come-from-behind victory in the single sculls at the 1956 Olympics in Melbourne that he tossed his gold medal high in the air after the official presentation ceremony. Unfortunately, Ivanov had misjudged the trajectory, and the medal fell into Lake Wendouree. Ivanov jumped in after it, and later a corps of trained divers scoured the lake bottom, but it was never found.

Ivanov was given a second medal and went on to win two additional golds in the single sculls in 1960 and 1964.

Boxer Muhammad Ali claims he hurled his Olympic gold medal into the Ohio River in anger one night in 1960 from a bridge in Louisville, Kentucky. He had just been refused service in a whites-only restaurant and then harassed by a mob of racist bikers. "The medal was gone, but the sickness was gone too," he wrote in his autobiography, *The Greatest*. "I felt calm, relaxed, confident. . . . I felt a new, secret strength."

The only athlete to win a gold medal in both the decathlon and another event in the same Olympics

Representing the United States, Harold Osborne won the high jump at the 1924 Olympics in Paris, clearing every height on his first attempt. Five days later he came from behind in the final events to nose out Britain's Emerson Norton and win the decathlon.

All told, Americans won twelve track and field gold medals that year. Finland placed second with ten.

The only nation to compete in every modern Summer and Winter Olympics

England has been represented in every Summer Olympics from 1896 (Athens) to 1988 (Seoul), and in every Winter Olympics from 1924 (Chamonix) to 1992 (Albertville, France). And as of this writing, the Britishers have every intention of competing in the 1992 Summer Games in Barcelona.

The only gold-medal winner in both the Summer and Winter Olympics

A graduate of Yale, and Harvard Law School as well as a Rhodes Scholar at Oxford, Eddie Eagan won the light-heavyweight title at the 1920 Olympics in Antwerp. He stayed with boxing through the 1920s, competing as a heavyweight in the 1924 Olympics, and winning several additional titles, including the U.S. and British amateur-heavyweight championships.

By 1932 Eagan had married the former Margaret Colgate (of the soap and toothpaste Colgates) and embarked on a successful career as a New York lawyer. When he turned up at the 1932 Winter Olympics at Lake Placid, New York, Eagan earned a second gold medal as a member of the U.S. four-man-bobsled team. Among his teammates were Bill Fiske, who became the first American pilot to enlist in Britain's RAF during World War II, and songwriter Tippy Gray, whose songs included "If You Were the Only Girl in the World" and "Got a Date with an Angel."

It seemed like a good idea at the time: sports played only once at the Olympics:

1. *Cricket (Paris, 1900).* Great Britain, represented by the Devon Wanderers Cricket Club, trounced France, 262–104. No other countries competed.
2. *Croquet (Paris, 1900).* France was the only participant in this one-time-only event. Both singles and doubles versions were played.
3. *Motorboating (London, 1908).* Great Britain won two gold medals, France one.
4. *Pigeon shooting (Paris, 1900).* That's *live* pigeons—not the inert, clay variety. Marksman Léon de Lunden, of Belgium, was the gold medalist, picking off twenty-one birds; Maurice Faure of France won the silver medal with twenty. This was the only event involving the deliberate killing of live animals in the history of the Games.

The only professional coach fired and replaced by his brother

Midway through the 1989–1990 National Hockey League season, the Washington Capitals were dead last in the Patrick Division and just coming off an eight-game losing streak when the team's management decided a change was in order. So they sacked head coach Bryan

Murray and brought up his brother Terry, who had been coach of the Capitals' farm club, the Baltimore Skip-jacks. It was the first and only time a coach in any major professional sport had ever been dumped for a sibling.

The only major regular-season National Hockey League record tied in a playoff

No important regular-season pro hockey record has ever been broken in postseason play, but one has been equaled.

It's the record for most goals in a period by a player—four—held by nine different men, including Busher Jackson (Toronto, 1934), Red Berenson (St. Louis, 1968), Wayne Gretzky (Edmonton, 1981), Bryan Trottier (New York Islanders, 1982), and Joe Nieuwendyk (Calgary, 1989).

The Philadelphia Flyers' Tim Kerr was the first player to score four times in a period in a playoff game. He did it against the New York Rangers on April 13, 1985, helping the Flyers to a 6–5 victory. Mario Lemieux of the Pittsburgh Penguins matched the feat in the first period of a 1989 playoff game against Philadelphia. Pittsburgh came out on top, 10–7.

The only NHL goalie to post a season goals-against average below 1.00

George Hainsworth, who tended goal for the Montreal Canadiens from 1926–1933, allowed an average of less than a goal a game during the 1928–1929 season, appearing in forty-four games and shutting out the opposition in twenty-two.

In one 1929 outing, he took on the Toronto Maple

Leafs despite a pregame practice encounter with a flying puck that knocked him unconscious and swelled an eye shut. Though the Maple Leafs hammered the stricken Hainsworth mercilessly, he held them to a single score. Despite such heroics, Hainsworth was traded to Toronto in 1933. He was later elected to the Hockey Hall of Fame.

The only jockey to ride two Triple Crown winners

The first time Eddie Arcaro achieved horse racing's most elusive goal was in 1941; the horse was Whirlaway. Having already won the Kentucky Derby and the Preakness, the chestnut colt took the Belmont Stakes before a crowd of thirty thousand in an almost effortless 2:31, becoming only the fifth horse to win the Triple Crown.

Riding Citation, Arcaro galloped to a second Triple Crown in 1948, winning Belmont by over six lengths in the extraordinary time of 2:28. Citation showed even less exertion than Whirlaway had. "He's the greatest horse I've ever seen," said Arcaro after the race.

The only Triple Crown winner to sire a Triple Crown winner

The three-year-old Gallant Fox galloped to victory at the Belmont Stakes on a drizzly June day in 1930 to capture racing's Triple Crown. Five years later, Gallant Fox's son Omaha repeated the feat in a drenching downpour. The victory made William Woodward the only person ever to breed and own two Triple Crown champions.

The only person ever to pick ten out of ten races correctly

A racing reporter for the Baltimore *News American*, Charles Lamb correctly predicted the winners of all ten races run at Delaware Park, in Wilmington, Delaware, on July 28, 1974.

One-of-a-kind holes in one:

1. Otto Bucher shot a hole in one on the 130-yard twelfth hole at La Manga Golf Club in Spain in 1985. He was four months shy of his one hundredth birthday.
2. On July 30, 1962, Scott Statler aced the seventh hole of his father's par-3 golf course in Greensburg, Pennsylvania. He was four years old.
3. U.S. Open challengers Jerry Pate, Nick Price, Doug Weaver, and Mark Wiebe all shot holes in one on the sixth hole at Oak Hill Country Club in Rochester, New York, on June 16, 1989.
4. Joseph Boydstone shot back-to-back holes in one at Bakersfield Golf Club in California on October 10, 1962, and added a third later in the game.
5. Sue Press became the only woman ever to shoot consecutive holes in one at Chatswood Golf Club, in Sydney, Australia, on May 29, 1977.
6. Scott Palmer shot his one hundredth hole in one on May 20, 1989.
7. Former president Dwight D. Eisenhower scored a hole in one at Palm Springs, California, on February 6, 1968.
8. In a 1983 match at Elfordleigh Golf Club, in Devon, England, Richard Ingerson aced the second hole twice in a single game. He did it playing back-

to-back rounds of the club's nine-hole course.

9. L. Bruce's tape-measure hole in one at Hope Country Club, Arkansas, on November 15, 1962, traveled 480 yards—the longest ever recorded.

10. A duffer on a Livermore, California, golf course sent a ball crashing through the cockpit of an airplane as it was about to touch down at a local airport. Although the ball struck the pilot on the head, the plane landed safely.

The only racing-car driver to win the Indianapolis 500 and the World Grand Prix Championship in the same year

The Indianapolis 500 and the ten races that make up the World Driving Championship in Grand Prix racing pose such different challenges that many drivers won't even attempt both in the same year. The Indy involves two hundred laps around a flat two-and-a-half-mile oval track; the European races feature meandering country roads, sharp turns, and lots of hills.

Twenty-nine-year-old Jim Clark of Great Britain had already held—and lost—the Grand Prix championship when he regained it in 1965. Then he made his third appearance in the Indianapolis 500, driving a rear-mounted Lotus-Ford, and won that too. A quiet-spoken Scot, Clark attributed his double success to "not letting my emotions run away with me."

The only woman ever to compete in the Indianapolis 500

Thirty-nine-year-old Janet Guthrie made it as far as the qualifying rounds for the 1976 Indianapolis 500, but when her car, a Vollstedt-Offenhauser, developed mechanical problems, she was prevented from entering the race.

She qualified in 1977, but during the time trials three weeks before the race, she all but demolished her Lightning-Offenhauser and sustained minor injuries when the vehicle spun out of control at 191 miles per hour and slammed into a wall. The car was somehow repaired, and despite a broken wrist, Guthrie showed up at the starting line of the Indy 500 and made it to the twenty-seventh lap, when her engine died and she was forced to leave the race.

Finally, in the 1978 Indy, she went all the way, finishing in ninth place.

The only nation to send a team to every World Cup competition

The World Cup has been played every four years since 1930—with time out during World War II—and Brazil has never failed to qualify for a first-round berth.

Brazil won the Cup in 1958, 1962, and 1970. In their last outing—1990—they were eliminated in the first round.

The United States, incidentally, has never won.

The only Oxford vs. Cambridge air race

Airplane racing isn't most people's idea of a varsity sport—and for that matter, neither is it Oxford's or Cambridge's. But in the early years of aviation, both schools briefly fielded varsity flying teams, and on one occasion competed against each other.

On July 16, 1921, three pilots for Cambridge and three for Oxford, all manning identical SE5 prop planes, took off from an airfield in Hendon, just outside London. The course: three 129-mile laps out to Hertford and back. Oxford ate Cambridge's dust from the start, one of its pilots never even making it to the finish line. With an average speed of 118.55 miles per hour, Cambridge won the event handily.

The only person to play two world-champion chess masters in a single day

During a 1938 tournament in Plymouth, England, R. M. Bruce took on Vera Menchik-Stevenson in the morning and Alexander Alekhine in the afternoon. Menchik-Stevenson, perhaps the greatest female chess player of all time, was the women's world chess champion from 1927 until her death in 1944. Alekhine held the world chess championship from 1927–1935 and from 1937–1946.

Bruce lost to both.

The only competitive team sport in which the players wear blindfolds

Like soccer, lacrosse, and field hockey, the idea of goalball is to put the ball into the opposing team's net. It's played on an indoor surface about the size of a basketball court by two teams of six, though only three are on the court at a time. Every player is blindfolded.

The reason for this is that goalball is a game for the blind and visually impaired; the blindfolds "allow sighted people to play with the blind on an equal footing," explains Roel Moberts, who is goalball chairman of the International Blind Sports Association.

Bells inside the ball enable the players to keep track of it. Once a team takes possession, it has eight seconds to roll the ball into the net. Defensive players can block the ball with any part of their body.

A game consists of 2 seven-minute periods, and the action can get intense, with players diving to block shots that seem to travel as fast as a sharply kicked soccer ball. When two evenly matched top-ranked teams face each other, scores are usually in the low single digits.

Goalball originated in Germany after World War II as a way of rehabilitating blind veterans. It was introduced in the United States in 1976, and today there are about fifteen hundred players in about thirty-five countries, most of whom participate in the World Goalball Championship Games every June.

The only worldwide school recess

Imagine—five million grade-schoolers all sprung from class and racing for the jungle gym at exactly the same moment.

It happened on May 8, 1991, thanks to Lenny Saunders, a teacher at Valley View School in Montville, New

Jersey. To dramatize the importance of regular exercise for children, Saunders recruited 5 million kids from 8,000 schools in 50 states and 40 countries to join in Project ACES. That's "all children exercising simultaneously."

Admittedly, in the interests of simultaneity, kids in such distant outposts as Japan and Australia had to be rousted from bed and delivered to the schoolyard in the middle of the night. But the exertion was worth it, said Saunders. The monster recess "promotes youth fitness and it doesn't cost anything."

Easy for him to talk. He wasn't the teacher on yard duty that day.

Holy cow!

1. Comedian Lenny Bruce said he attended only one baseball game in his life—the seventh game of the 1960 World Series.
2. Only one spectator braved sub-zero temperatures and high winds to show up for a football game between Washington State and San Jose State at Pullman, Washington, on November 12, 1955.
3. A horse called Broker's Tip won only one race in its life—the 1933 Kentucky Derby.
4. Pitcher Mike Parrott of the Seattle Mariners won only one game in 1980—on opening day. He finished the season with a 1–16 record.
5. Dave Krieg is the only graduate of Wisconsin's Milton College to play pro football.
6. Harvard-St. George, a private high school for girls in Chicago, scored only one point

in a 1978 basketball game against Chicago
Latin. The lone scorer was Jeanine
Griffith, who sank a foul shot in the fourth
quarter. A teammate had twelve fouls,
and only one girl knew how to dribble.
"We only have ten girls in the school, and
six are on the team," coach Lynn Hudson
said afterwards. "Things were so bad, I
had my eyes closed from the opening
seconds." Final score: Chicago Latin 117,
Harvard-St. George 1.

MOVIES, TV, AND POPULAR CULTURE

The only feature film ever made in Esperanto

Star Trek's William Shatner starred in *Incubus,* a dreary 1966 tale of a good man tormented by evil forces. Czech actor Milos Milos played the incubus—a demonic spirit who seduces women while they sleep and steals their souls.

In order to give the story a properly eerie feel, the directors insisted that all the dialogue be spoken in Esperanto, the universal language concocted by Dr. Ludwig L. Zamenhof in the nineteenth century. The effect *was* pretty strange, given that none of the actors had even a smattering of Esperanto, and all had to learn their lines phonetically. Though *Incubus* left most critics yawning—or scratching their heads in bewilderment—it holds the distinction of being one of the few made-in-America movies ever to rely entirely on subtitles. (See also **the only film in which Trevor Howard spoke all his lines in the Cheyenne language,** page 227.)

The only feature film ever made in Latin

It was Saint Sebastian's singular misfortune to be lashed to a tree and shot so full of arrows that he resembled a pincushion. Appropriately, he later became patron saint of both archers and pinmakers.

In 1976 British director Derek Jarman gave a homoerotic spin to Saint Sebastian's martyrdom in his movie, *Sebastiane*. Since it was set in the Roman Empire in the third century A.D., Jarman decided that having the actors speak their lines in Latin would add a touch of authenticity.

Translator Jack Welch took pains to use street Latin rather than schoolbook Latin, liberally lacing the dialogue with tangy colloquialisms. But he was unable to find a Latin equivalent for *motherfucker*, so he translated it into Greek as *Oedipus*.

The only uncomical Marx Brother

Minnie and Sam Marx had five sons, of whom four—Julius, Leonard, Arthur, and Herbert (a.k.a. Groucho, Chico, Harpo, and Zeppo)—went on to glory as the Marx Brothers. The fifth was Milton, better known as Gummo. He made his fortune in women's wear.

As a child, Gummo did have a decent singing voice, and ironically, he was the first to perform on stage. (There is no record of his ever having been billed as the Marx Brother.) Later, Groucho joined him, and then Harpo and Chico followed suit, and the four Marx Brothers became the toast of New York vaudeville.

But right after World War I, Gummo, who claimed he'd never liked show business, stepped aside and was replaced by Zeppo. Gummo became his brothers' busi-

> **Only one full-length feature film has ever been made in**
>
> 1. *Iban.* (The language of coastal Dayaks of Sarawak, Malaysian Borneo). *Bejalai,* 1987.
> 2. *Lapp. Ofelas.* A family project, directed by Nils Gaup, and starring Mikkel, Ailu, and Sara Marit Gaup. Set in the Arctic Circle, c. 1100. Much of the action was shot in − 40°F temperatures. Released in 1987.
> 3. *Frisian.* (Spoken in the Frisian Islands.) *De Droom,* 1985.
> 4. *Pidgin English. Wokabout Bilong Tonten.* Filmed in New Guinea, 1973.

ness manager and later operated Gummo Marx, Inc., a New York City dress manufacturer. He never performed on stage again.

Why *Gummo?* He told a reporter he was given the tag because he'd wear rubbers, or gumshoes, even when it wasn't raining, to cover the holes in his shoes.

"I attribute my brothers' success entirely to me," he said. "I quit the act."

The only movie to inspire a brand of condom

Actress Sylvia Sidney was once adjudged the most popular movie star of her day—at least among Japanese birth-control practitioners.

Sidney acquired an intense, if short-lived, cult following in Japan for her performance in the title role in the 1932 nonmusical film version of Puccini's *Madame Butterfly*. (Cary Grant played Pinkerton.) Inevitably, several marketers got rich quick with a range of movie spin-offs—among them, a brand of condoms with the actress's picture as the trademark. They were called Sylvia Sidneys.

"Not only could we not stop them, I never got a penny in royalties," she said. "And I'm told they sold extremely well."

The only all-midget western

In the depths of the Depression, Hollywood schlock-meister Jed Buell got the idea that he could produce a full-blown western—a musical western at that—for a fraction of the usual price if he hired actors a fraction of the usual size. With an ad offering "Big Salaries for Little People," Buell quickly recruited some sixty midget actors who became the cast of the 1938 film *The Terror of Tiny Town*.

Terror bears similarities to many other Hollywood westerns of the time, but for several concessions to the players' size. Gunslingers ride Shetland ponies and walk under the swinging doors of the local saloon, where they heft massive beer steins with both hands. Billy Curtis plays the hero; an actor known as Little Billy is the villain, and Nita Krebs is the lovesick barmaid. Her big number: "Let's go way up on the hill. You can be Jack and I'll be Jill."

No sooner had the final edits been made on *Terror* than producer Buell signed to shoot a second all-midget film, this one to be set in a lumber camp, with a normal-sized human playing Paul Bunyan. It was never completed.

The only film in which Trevor Howard spoke all his lines in the Cheyenne language

The very British Trevor Howard was the unlikely but felicitous choice for the lead in the 1981 Keith Merrill western, *Windwalker,* filmed against the background of Utah's Wasatch Mountains. Cast as a dying Cheyenne chief who defends his family against the hostile Crow, Howard speaks his lines, as do all the characters, in native American languages. Like *Incubus* (see **The only feature film ever made in Esperanto,** page 223), it is one of the few American made films to use subtitles.

The only feature-length movie starring Evel Knievel

Stuntman Evel Knievel's most wretched excess was *not* his bungled attempt to cross Snake River Canyon in a rocket in 1974. Rather, it was his one and only attempt at serious acting—*Viva Knievel*—a 1977 film in which he portrayed himself as a crash-helmeted miracle worker who battles drug dealers, cures alcoholics, and hands out gifts to children in a Mexican orphanage. (The gifts are hobby-shop models of Evel himself. One crippled child in the film is so moved that he throws away his crutches and walks.) Not even the presence of Gene Kelly, Dabney Coleman, and Leslie Nielsen could save this turkey. One critic gave it such a merciless panning that Knievel hit him with a baseball bat and got hauled off to jail.

Though Knievel never acted again, he did figure in two other movies. One was an earlier film bio, *Evel Knievel,* starring George Hamilton; the other was a documentary about him, *The Last of the Gladiators,* made in

1977. That's three Knievel-related movies in all—probably enough for some film student to base a graduate dissertation on.

The only silent-film version of Bizet's *Carmen*

Carmen has been brought to the screen at least a dozen times over the past eighty years, in both silent and talking versions. Most of the silent treatments, not surprisingly, followed the Prosper Mérimée novella rather than the Bizet opera.

Even Cecil B. De Mille's 1915 *Carmen*, starring soprano Geraldine Farrar, went with the novella rather than the opera. One reviewer likened a Farrar performance without music to "the Mona Lisa without the smile, a Stradivarius without its strings," but the movie got overwhelmingly positive notices.

One dissonant note came from the estate of Georges Bizet, which threatened to sue De Mille for copyright infringement. As a precaution, De Mille dropped plans to have a piano accompanist play excerpts from the score.

Strangely, the day it opened, the Fox studio premiered a rival *Carmen*, with screen siren Theda Bara, a.k.a. "the Vampire Woman," in the title role. Theda Bara was *not* a singer, but the version in which she appeared, directed by Raoul Walsh, *did* follow Bizet's opera, using the libretto as the script. Despite Bara's fabled screen allure—and her off-screen escapades—*The New York Times* found her Carmen much less sexy than Farrar's. Indeed, most critics panned the Walsh *Carmen*, recognizing it as a cheap attempt by Fox to scoop De Mille. It was quickly withdrawn from circulation.

Postscript: Because of problems with both the lighting and the photo emulsion, Farrar's pupils did not reg-

ister on the film, and her eyes photographed as blank disks. The effect was dramatic, but Farrar is said to have freaked when she saw the first rushes of herself, and to have begun screaming and clawing at the screen.

The only movie featuring Edward G. Robinson and James Cagney

Cagney and Robinson have been lampooned by so many stand-up impressionists that it's hard to believe they worked together only once—and not very memorably at that. The vehicle was *Smart Money*, a 1931 Warner Bros. crime drama about a barber turned gambler who hits it big, only to wind up in jail.

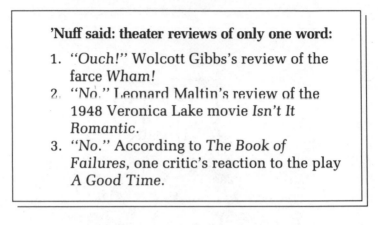

'Nuff said: theater reviews of only one word:

1. *"Ouch!"* Wolcott Gibbs's review of the farce *Wham!*
2. *"No."* Leonard Maltin's review of the 1948 Veronica Lake movie *Isn't It Romantic.*
3. *"No."* According to *The Book of Failures*, one critic's reaction to the play *A Good Time.*

Smart Money also marked the screen debut of Boris Karloff.

The only movie in which Doris Day was murdered

Who would kill cheerful, pillow-talking Doris Day? Steve Cochran, that's who. He plays her boorish, red-neck husband in *Storm Warning*, a 1951 melodrama set in the Deep South. A kard-karrying Ku Klux Klansman as well as a depraved lout, he's driven to murder by his lust for Doris's sister, a fashion model visiting from up north, played by Ginger Rogers. Ronald Reagan is the district attorney.

The only movie costarring Bob Hope and Katharine Hepburn

Hepburn-Tracy was magic. So was Hepburn-Grant. Even Hepburn-Fred MacMurray wasn't bad. But Hepburn-Hope was another story. The two were matched up in *The Iron Petticoat*, a 1956 rip-off of *Ninotchka*, in which Hope is cast as a U.S. military officer trying to woo Hepburn, a Soviet flier, over to American ways. The movie was panned by critics and sank without a trace, although it is still available in video form.

The only X-rated movie to win an Oscar for Best Picture

Midnight Cowboy, a disturbing 1969 film starring Dustin Hoffman and Jon Voigt as two drifters attempting to negotiate New York City's seamy underside, was X-rated when it opened. It won an Academy Award that year not only for Best Picture but also for Best Director (John Schlesinger) and Best Screenplay (Waldo Salt). It was rerated R in 1971.

The only movie title with two errors

A band of fortune hunters searches for sunken treasure in *Krakatowa, East of Java*, one of the worst Cinerama epics ever filmed. The proper spelling of "Krakatowa" is "Krakatoa" or "Krakatau." It's an Indonesian volcano that erupted in 1883.

And it's *west* of Java.

The only movie in which Ronald and Nancy Reagan costarred

Although Ron and Nancy both had Hollywood careers, they appeared together only once—in the 1957 film *Hellcats of the Navy*. Ron plays a World War II submarine commander accused of leaving a frogman to drown; Nancy plays his girl. Of course, the charges aren't true, and in the end Ron proves himself a brave and honorable man, winning Nancy's undying love in the bargain.

Big screen, small titles:

1. M. Fritz Lang's creepy 1931 melodrama about a child killer, played by Peter Lorre.
2. O. A prehistoric flying reptile terrorizes Manhattan in this 1982 movie starring Michael Moriarty.
3. V. Aliens terrorize the earth. Made in 1983, it remains one of the most expensive TV movies ever.
4. W. Mediocre 1974 thriller starring Twiggy.
5. Z. Highly acclaimed 1969 Costa-Gavras political thriller set in Greece.

The only way to watch *The Sound of Music*

In Seoul, South Korea, in the late 1960s, a movie theater manager decided the running time of *The Sound of Music* was too long. He shortened it by cutting out all the songs.

The only federal law-enforcement agent to burp on network radio

Well, ex-c-u-u-u-se me! FBI agent Melvin Purvis and sixteen of his men staked out Chicago's Biograph Theater for two hours on July 24, 1934, waiting for the show to break and John Dillinger to emerge. When he did (after viewing *Manhattan Melodrama*, starring Clark Gable and William Powell), Purvis's men gunned him down. Acclaimed a national hero, the G-man later appeared on the *Fleischmann's Yeast Hour*, where he burped loudly into a live microphone. The coast-to-coast eructation was heard by millions of listeners, grossed out executives at the J. Walter Thompson advertising agency, and earned Purvis a dressing-down from FBI boss J. Edgar Hoover. He was not invited back on the show.

Actor Richard Burton burped the first time he kissed Elizabeth Taylor during the making of *Cleopatra*. The scene had to be refilmed.

The only Finnish-language TV program in the United States

Some 616,000 Americans claim Finnish roots, according to the 1980 census, and 112,000 of them live in Michigan. Most are concentrated in the Sauna Belt on Michigan's upper peninsula, where even the churches have saunas, street signs are in Finnish, and *Finland Calling* is broadcast every Sunday morning on WLUC-TV, Channel 6, in Negaunee. It claims to be the nation's only regularly broadcast Finnish-language TV show.

The only Hollywood cowboy to stuff and mount his horse

By his own account, Roy Rogers lost a piece of himself when his horse Trigger died. Small wonder: unlike other movieland horses, Trigger could count to twenty-five and draw an X with a pencil clenched between his teeth. He was even housebroken. So instead of burying

the animal, Roy and his wife, Dale Evans, had him
stuffed, mounted, and enclosed in a glass case.

In fact, he did the same for Trigger, Jr., as well as
Dale's horse, Buttermilk, and Bullet, his dog. All are
tastefully displayed at the Roy Rogers-Dale Evans Museum in Victorville, California, where you can also see
virtually every pair of boots, lasso, and saddle the cowboy couple ever owned, as well as an impressive collection of antique cars, rodeo awards, trophy heads from
African safaris, family photos, and household furniture.
Many visitors come away with the sense that Roy and
Dale never threw anything out. The collection was inspired by a depressing visit Roy made years ago to the
Will Rogers museum.

"It didn't have anything in it," he remembered. "Just
a couple of ropes and things. I made up my mind right
then that if I ever got anyplace in this business, I was
gonna keep everything. Well, I sure did."

The only lasting contribution to popular culture made by *The Hank McCune Show*

A primitive slapstick sitcom that ran for seven weeks
in 1950, never to be seen again, *The Hank McCune Show*
has one claim to posterity: It was the first TV show ever
to use canned laughter.

The only play performed before a paid audience

The New York critics didn't take kindly to *The Ladder*, a drama about reincarnation that opened on Broadway in 1926. With theatergoers staying home in droves,
the play's chief backer, an eccentric Texas oilman
named Edgar B. Davis, attempted to boost attendance by

not charging admission. He kept the play going on that basis for 789 performances, losing $500,000 in the process before closing it down in 1927.

Undaunted, Davis attempted to reincarnate *The Ladder* in Boston a few years later. But the critics there were no kinder or gentler, and attendance was even sparser, despite Davis's free-admission policy. So he dispatched squads of men throughout Scollay Square every evening with instructions to pay seventy-five cents to anyone who would come to the theater and watch. (He prudently held off payment until after the final curtain.) According to no less a source than *Playbill*, *The Ladder* "may be the only play in history to pay its audience."

Watch carefully, there won't be another one: TV series that lasted only a single episode:

1. *You're in the Picture.* This 1961 audience participation show, hosted by Jackie Gleason, was panned so mercilessly after it premiered that a second episode never materialized. Instead, the following week Gleason spent the entire allotted half hour apologizing for the fiasco.

2. *Turn-on.* Patterned loosely after Rowan and Martin's *Laugh-in* and premiering in 1969, *Turn-on* was big on animation, short videotaped blackouts, computer graphics, and synthesizer music. Its heavy reliance on sexual innuendo frightened off many ABC affiliates after the first week, forcing Bristol-Myers to drop its sponsorship.

The only visit Sonja Henie ever made to Omaha, Nebraska

Following her gold-medal performance at the 1936 Olympics in Berlin, figure skater Sonja Henie became an overnight sensation in the United States. When she brought her ice show to Omaha, Nebraska, on the eve of Valentine's Day, 1941, a local booster commissioned an eighty-pound ice sculpture of the skater's heart, vowing that the city would keep it until Sonja returned.

But Sonja reacted lukewarmly to the frigid valentine and, for that matter, to Omaha; she died in 1969 without ever going back. As for the heart, it reposes safely in the Omaha Cold Storage Terminal. Visitors are welcome during business hours, but hurry. As of this writing, the heart was down to sixty pounds.

The only female Smurf

There are over one hundred Smurfs, all of them created by Belgian cartoonist Peyo Culliford, beginning in 1957. All but one—the heroine Smurfette—are male. The oldest, at 543, is Papa Smurf.

The only two-time winner of the Miss America contest

Sixteen-year-old Mary Katherine Campbell was the second Miss America. The auburn-haired, hazel-eyed high-school student was crowned in Atlantic City, New Jersey, on September 8, 1922, and again, on September 7, 1923. She had previously been Miss Columbus, Ohio.

The only fashion trend inspired by a method of execution

Coiffure à la victime was all the rage during the Reign of Terror. Fashionable young women in England and France bobbed their hair and shaved the napes of their necks in imitation of the tonsures given to Marie Antoinette and other victims of French revolutionary justice preparatory to being guillotined. For an added touch of drama, some women wore blood-red ribbons around their necks.

The only sign of the zodiac represented by an inanimate object

Eleven of the twelve signs of the zodiac are named for animals, people, and mythical beasts. The exception is Libra, which is represented by a pair of scales.

Why scales? No one knows for certain. The easy answer is that each sign is named after the constellation with which it originally coincided—a scheme worked out, most likely, by the ancient Sumerians. Still, that doesn't stop some astrologers from asserting that people born under the sign of Libra (September 23–October 23) are *balanced* in their views and tend to *weigh* matters carefully before making a decision.

If the sign of the scales has any special significance at all, most likely it's because the autumnal equinox, when day and night are in equal *balance,* originally occurred in the constellation of Libra. It no longer does, of course: Because of a phenomenon called the precession of the equinoxes, the constellations no longer match up with their zodiacal namesakes.

THE ORAL TRADITION

The only breakfast cereal publicly endorsed by T. S. Eliot

Do I dare to eat it with a sliced peach? When T. S. Eliot was lecturing to undergraduates at Harvard in the 1930s, a couple of back-row pranksters who had difficulty hearing him sent him a large box of Wheaties with a note to eat up to give his voice more carrying power.

Eliot thanked them for the gift—in an uncharacteristically booming voice—in a subsequent lecture.

The only conclusive proof that desserts have feelings

A Canadian neurologist ran an electroencephalogram (EEG) test on a serving of lime Jell-O in 1976 and found the shimmering dessert to be bristling with brain waves.

The physician, Adrian R. M. Upton, conducted the EEG test by attaching electrodes to the Jell-O in the intensive-care unit of McMaster University Hospital, in Hamilton, Ontario. The experiment was not a prank, nor was it designed to verify whether powdered gelatin can be trained to perform simple but useful acts. Rather, he said, the presence of brain waves in an EEG reading taken on a dish of Jell-O is evidence of the basic faultiness of EEG readings in general.

"Even in the presence of brain death," Dr. Upton explained, "it's extremely difficult to get a flat EEG" because of stray electrical impulses emitted by nearby surgical equipment, pagers, etc., which are picked up by the EEG machine and recorded as brain waves. "However," he said, "a good technologist is well aware of them."

The only fruit named after a reproductive gland

The word *avocado* derives from *ahuacatl*—the Nahuatl word for "testicle." When Cortés arrived in Mexico, the Aztec chief Montezuma introduced the luscious green fruit to him, explaining that its name derived from its aphrodisiac properties rather than its appearance. (No argument there; how many people have pear-shaped testicles?) There is no proof that avocados have any restorative effect on the libido, although many people, including King Louis XIV, have eaten them in the hope of curing impotence.

The etymology of the word *orchid*, by the way, is similar: It comes from the Greek word *orchis*, or "testicle." In fact, orchids have also been called ballock-worts, dogstones, and *testiculus canis*. The reason: The flower's twin tubers look somewhat like testicles.

The only ten-foot-wide nonstick frying pan

You *need* a ten-foot-wide pan to fry fifty dozen eggs at once. That's a typical serving at the Central Maine Egg Festival, held every July in Pittsfield, Maine. The festival switched to a nonstick pan some years back in what would appear to be a well-intentioned effort to hold cho-

lesterol levels down. Not all the eggs are fried and eaten at the annual eggoree; many are thrown, decorated, and carried in races.

The festival also features some of the world's biggest spatulas.

The only state with two state vegetables

Unable to choose between the pinto bean and the chili—staples of Native American and Mexican American cuisine, respectively—the New Mexico state legislature declared both the official state vegetables in 1965.

The only low-cost, radioactive dinnerware

Fiesta Ware was a popular brand of tableware introduced by the Homer-Laughlin China Company in 1936. The dishes were available in five vivid decorator colors, but the orange dishes were discontinued in the 1940s because of rumors that they were radioactive.

They really were—sort of. In 1981 the New York State Department of Health reported that orange Fiesta Ware, as well as eight other brands of vintage tableware, contained traces of lead as well as uranium, which emitted low levels of radiation. While the other colors posed no health threat, the report said, repeated use of the orange dishes over time could cause dangerous buildups of uranium and lead in the body. Kidney and stomach damage could result.

The health officials noted, however, that there was no danger in merely collecting the plates, still found in thousands of U.S. homes. Just don't eat off them, they advised.

The only New York City Automat to survive into the 1990s

Not so long ago, Horn & Hardart Automats were as much a New York City institution as the subway and the Empire State Building. This was fast-food dining at its most leisurely—a level of elegance on the cheap, says architecture critic Paul Goldberger "that McDonald's and Burger King will never equal."

The original Automats, created by Joseph V. Horn and Frank Hardart, were opened in Philadelphia in 1899; New York didn't get its first until 1911. The idea was simple, yet remarkably forward-looking: Dishes were served *automatically* from little compartments, each with a glass door. You surveyed the choices, fed in the appropriate coins, turned the knob, and the door sprung open. Coffee was dispensed from a brass spout shaped like a dolphin's head. The need for waiters was eliminated—and with it, tipping dilemmas, botched orders, and "Hi, I'm Todd, your waitperson."

Automat food was uniformly middlebrow and reasonably priced, yet there was an opulent feel to the Art Deco interiors, with their marble paneling, polished granite floors, and brass ornamentation. If you were really looking to economize, you could dawdle the whole day over a cup of free tomato soup—hot water mixed with ketchup and saltines.

"This is what my mother told me," former New York City parks commissioner Henry Stern told *The New York Times.* "One day in the Depression, a man came to the Automat and wanted to commit suicide. So he found a roll—his last nickel for a roll—and spread it with J-O Paste, which is rat poison. But at the last minute he lost his nerve and walked out. Someone else came in and saw the roll. It looked like it was buttered. He ate the roll and died. The moral, according to my mother, was Don't eat from other people's plates."

The Automats began vanishing in the early 1970s. The last one to go was located at 200 East Forty-second Street; it was closed in 1991, a victim of competition from fast-food eateries and changing eating habits. "That's dreadful," Henry Stern said. "It was equivalent to the Woolworth Building and Macy's windows as the most public place in town. It was everything."

The only Chinese-Norwegian restaurant in the United States

The Sunset Park and Bay Ridge sections of Brooklyn, New York, have historically been home to one of the largest concentrations of Norwegian Americans in the United States. Among the area's best-known landmarks was the Atlantic restaurant, a diner serving Norwegian cuisine to a predominantly Norwegian clientele.

But the neighborhood has changed in recent years, with the arrival of hundreds of Asian and middle-eastern families. To reflect this shifting cultural mix, the Atlantic changed its name to WeeKee's in 1990 and installed a large sign outside that says CHINESE-NORWE-GIAN-AMERICAN CUISINE.

WeeKee's patrons are served by both Chinese and Norwegian waiters, and the menu features pork fried rice and moo goo gai pan as well as fish pudding and *stekte middagspoiser* ("fried sausage"). Says Bjorg Nilsen, who has worked at the restaurant for several years, "It's good that people can order different things now."

The only restaurant required by law to serve bean soup every day

On a sultry summer's day in 1904, Speaker of the House Joseph G. Cannon showed up at the House of Representatives Restaurant in Washington, D.C., ready for Yankee bean soup. But it was too hot for soup, he was told, and none had been prepared.

"Thunderation!" he bellowed. "I had my mouth set for bean soup. From now on, hot or cold, rain, snow, or shine, I want it on the menu everyday."

And so it has been, every day since; by federal mandate, Speaker Joseph G. Cannon Memorial Bean Soup must always be served at the House of Representatives Restaurant, Room H118 in the Capitol. Still a bargain at ninety-five cents a bowl.

The only sugared breakfast cereal you could eat with a magnet

Virtually all breakfast cereals have iron, some more than others. Sufficient iron is essential to the diet; it enables oxygen to be delivered to the muscles and properly transported by the blood.

But a little iron goes a long way. When Kellogg Co. introduced Frosted Rice in 1977, it received letters from consumers who had discovered it was possible to pick the stuff up with a strong magnet.

According to a company spokesman, "We had problems evenly distributing the product's sugar coating," wherein most of the iron was concentrated. Rather than attempt to even out the iron content, Kellog simply reduced it from 25 percent of the FDA recommended daily allowance to 10 percent. In a statement to *The Wall Street Journal*, Kellogg promised that the new, improved—and demagnetized—version could not be lifted with magnets "unless they are very, very strong."

The only beverage to receive the papal seal of approval

Coffee was introduced to Europe by Arabian traders in the sixteenth century and promptly condemned by many Roman Catholic clerics as an infidel's drink, "the wine of Islam." Its stimulating effects, they believed, proved that the beverage was bewitched. But Pope Clement VIII, an insatiable coffee drinker himself, dispelled clerical resistance in 1592 when he issued an edict officially recognizing coffee as a Christian drink.

The only meat store in the United States that sells fresh rhinoceros steaks

Got a hankering for fresh snapping turtle—or breaded leg of llama? Then get on the horn to Czimer Foods, in the Chicago suburb of Lockport. Established in 1914, it's the only bona fide purveyor of such delicacies as hippo roast, bear, wild hare, peacock, elk, buffalo, rhino, and elephant in the United States. Probably in the world.

Czimer's clientele includes restaurants and organizations as well as individuals with a taste for the bizarre. A Michigan electrical-supply company recently placed an order for 150 pounds of hippo stew and 300 pounds of reindeer roast for a company dinner.

"The big problem is supply," says Arthur Czimer, one of three Czimer cziblings who run the business. "We haven't been able to get elephant for five years. There's a scarcity of alligators and bear because of tightened conservation rules. But we're expecting ten lions in a few months. Lions we need badly."

The only food that doesn't spoil

Even if you rarely use honey, chances are there's a half empty jar of the stuff somewhere in your pantry, purchased ten or fifteen years ago for some reason or another. Fish it out and you may find that it has crystallized somewhat, but don't make the mistake of thinking it's gone bad: Honey contains natural enzymes that keep it fresh forever, without artificial preservatives. Supplies of honey disinterred in this century by archaeologists from the Egyptian pyramids proved as fresh as the day they were bottled, three thousand years ago.

Honey may in fact be the single oldest processed food known to humankind. It was introduced to the world by the nomads of central Asia, who harvested it by smoking bees from their hives. Later, the ancient Romans prescribed a mixture of honey and coriander as a cure for childbirth fever. In medieval Europe it was also used as an antidote to snakebite and rabies, and a poultice of honey and ground garden slug was said to be effective against warts.

Over the centuries honey has been used not only as a sweetener but as an antiseptic, an intoxicant, an energy source, and a laxative. It has also been known to cause cavities in the teeth of honey bears.

The only food adult koalas eat

Koalas are cuddly and appealing, but don't get too close to one; every last one has a fierce case of cough-drop breath. The reason: the koala (*Phascolarctos cinereus*) will not even consider eating anything but the leaves of the eucalyptus tree.

And not just any eucalyptus leaves. Indigenous to eastern Australia, these nocturnal tree dwellers are un-apologetic homebodies who typically keep to a turf of three hundred to four hundred acres and a handful of favorite trees. Some koalas will eat *spotted* eucalyptus and nothing else; others will eat only the red gum variety.

Even then their pickiness doesn't stop. Give a hungry koala the right brand of eucalyptus, and he still may walk off in a huff without so much as a nibble. That's because some leaves contain prussic acid, a deadly toxin. Koalas know which ones to avoid.

The question then: What does a koala eat when he's trapped in a Wendy's or a sushi bar with nary a eucalyptus tree for miles? Will he break down and order a burger?

Not ordinarily. To be sure, under extreme duress, adult koalas may eat other foods such as mistletoe and box leaves. They will also come down from their trees from time to time to snack on gravel and soil, though as an aid to digestion rather than for nourishment. But without eucalyptus adult koalas will die. And with the destruction of vast areas of forest in Australia by fire and man, millions of koalas have starved to death in this century.

The only major automobile company to manufacture edible cars

Henry Ford believed that soybeans were America's last best hope for nutritional salvation, and that people should eat them at every meal.

He also believed they should drive soybean automobiles.

Ford began puttering around with soybeans and soybean oil in his Dearborn, Michigan, workshop in 1929. In the mid-1930s he went a giant step farther, building full-scale soybean processing plants in River Rouge, Saline, and Milan, Michigan. From beans grown on Ford-operated farms and also purchased from local farmers, the factories extracted millions of gallons of soybean oil, which was used in the manufacture of horn buttons, control knobs, switch handles, housings for distributors, and paint.

Ford hoped someday to manufacture an all-soy car—the world's first true soymobile. But his dream never came to pass, and by the end of World War II, the company had closed its soybean factories for good.

MUSIC
AND DANCE

The only bandleader to patent a major kitchen appliance

In 1922 Stephen J. Poplawski of Racine, Wisconsin, developed a new type of electric food mixer whose principal operative features were rotating blades at the bottom of a removable glass carafe.

In 1936 bandleader Fred Waring saw a demonstration of the Poplawski vibrator, as it was called. Waring and The Pennsylvanians were among the most popular bands of the day; millions of fans bought their records, heard them in concert, and tuned into their weekly broadcasts from New York's Vanderbilt Theater. Waring, who had majored in architecture and engineering at Penn State, loved gadgeteering as much as bandleading. He took Poplawski's device, made some adjustments, and applied for a patent. Voilà: The Waring blender was born.

A natural salesman, Waring toured the country promoting his brainchild, touting it as a bartender's aid—a no-muss, no-fuss way to mix drinks and influence people. Ironically, his father, a banker, often spoke at temperance rallies, and Waring himself had supported Prohibition. Small wonder some Waring fans claimed he designed the blender for the benefit of an ill relative who couldn't swallow.

In time the Waring company brought out new models of the blender in a range of designer colors, marketed it as an indispensable kitchen aid, and added more buttons—chop, grate, liquefy, mangle, maim, etc.—than are found on a concertina.

Waring also invented the travel iron.

The only available recording of a castrato

Castration for dollars was a common practice in seventeenth- and eighteenth-century Italy. In exchange for payment and the promise of future glory, poor families would often sign their male children over to choirmasters and opera directors who would have the boys emasculated in order to preserve the youthful quality of the voice.

Castrato sopranos were among the most celebrated and highly paid performing artists of their day. Following an especially moving aria, the audience would often cry, *"Evviva il cotello!"* ("Long live the little knife!"). But the inhumane practice performed for the good of music declined in the 1800s, with Pope Pius IX hastening its end by condemning it in a papal bull in 1851. Nonetheless, the Vatican continued to give refuge to existing castrati and remained the only place in the world where castrati sang regularly in the latter half of the nineteenth century.

By the time the director of the Sistine Chapel choir, Domenico Mustafa, died in 1912, only a single castrato remained—Alessandro Moreschi (1858–1922). A member of the choir since 1883, Moreschi was known to devotees as *"l'angelo di Roma"* His exquisite voice can still be heard, albeit faintly and scratchily, on a unique series of ten primitive gramophone recordings he made in

1902–1903. No other recordings like it were ever made. The label describes him as "*Soprano della Capella Sistina.*"

The only ballet dancer to execute an entrechat douze

In executing an entrechat, a ballet dancer leaps into the air and crosses and uncrosses his or her legs at mid-calf. A single midair entrechat is a feat worth noticing; Marie Camargo (1710–1770) was the first dancer to have executed two. (In her day, entrechats were the exclusive province of male dancers; in order to bring it off, she first had to cut several inches off her skirt.) In this century, the great Waslaw Nijinksy (1889–1950) was for years the only dancer capable of an entrechat-dix—five complete entrechats, or ten movements in all.

But on a BBC broadcast in January 1973, Wayne Sleep, the diminutive principal dancer of the Royal Ballet, performed the world's first and only entrechat-douze—six complete entrechats between takeoff and landing. The feat was replayed in slow motion several times.

The only well known female operatic role meant to be sung by a man

There are many operas in which women sing male roles—Cherubino in *The Marriage of Figaro*, for example, or Feodor in *Boris Godunov*. But the gargantuan Cook in Prokofiev's farcical opera, *The Love for Three Oranges*, is the only female character normally played by a man.

Small wonder, since not even the best-fed coloratura could measure up to the part. The Cook (she's actually a witch named Creonte) is built like Primo Carnera, with a voice to match, and spends much of her time on stage terrorizing the rest of the cast with a ladle the size of an oar. The part is scored for a bass and is always sung by a man.

The only composer to sign the Declaration of Independence

Thomas Jefferson wasn't the only founding father to fit the description *renaissance man*. Francis Hopkinson (1737–1791) was every inch his match.

A lawyer, jurist, author, poet, inventor, musician, and dry-goods retailer, Hopkinson composed works for harpsichord and fortepiano, as well as songs and choral pieces. His "My Days Have Been So Wondrous Free," set to a poem by Thomas Parnell, is the earliest secular song by an American extant today. *The Temple of Minerva*, which he described as an "oratorical entertainment," was a favorite of Jefferson's and George Washington's. At its best, Hopkinson's compositions are evocative of the chamber pieces of Henry Purcell.

An outspoken advocate of independence from Great Britain, Hopkinson represented New Jersey at the Second Continental Congress and was one of fifty-six men to put his John Hancock on the Declaration of Independence. (He signed as "Fras. Hopkinson.") He later served as a U.S. district-court judge and helped frame the U.S. Constitution.

The only piano with a built-in staircase and balcony

The unique Klavins piano *needs* a staircase and balcony; otherwise, the only way a pianist could reach the keyboard would be by sitting on an eight-foot-high stack of Chopin scores—or on the shoulders of another pianist. Standing thirteen feet high and weighing two tons, it's the tallest piano ever built. A guardrail on the balcony prevents the pianist from toppling over the side during especially frenzied allegros.

According to *Clavier* magazine, German designer David Klavins created the instrument to correct tonal problems arising from traditional stringing methods. In conventional concert grands, the strings are stretched from front to back; in Klavins's piano, they're stretched vertically. The bass strings are nearly ten feet long.

The only character to appear in two Gilbert and Sullivan operettas

In the final act of *H.M.S. Pinafore*, which premiered in 1878, Little Buttercup reveals with much embarrassment that she accidentally switched Captain Edward Corcoran with Able Seaman Ralph Rackstraw when they were infants in her care "a-many years ago." The two exchange ranks to correct the error, and Corcoran closes out the play demoted but happier than ever.

However, fifteen years later he resurfaced in Gilbert and Sullivan's *Utopia, Limited,* his old rank fully restored. No mention is made of his demotion, and he is listed in the dramatic personae as Captain Sir Edward Corcoran, KCB, RN. The only G & S figure ever to be recycled, Corcoran appears principally to sing the praises of industrial progress: "We can steer and we can stoke, and, thanks to coal, and thanks to coke, we never run a ship ashore!"

At the height of *Pinafore*'s popularity, the lines, "What, never? . . . Well, hardly ever," were so frequently sung, quoted, and lampooned, that one London editor grew sick of hearing them and is said to have ordered his staff never to print them in his newspaper. Asked one subeditor, "What, never?" And his superior groaned in resignation, "Well, hardly ever."

The only decemet ever composed

A decemet is a musical monstrosity—a chamber piece for ten string instruments. The only reason the word even exists is because German composer Franz Xaver Gebel (1787–1843) wrote one.

Gebel was born in Austria but lived most of his life in Moscow. Though the score of his Decemet, Op. 28, survives, his reasons for composing it remain obscure. There are no known recordings of the decemet, and few of his works are ever played at all.

The only opera about baseball

The outlook was actually quite rosy for William Schuman's one-act opera, *The Mighty Casey*, when it premiered at a high-school auditorium in Hartford, Connecticut, in 1953.

Based on Ernest Thayer's 1888 narrative poem, *Casey at the Bat*, the opera revealed such long-suppressed facts as Casey's batting average (.564), his home-run total (99), his runs batted in (200), his position (right field), and his appetite for inside fastballs. Casey's sweetheart also makes her debut, and there is a bench-clearing brawl that Thayer forgot to mention in the poem.

But somehow *The Mighty Casey* never got to first base. The hero himself never sang or spoke, the libretto lacked buoyancy and wit, and most critics found the music more clangorous than melodic. According to *The New York Times*, the musical accompaniment to Casey's bottom-of-the-ninth strikeout carried suggestions of "Prokofiev's *Scythian Suite*, Beethoven's 9th Symphony, Times Square on Saturday evening, and the Queen Mary coming into dock, all rolled into one."

The only true excitement generated by the 1980 Kuhmo Music Festival

To the cheers of a packed house, Soviet cellist Augustinas Vassiliauskas stumbled on his way to the podium to take his bows following a concert at the Kuhmo Music Festival of 1980, held in central Finland, and fell on his three-hundred-year-old instrument, shattering it beyond repair.

The only country with a national anthem written by a major composer

Following two visits to England in the early 1790s, Franz Joseph Haydn returned home to Austria determined to give his country as stirring and stately a national anthem as "God Save the King." In January 1797, he completed work on the "Gott erhalte Franz den Kaiser" ("God Save Emperor Francis"), which received its official premier on February 12—the birthday of Emperor Francis I.

For reasons not altogether clear, the state authorities combined Haydn's sublime music with a third-rate text by one of the most notorious hack poets of the day, a former Jesuit priest turned police informer named Lorenz Leopold Haschka. Nonetheless, the "Gott erhalte" touched off a fervent new wave of Austrian patriotism. Later, Haydn worked it into his *Emperor* Quartet (in C Major, Op. 76, No. 3), and it was even sung as a hymn in churches throughout Europe and the United States.

"Gott erhalte" remained at the top of the charts in Austria for well over a century. But when Hitler retitled it "Deutschland, Deutschland über alles" and turned it into a Nazi fight song, the Austrians lost their taste for it. After the war, Austria scrapped the tainted "Gott erhalte" and held a nationwide contest to find a replacement. Two thousand lyricists entered. The winner was poet Paula Preradovic. The melody for the new anthem, titled "Land of Music, Land of Streams," was taken from *The Little Freemason* Cantata, K. 623—one of the last compositions by another great Austrian composer, Wolfgang Amadeus Mozart, who died a month after completing it.

The only musical rendering of the United States Constitution

An obscure Boston composer named Joseph Greeler set the entire U.S. Constitution—Bill of Rights, the rest of the amendments, and all—to music in 1874.

This strange oratorio took over six hours to perform, beginning with the preamble, which was scored as a recitative, sustained principally by altos and double basses. The amendments were treated as fugues; the passages on states' rights were set in a minor key for bass and tenor.

According to *Music World*, Greeler's *Constitution*

was performed several times before enthusiastic audiences. The score has long since disappeared.

The only key in which Irving Berlin could play the piano

"American music was born at his piano," violinist Isaac Stern once said of Irving Berlin. He might have added that it was a piano like no other—a custom-made affair equipped with a hand clutch that enabled Berlin to pick out tunes in any key, even though the only one he knew was F-sharp. He took it with him wherever he traveled, and when he retired from songwriting in 1974, he donated it to the Smithsonian. He called it his "Buick."

Between 1911 and 1972, Berlin wrote 1,500 songs, 19 Broadway musicals, and 18 Hollywood film scores without really knowing how to read or write music or play an instrument. "Oh, I can pick out the melody of a song with one finger, but I can't read the harmony," said the man who has been described as the single most powerful influence on the course of modern American music. "I feel like an awful dope that I know so little about my trade." The critic Alexander Woollcott called him "a creative ignoramus."

After composing a melody, Berlin left it to arrangers to work out the harmony and orchestration—and, usually, to transcribe it into a key other than F-sharp.

The only recording artist whose work is protected from pirating in Thailand

They call Thailand the music piracy capital of Southeast Asia. Despite pressure from foreign embassies and musicians' groups to start showing a little respect for international copyright laws, the pirating of recorded music is thirty-three-million-dollar-a-year business there.

No strings—almost: musical instruments with only a single string:

1. *Monochord.* More of a teaching apparatus than a musical instrument. Consisting of a single string stretched across a soundboard, it was used in eleventh-century music schools to demonstrate intervals in plainchant.
2. *Dactylomonocordo.* A kind of single-stringed lute invented by the Neapolitan composer Guida in 1877.
3. *Trombo marina.* Literally, "sea trumpet," though it is neither a trumpet nor connected in any way with the sea. Also called the nun's fiddle, it has a narrow tapered body, sometimes over seven feet long, with a single string running its length. Originating in Slavic Europe in the Middle Ages, it peaked in popularity—mostly as a street instrument—around 1700.
4. *Kalumbo bow.* Your basic central African zither, consisting of a string stretched tightly over a hollow gourd. Its resemblance to a hunting bow is unmistakable.

On almost any street in Bangkok you can find a store selling knockoffs of top-selling cassettes, many going for as little as eighty cents each. In fact, legitimate recordings are the exception in Thailand: Close to 99 percent of all tapes sold there are pirated. The works of virtually no artist, from Mozart to Metallica, are protected. The sole exception is the king. And we don't mean Elvis.

Educated in the United States, Bhumibol Adulyadej assumed the throne in 1946 at nineteen and is the only monarch many Thais have ever known. He's also the only Dixieland musician most Thais have ever heard; one British journalist called him "a keen jazzman who blows up a storm on clarinet and trumpet." If you're caught stepping on a coin that bears the king's likeness, or making a wisecrack at his expense—or passing a counterfeit edition of his celebrated palace jam session with New Orleans trumpeter Kid Sheik Cola—you will wind up in jail. Most Thais know better.

The only opera by Beethoven

Although he lived to see it critically acclaimed, Beethoven swore that his one and only opera, *Fidelio*, was the work that inflicted on him "the worst birth-pangs and brought me the most sorrow." Getting it composed, staged, and produced cost him so much time and effort that there's no wonder he never wrote another opera.

When *Fidelio* premiered in Vienna in 1805, the house was barely half full, and many of those in attendance were officers of Napoleon's invading army. The notices were indifferent, and even one of the lead singers, Herr Meyer, is said to have muttered during the performance. "My brother-in-law would never have written such damned nonsense." His brother-in-law was Mozart, and it was no secret that Beethoven hated being unfavorably compared with him.

Beethoven reworked some of *Fidelio*, and it was next staged the following year—again to so-so reviews.

Worse, the composer got into a shouting match with the theater manager over the receipts. According to Emil Ludwig in his biography of Beethoven, the manager noted that the gallery had been half empty. "I don't compose for the masses," Beethoven retorted.

"Even Mozart was not ashamed to write for the gallery," answered the manager, touching a nerve.

Beethoven snatched back his score and stormed out, thus ending *Fidelio*'s second run. It wasn't until 1814 that the opera, largely revised, was heard again. This time the critics loved it.

Fidelio is set in eighteenth-century Seville. The title character is a Spanish noblewoman disguised as a man, determined to liberate her husband Florestan, who languishes in a dungeon. Florestan may be the only operatic character to share his name with a twentieth-century toothpaste additive: Several years ago, TV commercials sang the praises of fluoristan, a potent decay-bashing ingredient in Colgate toothpaste.

The only major opera with no roles for females

Try to imagine *La Bohème, Aida, The Marriage of Figaro, Porgy and Bess,* or any other grand opera without a love interest. Not much fun, is it? Take sex out of opera, and the patrons will stay home in droves.

But there is a popular opera without sex—and without women. It's Benjamin Britten's 1951 four-acter, *Billy Budd,* based on Herman Melville's novella.

Set aboard the H.M.S. *Indomitable* in 1797, during the Napoleonic Wars, it is the story of the persecution of young Billy, an "able seaman," by the sadistic Claggart—and Billy's tragic martyrdom. In the opera, as in the novella, virtually all the characters are naval officers and enlistees; none are women.

Billy Budd is also one of the few operas with a prose libretto (cowritten by novelist E. M. Forster).

The only nonnative dance permitted in the Republic of Kiribati

Watch those dancing feet if you happen to set them down in Kiribati. Virtually all foreign dance steps—from the hula to the hora—are illegal in this tiny Pacific archipelago.

Independent since 1979, Kiribati, originally called the Gilbert and Ellice Islands, permits only native Kiribatian dances—at least in public, according to chief cultural officer Bivere Eritaia. Twisters, however, are exempt.

The only major opera to require a singer to hit a low D

There is actually more talking and less singing in *Die Entführung aus dem Serail*, or *The Abduction from the Seraglio*, than in Mozart's other operas. First performed in Vienna in 1782, it has never been ranked among his best work and did not premiere in the United States until 1946. However, it does contain many sublime moments that challenge the art of the virtuoso. In Act III, Osmin, the ruler of the harem, hits a bottom D—that's three octaves below middle C on a piano—a frequency of 73.4 Hz.

The only work scored for two armless pianists

While there is a fairly extensive literature of piano music for one hand—Ravel's *Concerto in G for Left Hand* is the best-known example—the *Bombardo-Carillon* by Alkan (pseudonym of Charles-Henri-Valentin Morhange) is the only piano duet we know of scored for

no hands. It's meant to be played on a pair of pedal pianos, a nineteenth-century keyboard instrument equipped with two keyboards—one for the hands, one for the
feet. The piece is rarely heard these days—a reflection, no
doubt, of the current scarcity of pedal pianos (and armless
pianists). (See also **The only composer crushed to death
by the Talmud,** page 315.)

The only opera star hired full-time to sing a head of state to sleep

Carlo Farinelli (1705–1782) was one of the most celebrated castrati of the eighteenth century. A soprano of
dazzling range and clarity, he was said to be the only
singer of his day who could do justice to the notoriously
difficult *Concerto for Larynx.* But at the peak of his career, he retired from the stage to accept a position as official lullabist to King Philip V of Spain.

The king, grown morose and unstable, was plagued
with horrendous insomnia. At the invitation of the royal
consort, Queen Elizabeth Farnese, Farinelli moved into
the royal palace in 1737 for the sole purpose of singing
the troubled ruler to sleep.

For the next ten years, he tucked Philip in with the
same four songs every night—two arias from Johann
Hasse's opera, *Artaserse,* a minuet by Attilio Aristi, and
"The Nightingale Song," by Geminiano Giacomelli. When
Philip died in 1746, Farinelli retired a wealthy man.

The only major symphonic orchestra to perform regularly without a conductor

Pervyi Simfonicheskii Ansambol—Persymfans for
short—made its debut in Moscow in 1922—the premiere
engagement of the world's only major symphonic orchestra to perform regularly minus a conductor.

Though critics applauded the Persymfans interpretations of Mozart, Beethoven, and Bach, politics figured as importantly as tempi in the program. The idea of a conductor—a supreme dictator controlling every musical nuance—seemed contrary to the collectivist aims of the Russian Revolution. And so the musicians began an experiment to see if they could collectively lead and keep time for themselves.

After four seasons, however, the Persymfans began to be troubled by dissension and infighting. Some of the musicians accused the first violinist of abusing his power by setting the tempo for each piece and keeping time by nodding his head. Others challenged the propriety of such class distinctions as *first* and *second* bassonist.

Increasingly, rehearsal time was taken up by no-win ideological bickering. Finally, in 1928, the Persymfans disbanded, and most of its members joined conventional orchestras.

MONEY (AND WHAT IT BUYS)

The only U.S. currency minted from a president's silverware

In 1791 Congress gave President George Washington the go-ahead to establish a national mint, equip it with stamping machines, and commission artists to design its first coins. The building was erected in Philadelphia the following year. As a gesture of good faith, the president contributed about one hundred dollars of his wife's silver, including a prized tea service, to the new venture. It was melted down and stamped into fifteen hundred "half-dismes," or silver five-cent pieces, in July 1792.

Despite the graciousness of the Washingtons' gesture, the coins were exceedingly ugly, "with one of the worst renderings of an eagle ever seen," according to Ted Schwarz in *A History of United States Coinage*. "The bird is scrawny and, though defiant, looks physically as though he might easily be defeated by a hummingbird."

The only federally authorized coin never minted

On August 8, 1776, the U.S. Congress drafted a list of proposed coins for the new republic. Among them was the mill, "of which 1,000 shall be equal to the federal dollar." Though there have been times in the nation's past when a one-mill coin might have come in handy, the government has never minted anything lower than a half cent.

However, the absence of a mill didn't stop many towns from levying taxes in mills well into this century, and in 1935, Secretary of the Treasury Henry Morgenthau, Jr., proposed the coining of one-mill pieces. A "midget-coin bill" was even introduced in Congress, but to the dismay of penny-pinchers and low tippers everywhere, it was never voted on.

The only U.S. paper currency bearing a woman's likeness

In these liberated times, women can run for public office, prowl the Yale Club, manage ball teams and orchestrate hostile takeovers. About the only thing they can't do is get their portrait on a United States currency note. In fact, only one female U.S. citizen has ever managed to crash currency's gender barrier—Martha Washington.

From 1886–1891, the one-dollar U.S. Silver Certificate carried a Charles Burt engraving of the first First Lady, based on a portrait of her by Jacobert. The same portrait, flanked by a picture of Martha's husband, also appeared on the reverse side of the 1896 certificate.

Except for Pocahontas, whose picture adorned an

1875 twenty-dollar bill, and female personifications of such abstract virtues as Liberty and Justice, everyone else ever pictured on paper money in the United States has been a man.

Ironically, of all the First Ladies, Martha Washington was among the least political—and the least likely to be commemorated on a currency issue. Barely literate, she kept her nose resolutely out of all affairs of state and occasionally appeared at official dinners with a ring of kitchen keys dangling from her waist.

The only time in U.S. history when the federal government was not in debt

The United States government has been in hock to individuals, banks, and other creditors almost continuously since the Revolutionary War. But there was one momentary respite during the administration of President Andrew Jackson when the government didn't owe a cent.

To be sure, history was on Jackson's side: Every chief executive back to Washington had tried, unsuccessfully, to wipe out the national debt. But the country had been in a prolonged growth spurt since the close of the War of 1812, and the federal government was raking in money faster than it could fold it, mostly from import tariffs and the sale of public lands.

On January 8, 1835, the government paid off the last of its debts and subsequently reported a surplus of thirty-seven million dollars. Worried that the administration would squander it, Henry Clay pushed a bill through Congress mandating that the money be distributed among the states. Most used it for things like education and public works; one state actually divided it up among all its citizens.

> **The only U.S. coin in circulation**
>
> 1. on which a president faces left is the Lincoln-head cent.
> 2. noncircular U.S. coin in circulation is the Susan B. Anthony dollar. (Production was discontinued in 1981, but Anthony dollars still turn up.)
> 3. with two images of the same president is the redesigned Lincoln-head cent.

But the good times were short-lived. The surplus helped fuel a period of speculation, inflation, and financial chaos that make the 1980s look tame. Then came the panic of 1837, and the surplus vanished overnight. The country has been in the red ever since.

These days, the national debt is well over one *trillion* dollars, and getting bigger by the minute. If you'd like to know at a glance exactly how grim the picture is, consider purchasing the new Debtman Calendar Clock, available from Warren Dennis, of Pasadena, California. Along with telling the time and date, it registers the minute-by-minute increase in the amount Washington owes.

The only pornographic, yet legal tender U.S. coin

In 1916, the United States Mint commissioned sculptor Hermon MacNeil to redesign the twenty-five-cent piece. MacNeil decided on a classical representation of Liberty and hired actress Irene MacDowell to pose for him. The two took pains to conceal their working arrangement from the public and from Miss MacDowell's husband, who was dead set against her career as a model. He also happened to be MacNeil's tennis partner.

But the risk of being found out turned out to be the least of MacNeil's worries. As soon as the new coin went into circulation, many taxpayers felt the sculptor had taken some uncalled-for liberties with Miss Liberty: Both her right breast and right thigh were completely exposed.

Letters poured into Washington by the sackful to decry the monetary lewdness, and Anthony Comstock, self-appointed guardian of public morals and founder of the Society for the Suppression of Vice, clamored for the coin's quick demise. There could be no possible argument, he said, for any form of currency that "showed the bared nipple and areola of an adult female."

Thus pressured, Congress, in 1917, sent MacNeil back to his drawing board, although the lawmakers decorously avoided any mention of Miss Liberty's undress. Instead, they asked the sculptor to rework the coin to make it more aesthetically appealing and easier to stack.

MacNeil obliged, also covering Liberty's breast and neck with a kind of chain-mail bra—an absurd anachronism—and chastely draping her thigh. Now properly attired, the Liberty quarter remained quietly in circulation until 1930.

The model for the Mercury dime and the Walking Liberty half-dollar, both minted from 1916 until the end of World War II, was Elsie Noll Stevens—wife of poet Wallace Stevens. Introduced to the poet at a gathering, pianist-wit Oscar Levant said, "Why shouldn't you be a great poet? I'd be inspired too if my wife had little wings where her ears should be."

The only opportunity to get a great deal on the Great Wall

Looking to buy Chinese real estate cheap? Since 1989 the Jing Ao Great Wall Souvenir Co. has been officially licensed to remove loose pebbles from the fifteen-hundred-mile-long wall and mount them on wooden stands for sale to tourists. "If I can just sell a tiny fraction of what I want," says Australian owner of the company, Sydney Parmenter, "I'll be a very rich man."

Why would Beijing's leaders sanction the deliberate pillage of China's most revered landmark? Evidently, because it makes them looks good. In June 1989, Following the Tiananmen Square uprising, the government wanted to show the world that foreign businesses were still welcome to set up shop in the People's Republic. Parmenter's off-the-wall idea fit the bill perfectly.

Besides, except for a few nicely restored showcase stretches, most of the fifteen-hundred-mile Wall is in grievous disrepair anyway—little more than a disordered mound of small stones and rubble. But Parmenter is anything but blasé.

"It's overwhelming when you sit down and think of the Great Wall of China, and you are selling the bloody thing," he says.

The only over-the-counter medication for the prompt relief of hemorrhoidal pain *and* facial wrinkles

WOMAN 1: It's a hemorrhoid ointment!
WOMAN 2: No—it's a face cream!
Announcer: No need to argue, ladies—you're *both right*! Preparation H is a leading hemorrhoid ointment *and* a face cream! It's actually two ointments in one.

Granted, you've never seen this commercial, but there's no telling what the future may bring: Preparation H, the mother of all hemorrhoid ointments, is also used as a facial cream.

Reports from the cosmetic grapevine indicate that small dabs of the viscous gunk will mask wrinkles and impart a youthful look to the complexion. The idea of using Preparation H for that purpose seems to have taken root in the 1970s and is still going strong.

One Beverly Hills woman told *Newsweek* that she saves the ointment for chic gatherings "when I want to look extra special." A New York City druggist told of selling out her entire stock in one day soon after the craze hit the East Coast.

"Everybody left with one lipstick and one tube of Preparation H," she said. "Nobody with hemorrhoids could buy it because everybody with wrinkles had grabbed it up."

Nonetheless, whatever its immediate positive effects, Preparation H users would do well to remember which end is up. Says one New York dermatologist, "Women could become sensitized to it after not much use. The skin could redden, burn, scale, and blister after a week of use."

The only vitamin-enriched pantyhose

Well-dressed legs can also be well-fed legs, thanks to Kanebo Ltd.

The Japan-based company manufactures and markets a line of women's nylon pantyhose embossed with tiny capsules of seaweed fibers, vitamins, and other nutrients. The capsules break on contact with the skin, and their contents are absorbed through the pores, explains Kanebo USA president Hiro Jimbo. The result: smoother, healthier, more wrinkle-resistant legs.

The only scalene-triangle-shaped postage stamp

There is no law in any country mandating that post-age stamps must have four sides. The Kingdom of Tonga once printed a series of round stamps intended to look like coins; Sierra Leone printed a stamp in the shape of Sierra Leone. Some countries have pushed creativity even further: Bhutan has issued perfumed stamps, holographic stamps, and sound-sheet stamps imprinted with miniature phonograph recordings of the Bhutanese national anthem.

Triangular stamps, though novel, are by no means unique. Scores of countries, from Malaysia to the Maldives, have issued them. However, triangular stamps always have two or, more typically, three equal sides. The only scalene, or assymetrical, triangular stamp was a two-and-a-half-centavo issue printed by Colombia in 1869.

(Colombia, incidentally, is also responsible for the world's smallest stamps—a series of .31″ × .37″ mini-specks issued between 1863 and 1866.)

The only major country that still issues glueless stamps

Great Britain introduced self-sticking postage stamps in 1840, and most of the world has since latched on to the idea. The lone holdout is China, where stamps are still printed and sold without an adhesive backing. However, glue pots are supplied at most post offices for users' convenience.

Well into the nineteenth century, Korea clung fiercely to the idea of glueless stamps. When Japan attempted to introduce the preglued variety there in 1884, the Koreans revolted, setting afire the main post office in Seoul and littering the streets with the alien postage. Japan sent troops in to quell the disturbance and annexed Korea a few years later.

Israel, by the way, is **the only country in the world that prints stamps with kosher glue.**

The only deliberate use of gibberish on a postage stamp

The Portuguese overseas province of Macao issued a 1936 airmail stamp that bore two lines of Greek characters liberally peppered with accents and diacritcal marks. Though the inscription looked legitimate, it was pure twaddle. Its purpose was to thwart forgers.

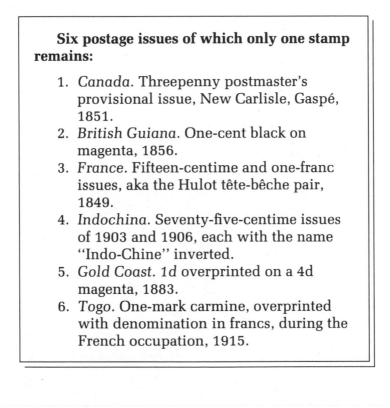

Six postage issues of which only one stamp remains:

1. *Canada.* Threepenny postmaster's provisional issue, New Carlisle, Gaspé, 1851.
2. *British Guiana.* One-cent black on magenta, 1856.
3. *France.* Fifteen-centime and one-franc issues, aka the Hulot tête-bêche pair, 1849.
4. *Indochina.* Seventy-five-centime issues of 1903 and 1906, each with the name "Indo-Chine" inverted.
5. *Gold Coast.* 1d overprinted on a 4d magenta, 1883.
6. *Togo.* One-mark carmine, overprinted with denomination in francs, during the French occupation, 1915.

NIMALS AND INSECTS

The only land animal other than man that commonly mates face-to-face

Sometimes they do it in the road, but two-toed sloths (genus *Choloepus*) are much happier mating—and doing everything else—in trees. The reason for this is that they are equipped with outlandishly long toenails, which aid climbing but make getting around on the ground more trouble than it's worth.

Moreover, the position of the genitalia and the forward tilt of the pelvis pretty much limit amorous sloths to belly-to-belly coupling—though rarely in the missionary position. Typically, the two partners mate vertically, each hanging by its arms from a branch.

Sex may well be the most strenuous activity a two-toed sloth will agree to. Living mostly in the tropical forests of northern South America, it spends most of the day sleeping and, even when awake, doesn't exactly maintain a feverish pace. The sloth has a sluggish nervous system and no reflexes to speak of. It can turn its breathing on and off at will without suffering any physical harm, and ingested food takes a good two weeks to make its way from one end of the alimentary tract to another. Sometimes a sloth will remain stationary long enough for moss to grow on its back.

The only animal other than man capable of getting sunburned

You may not like hearing this, but the pig bears closer physiological similarity to humans than any other mammal, with the possible exception of primates. Porcine teeth, blood, digestive organs, and skin are strikingly akin to their human counterparts. Pigs—and this you *will* appreciate—are by and large exceptionally clean, intelligent, easily trained, and moderate in their appetites (although the pig is **the only animal other than man that will willingly drink enough alcohol to be classified as an alcoholic).**

Porcine tissue and secretions, totally compatible with human physiology, have become indispensable in the treatment of human disease. In particular, pigskin is used as a component in artificial heart valves and as a soothing natural covering for severe burns. Not surprisingly, the components in pigskin that make it so adaptable to humans also make it vulnerable to the destructive force of the sun. The same ultraviolet rays that turn your skin red on a summer's day wreak equal havoc with the skin of *Sus scrofa*—which is why most farmers provide their hogs with a place to get out of the sun.

The only breed of dog that suffers from blackheads

Good thing dogs don't date. If they did, the Chinese crested dog would spend every Saturday night home alone watching *Kojak* reruns. It's the only canine plagued with adolescent zits.

Entirely bald, except for a regal tuft of hair sprouting from his head, the Chinese crested is by and large a well-designed breed; tiny, odorless, and usually even-tempered, it makes an excellent pet, especially for children. But its skin is unusually sensitive and prone to rashes and irritations—and, during puberty, to acne and blackheads.

Unlike dogs, it isn't at all unusual for cats to suffer the heartbreak and embarrassment of facial acne. Flare-ups are typically caused by bits of food clinging to the chin, feline glandular secretions gone wild, and poor hygiene. Cats keep clean by licking themselves, but an overweight or badly designed animal may have difficulty doing a good job on its own face. Kitty zits may result.

The only animal other than man capable of getting leprosy

Since ancient times, leprosy has long been thought of as an exclusively human affliction; until 1976 no other species was known to be susceptible to it, and the very impossibility of inducing leprosy in laboratory animals made it difficult to learn more about the disease and discover a cure.

In 1971 two U.S. research scientists, Dr. Waldemar Kirchheimer and Dr. Eleanor E. Storrs, succeeded in infecting a nine-banded armadillo (*Dasypus novemcinctus*) with the leprosy bacterium. Their work paved the way for the discovery, in 1976, that armadillos, indigenous to South and North America, often get the disease on their own, without help from humans. In fact, once the leprosy bacillus finds its way into an armadillo's liver or spleen, it grows far more rapidly than it does in people.

Knowing that, the World Health Organization (WHO) attempted to breed armadillos in captivity for the purpose of growing enough leprosy bacilli to develop early detection tests and preventive therapies. The armadillo, predicted Dr. Hubert Sansarrico, chief of WHO's leprosy unit, "will be the prize animal in the fight against leprosy, just as the monkey is for poliomyelitis."

It seemed like a good idea at the time, but the armadillos wanted no part of the experiment and refused to breed. WHO asked Venezuela's National Institute of Dermatology to investigate the armadillo's uncooperativeness; meanwhile, the armadillists of the world rejoiced. Wrote one woman, angered by the WHO experiment, "It sounds as if the larger animals have very small brains and only trace amounts of compassion."

The only bird of prey that sings

It's probably just as well that birds of prey have no musical talent. After all, imagine what it would do to a vulture's macho image if word got out that it could sing like a nightingale.

But the pale chanting goshawk (*Melierax canorus*), a predatory bird indigenous to South Africa and Botswana, sings quite unembarrassedly despite its appetite for live game birds, mammals, and reptiles, as well as carrion.

During the day it often sits quietly and uncomplainingly for hours on a low perch in the hot sun, eyeing the ground for movement. When the goshawk spots a potential meal, it hops down and gives chase, often for hundreds of yards. Endowed with a strong pair of legs, it often catches its prey by running after it until the animal collapses in exhaustion.

But the mornings are made for music. The song of the pale chanting goshawk is a melodious string of piping notes that sound something like *kleeu, kleeu-kleeu-klu-klu-klu* . . . and often punctuates the dawn on the Kalahari. It is hauntingly beautiful.

But if you're a field mouse or a lizard, don't be fooled.

The only mammal smaller than a bumblebee

The Kitti's hog-nosed bat (*Craseonycteris thonglongyai*) is found only in about twenty limestone caves in northern Thailand. With its ears and wings tucked in, it is easily the world's tiniest mammal, though not necessarily the cutest.

Named for its porcine snout, the Kitti's behaves much like larger, more conventional bats, roosting upside down and emerging to feed only after dark. First spotted in 1973, the Kitti's faced extinction when its heavily forested stomping grounds were cleared for agriculture. The last time anyone counted, there were only about 160 left, although local observers say the Kitti's ranks have grown in recent years.

The only order of mammals that isn't color-blind

Don't buy a color TV or change the wallpaper on your Doberman's account: Dogs perceive colors differently from the way humans do, and possibly not at all. In fact, all mammals are color-blind, except for the primates.

The eyes of monkeys and apes are equipped with the same three types of color-sensitive cones humans have. But other mammals have only one or two out of the three. Dogs, cows, and cats are believed to see the world only in shades of gray. Other animals have some color vision but confuse red with green, or green with yellow.

Conversely, many birds, insects, fish, and amphibians are endowed with a degree of color vision attainable in humans only through massive doses of hallucinogens. The eyes of the stickleback fish, for example, have five different types of color-sensing cones, allowing it to see a lot more colors than primates can.

The only bird with nostrils at the end of its beak

Native to New Zealand, the kiwi (*Apteryx australis*) caused a stir in ornithological circles when it was first spotted in 1813. Endowed with a roly-poly physique, whiskers like a cat's, no tail, and a pair of tiny, useless wings hidden under its feathers, the kiwi looked less like a bird than a joke.

But the kiwi is nobody's fool. Though it can't fly, it can run like the wind. It lays the largest eggs of any species of animal relative to its size—often as heavy as one fourth its own body weight. And its long, curved bill, uniquely fitted with a pair of nostrils at the end, is perfectly suited for finding food—worms and grubs, mostly—and prying it out of the ground.

The only insect that dies after it stings

The worker honeybee (*Apis mellifera*) is the kamikaze pilot of the insect world. It will readily sting a human in defense of the hive, or if it is annoyed or threatened. But that first sting is always its last.

The reason for this is that when the bee pulls back after having buried its stinger in its target, the stinger is held in place by barbs, and the bee is disemboweled in the process. The stinger continues shooting venom into its victim for another minute or so; the maimed bee dies within a few hours. Nobody wins.

Queen honeybees, in contrast, have longer stingers with fewer barbs; though they rarely sting humans, they can do so repeatedly without harming themselves.

The only insect that can turn its head without moving its body

Insects don't have necks. Which means if they need to look behind them to keep tabs on a predator or change lanes, they have to turn their entire body.

Not so the praying mantis (*Sphodromantis lineata*), which can rotate its triangular head independently of its body, the same as a human—but in an even wider arc. That gift, combined with the mantis's exceptional eyesight and keen appetite for insect pests, makes it a friend to gardeners and farmers everywhere.

In fact, in many U.S. localities, killing a praying mantis is a punishable offense. New York designated the praying mantis the state insect in 1977—over the objections of state assemblyman John Esposito, who argued that an insect that eats its mate was not deserving of so lofty an honor.

The only species of bird discovered and rendered extinct by a cat

Stephens Island is a tiny point of land off the coast of New Zealand. In 1894 the island's lighthouse keeper, D. Lyall, found his cat tormenting an odd-looking flightless bird. Lyall packed it in dry ice and shipped it to England. There, Lord Walter Rothschild, of the British Ornithological Club, studied it with great interest, calling it the Stephens Island wren, and classifying it *Traversia lyalli*.

Meanwhile, back on Stephens Island, the cat killed another twelve specimens of the same bird over the next several weeks, and these Lyall also sent to Rothschild for safekeeping. Thereafter, neither Lyall's cat nor anyone else ever saw another Stephens Island wren. Most of the specimens the cat brought home, however, are on display at British museums.

The only quadruped that can kneel on all four knees

Remember elephant jokes? One went, How do elephants' knees get so wrinkled? Answer: From playing marbles.

That dotty comeback reflects an unusual fact about elephants—namely, that they can easily get down on all four knees. An elephant can also hunker down with its hind legs stretched out behind it and its front legs pointing ahead; not many animals can do that either. In fact, the surprisingly high degree of elasticity in elephantine limbs led many people to believe as recently as the seventeenth century that the species had no joints at all.

Because its legs are so sensibly jointed, an elephant can lie down—or kneel to shoot marbles—whenever it wants, though it appears that only Asian elephants ever do so. The English game hunter Frederick Selous once said that of the thousands of sleeping African elephants he'd seen in his time, not one was lying down. Nor had he ever seen an imprint in the soil to indicate that they ever did.

The only working robotic pig

For centuries, French pigs have proven perfectly competent at sniffing out truffles in the soil. But biochemist Krishna Persaud, of the University of Manchester Institute of Science and Technology, has designed a machine that he feels can put the porkers out of work.

The man-made truffler, which looks nothing like a pig and is totally lacking in porcine charm, is equipped with a sensing device that can detect the subtle aroma of a truffle at depths of up to ten inches. When it homes in on the prized fungus, a beeper goes off.

In field tests in the Manchester countryside, Persaud's robopig performed with 75 percent accuracy—about the same as that of an experienced porker. However, unlike its natural-born cousin, a mechanical truffler does not need to be fed, nor does it become sexually aroused by the scent of truffles.

The only canine paratroop corps

Guerrilla letter carriers, be warned: The Pentagon is training dogs to jump out of airplanes.

In 1980 the U.S. Army recruited forty German shepherds as part of a first- (and presumably last-) of-its-kind effort to turn them into paratroopers. The pooches

started off with easy jumps from an eight-foot tower, then graduated to flying leaps from the fantail of a Navy destroyer. The objective: to train them to parachute from planes with military police into danger zones.

In the first trial jumps, into a lake near Fort Bragg, North Carolina, each dog was strapped to the back of a human paratrooper, who would lower the animal to the ground on a tether from two hundred feet up. That way, dog and man landed a few seconds apart, thus avoiding tangling and collisions.

"I wouldn't ask my dogs to do anything a man wouldn't do," Sergeant, First Class Robert Meade, kennel master of the 16th Military Police Group at Fort Bragg, North Carolina, told the Associated Press. "I can't think of anything a man could do that a dog can't, except drive a jeep or operate a radio."

The only attempt to use camels to deliver mail in the United States

After winning the Mexican War, the United States found itself with an extra half million square miles of Mexican territory on its hands. The land was wide open and arid, and not served by railways; moving mail, people, and construction materials around would be next to impossible. Then, Jefferson Davis, secretary of war under President Franklin Pierce, came up with a near brilliant solution: camels.

At Davis's urging, Congress appropriated thirty thousand dollars for the purchase of seventy-six single-humped camels from Turkey and Egypt. They arrived at Indianola, Texas, in 1856, and twenty-eight were shipped to the deserts of California and the Southwest the following year.

It wasn't an altogether crackbrained idea. Uniquely suited to desert life, the camel has a double row of eyelashes and can close its nostrils and ears against wind-blown sand; the male even has a rear-facing penis, so that he doesn't urinate into the wind. Capable of carrying thousand-pound loads, traveling forty miles a day, and going without water a week at a time, the imported camels were used to cart road-building materials, do farm work, and deliver mail.

But the experiment was doomed. Horses freaked out whenever they saw the strange creatures; soldiers were afraid to ride them. Worse, the army hired a Turkish-born veterinarian as its camel expert, solely on the strength of his ancestry. Having no experience whatsoever with camels, he once tried to cure a sick animal by tickling its nose with a chameleon's tail.

Within a few years, the army gave up on the camels and sold them off to silver mines, zoos, and circuses. In the early 1860s, a German merchant named Otto Esche imported forty-five Mongolian camels to the United States with the hope of creating an east-west Camel Express. The project never materialized, and Esche sold his camels to a British mining company.

The only place where camels are found in the wild

Let's get this straight, for once and for all: Only single-humped camels, or dromedaries, are found in North Africa and the Middle East—and *all* are domesticated. Their double-humped cousins, the Bactrians, are limited to Mongolia—the Gobi Desert has the heaviest concentration. Living in the wild in packs of five and six, Bactrians tend to be heavier, hairier, and shorter than dromedaries. They are also more even tempered.

Another thing: Dromedaries didn't start out in the Middle East—they're an American import, just like blue jeans and Big Macs. Related to the llamas, dromedaries originated in South America, where they were much in demand as pack animals centuries before Columbus arrived. Eventually, they were imported to the Middle East, probably by the Romans and Carthaginians.

The only use of cats as letter carriers

At one time or another, horses, dogs, cows, pigeons, and even camels have helped move the mail (see **The only attempt to use camels to deliver mail in the United States,** page 287). But only once have cats been thus employed. That was in Liège, Belgium, in 1879. In a daring experiment, thirty-seven trained felines were engaged as mail couriers between the town's central post office and outlying villages, all within a radius of about eighteen miles.

The idea wasn't altogether daft. Given the extraordinary homing instincts of cats, delivering mail or even pizzas might seem a perfectly reasonable vocation for them. Indeed, many animal behaviorists believe that microscopic iron particles embedded in feline tissue actually give cats a kind of built-in compass that keeps them from ever getting lost. Nonetheless, the Liège cat-courier project was quickly disbanded because of the uncooperativeness of the participants.

The only purple land animal

If the poet Gillette Burgess never saw a purple cow, it wasn't because he was unobservant. There are virtually no truly purple animals of any species anywhere in the world. The one exception is the blesbok.

Like its cousin, the bontebok, the blesbok (*Damaliscus albifrons*) is a rare species of antelope native to southern Africa and found mostly on game reserves

---

Only one specimen has ever been recorded of a

1. *Townsend's bunting.* Spotted, recorded, and, unfortunately, shot by John K. Townsend in 1833 near West Chester, Pennsylvania.
2. *Brewster's linnet.* Captured in 1870 near Waltham, Massachusetts.
3. *Cincinnati warbler.* Also captured near Waltham in 1870. It may have been a one-of-a-kind hybrid of two more common species.
4. *Fontoynont's hedgehog-tenrec.* A rodentlike insectivore captured in Madagascar. Its preserved body is on display at the Museé National d'Histoire Naturelle in Paris.
5. *Garrido's hutia.* According to *The Guinness Book of World Records,* this rodent was collected in April 1967 on the tiny island of Cayo Maja, off the southern coast of Cuba.

---

these days. Averaging only 3'3" tall at the shoulder, the blesbok is recognized by the snowy patch of white covering half its face, its eighteen-inch horns, and a body the color of Welch's Grape Juice.

Blesboks move in herds, shun meat, and prefer fleeing to fighting. When they're threatened, writes naturalist Desmond Morris, "they usually run in single file upwind with their noses to the ground."

The only bird that hibernates

Everyone knows birds fly south for the winter. But as recently as the mid-1700s, humans hadn't yet caught on to the phenomenon of migration. Rather, it was generally believed that birds buried themselves in the mud and hibernated, as do land animals.

While we now know better, there is one bird that does hibernate—the poorwill (*Phalaenoptilus nuttallii*), a grayish-brown member of the goatsucker family found mostly in the western United States. The Hopi Indians have known about the poorwill's cold-weather napathons for centuries. In their language, the word for poorwill is *holchko*, or "sleeper."

The first documented sighting of a hibernating poorwill was recorded by biologist Edmund Jaeger in December 1946. He'd come upon a specimen burrowed into a crevice in the foothills of the Sierra Nevada. The bird was "dead to the world," Jaeger reported, its body temperature around 64°F—106° is normal—and its heartbeat virtually nil.

On a return trip the following November, Jaeger found the same bird sequestered in the same crevice. While he deftly slipped a band on its foot, the bird awoke and flew off. But the ID anklet enabled the biologist to track the bird over the next four winters. Rather than migrate, it stayed put and hibernated each year, stirring with the first thaw. It lost no weight and remained in robust health. Since then, bird-watchers and ornithologists have caught scores of poorwills napping.

The only animal that wrinkles its nose in disgust

"Man," Mark Twain wrote, "is the only animal that blushes . . . or needs to." No argument there. There may also be some validity to the often-heard claim that non-humans are incapable of smiling. But no animal other than man has ever been seen to wrinkle its nose in disgust.

Of course, many animals, especially primates, make their feelings known through a wide vocabulary of ritualized facial expressions. Chimpanzees, in particular, will communicate rage, fear, and curiosity through lip and eye movements; they even convey playfulness and contentment with a kind of open-mouthed, bare-toothed facial gesture closely related to smiling. Expose a chimp to the smell of boiled cabbage, or to the poetry of Rod McKuen, and he may indeed turn his face away. But he will not wrinkle his nose and brow the way humans do. It's just not in his repertoire.

The only freshwater shark in the United States

From the Just When You Thought It Was Safe to Go Swimming in the Mississippi Department: Not all sharks confine themselves to saltwater. The bull shark (*Carcharhinus leucas*) is comfortable in freshwater *and* saltwater. Seas, oceans, rivers, lakes—you can take a bull shark anywhere.

Bull sharks are routinely found all over the world, including the Atlantic and Pacific oceans, and in a number of inland waterways in the United States, such as the Mississippi, the Apalachicola River in Florida, and the Atchafalaya River in Louisiana, 160 miles from the sea. They feed mainly on porpoises, stingrays, turtles, and shellfish but are not above cannibalizing their own, or attacking humans. The largest ever measured was ten feet long and weighed in at four-hundred pounds.

The only use of a raccoon as a safety net

Cornell University undergraduate Lisa Nelson was hiking on a rain-slickened trail near the campus in 1990 when she slipped and plummeted seventy-five feet into Cascadilla Gorge.

Fortunately, Nelson chose her landing site wisely: the back of a napping raccoon. She was discovered by local police and rescue workers who found her, and her stunned savior, lying side by side at the foot of the rocky gorge.

Nelson was hospitalized briefly for treatment of a broken wrist and a few other minor injuries; the raccoon also survived.

The only cats that live in groups

Wild or domesticated, cats tend to be solitary creatures with a take-it-or-leave-it attitude toward social intercourse. The one exception is the lion (*Panthera leo*).

While all other wild cats are loners as well as jungle dwellers, lions live in organized groups, or "prides," on the grassy plains of central Africa. A typical pride includes between one and four male adults, several adult lionesses, and their cubs. Most females remain with the same pride permanently; most males are ousted or quit on their own after two or three years to take up a nomadic existence. Even then they continue to live and hunt in groups of two and three.

Why are lions so big on togetherness? Mostly it's a matter of survival. Given their taste for larger game—zebras, wildebeests, gazelles—lions hunt and kill more efficiently as a group. Once they've felled their prey, there is usually enough meat to go around. In contrast, leopards, pumas, cheetahs, and their ilk feed mostly on animals too small to share. Besides, the jungle isn't set up for cooperative hunting: The noise of several predatory animals thundering through the foliage would inevitably scare off their prey.

The only bird that can fly the moment it hatches

From the And You Think Your Kids Are Precocious Department: Rather than incubate her eggs the old-fashioned way—by sitting on them—a gestating Australian mound-builder bird creates a large compost heap of decaying grass, dirt twigs, and other debris that is several yards in width and as tall as a man. After allowing the mound to stew in the sun and rain for a few weeks, she buries her eggs in it, and that's where they wait till hatching day.

In the case of one species—the mallee fowl (*Leipoa ocellata*)—the male tends the mound carefully to maintain the interior temperature at a toasty 33° throughout the incubation period, which usually lasts about seven weeks. Mallee fowls, like other mound builders, are large, horsy birds, and even at birth, they are endowed with powerful linebacker's legs. As soon as they're out of the shell, they claw their way to the surface and begin to fly.

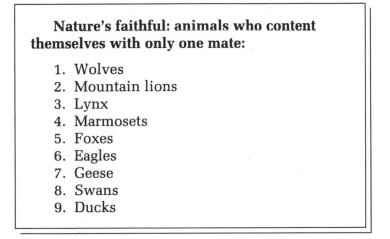

Nature's faithful: animals who content themselves with only one mate:

1. Wolves
2. Mountain lions
3. Lynx
4. Marmosets
5. Foxes
6. Eagles
7. Geese
8. Swans
9. Ducks

The only retrieving fish

You can train a dog to retrieve sticks, Frisbees, and felled birds. But the remora, or sharksucker (family *Echeneidae*), knows how to retrieve from birth.

Atop the remora's head is a ridged suction disk somewhat like the tips of toy arrows. The remora uses it to attach itself to sharks, turtles, whales, and even passing ships. Thus affixed, the remora feeds off the host and hopes the host doesn't return the favor. Usually, a remora can live in peaceful symbiosis with its host indefinitely.

Remoras can reach three feet in length, and since their suction disk can hold up to one hundred pounds, fishermen in many tropical areas will often tie a line to one, toss it in the water, and wait for it to latch on to something edible. According to James J. Parsons in *The Green Turtle and Man*, a remora's relationship with its host is much like that of a hunter and his retriever dog. "It is stroked, spoken to with . . . words of encouragement and thanks, and fed special food. When it fails to perform, it is . . . scolded, given the lash, or even bitten."

The only animal that moves on wheels

If you don't count bicycling bears and the Trojan Horse, the rotifer, a.k.a. the wheel animacule, is the one creature that can get around by rolling. A tiny organism found mostly in freshwater ponds and lakes, it is so named because of a cilia-covered rotary device at one end that sweeps in food and aids locomotion. But in one disk-shaped species, the device takes the form of a rotating belt that encircles the animal and enables it to move through the water like a Mississippi paddle wheeler.

The only animal able to crack open a coconut without assistance

The largest of all land crabs—some are as much as a foot wide across the shell and weigh up to nine pounds—the robber crab (*Birgus latro*) is indigenous to the southwest Pacific and Indian oceans. It has a clawspan wide enough for it to grab hold of a palm-tree trunk and shinny to the top. It is then an easy matter of plucking a coconut and letting it fall to the ground, where the crab's size and muscle are enough to break open the shell.

In their infancy, robbers are hermit crabs; by adulthood, there are no vacant shells big enough for them. In fact, mature robbers are so fully developed that they are equipped with a pair of lungs—and a corresponding need for oxygen. Keep one underwater for more than a few hours and it drowns.

The only land animal with an external backbone

Most animals have the good manners to keep their skeletal structures discreetly out of sight. Not the potto (*Perodicticus potto*). This small African primate wears part of its backbone on the outside.

Small, slow-moving, and covered with yellow fur, the potto spends much of its day hanging upside-down from tree branches and doesn't ordinarily go looking for trouble; West Africans call it the "softly-softly." But when threatened, it will curl itself into a ball and flatten the fur on its back to expose a row of sharp, bony points that extend from the thoracic and cervical vertebrae to form an impregnable shield. And by hurling itself at a predator, the gentle potto can inflict a lot of pain and suffering.

The only foolproof way to determine the sex of a penguin

The Southern Hemisphere is home to eighteen species of penguins, and in almost every case, males are all but indistinguishable from females. Ornithologists have found that the most reliable means of sexing a penguin—if not the most subtle—is to examine its anal vent during mating. Even then it's hard to be certain. The only sure way to know if you're dealing with a boy or girl penguin is to dissect it.

Sometimes you can guess at a penguin's gender by measuring its bill. In smaller emperor penguins, for example, the male's bill tends to be slightly thicker than the female's. In his 1951 book, *Sexual Behavior in Penguins*, L. E. Richdale lists eleven clues to a penguin's gender but cautions that none is totally reliable. At winter's end, for example, any unusually heavy penguin is likely to be a male; any unattached ones, especially during the breeding and incubation seasons, are also likely to be males.

But there are also plenty of svelte males and celibate females to make life difficult for the professional penguin sexer. In short, there is no way to establish a penguin's gender beyond a reasonable doubt other than by postmortem examination.

The only species of deer that grows horns regardless of its gender

Anytime you see a deer with antlers, you can bet the rent money it's a male; females never have them—except for female reindeer.

To be sure, male and female reindeer grow and shed their antlers at different times of year. But even to the trained eye, both sexes look astonishingly alike, and unless you keep close tabs on their rutting and calving seasons, you'd be hard-pressed to tell a boy from a girl. Evidently, the reindeer themselves have no such difficulty.

The only goat that can drive a truck

Donald Lee parked his Schwan Ice Cream truck in front of a house in Reelsville, Indiana, and knocked on the door to take an order. Meanwhile, a goat from a nearby farm scampered on to the driver's seat and released the parking brake. As Lee watched in horror, the truck careened 215 feet down a hill before crashing into a hickory tree. The truck sustained five thousand dollars in damage. The goat escaped without a scratch.

The only horse that can drive a car

The world's a pretty big place, and somewhere out there may be horses who can refinish furniture, fix a perfect margarita, or diaper an infant. But the only equine on record that can operate an automobile is Butterscotch, a palomino gelding owned by Dr. Dorothy Magallon, of Louisville, Kentucky.

According to *The Guinness Book of Pet Records*, the vehicle is a custom-fitted 1960 Lincoln, equipped with a raised steering wheel, outsize gas pedal and brake, and hoof-controlled gearshift and ignition. The 1,660-pound driver enters via a retractable ramp. He turns the steering wheel with his nose and sounds the horn by biting it. The car's maximum cruising speed is five miles per hour.

Butterscotch always wears a seat belt and never picks up hitchhikers.

The only breed of dog that perspires like a human

The tiny Mexican hairless has sweat glands throughout its body surface. When it's overheated, it sweats like a basketball player. The hairless also has real tear ducts and weeps openly when distraught, and is partial to fresh fruit and vegetables.

In Mexico, centuries ago, the Aztecs called the hairless Xolaizcuintl and revered him as a god who escorted dead souls to the afterworld. In life, too, hairlesses had unique gifts: Because of their high body temperature—104°—the Aztecs often used them like hot-water bottles in bed on frosty nights. And they believed that a hairless held against the body like a poultice would draw away asthma, rheumatism, kidney disease, malaria, and other ailments.

Non-Aztecs of the era also revered the hairless. Not as a god, though, but as a meal.

The only time the American flag was lowered to half-mast for a deceased zoo animal

When Samson the gorilla died of a heart attack in 1981, the Milwaukee County Zoo ordered all flags at the zoo flown at halfmast.

Many people phoned zoo director Gilbert Boese to say they found the gesture insulting to the flag.

"To a lot of people, Samson is a legend in Milwaukee County," he said. "But there are a lot of people who don't like the American flag being used that way."

Though Samson had been one of the zoo's most beloved tenants since 1950, lowering the flag was "a mistake," said Boese, "and I will take full responsibility for it."

WAR AND PEACE

The only transvestite Civil War hero

Loreta Janeta Velasquez was so caught up by the war fever that swept the south in 1860 that she left her husband and joined the Confederate Army as Harry T. Burford.

She served with distinction in many important battles, including Bull Run, and was highly praised by General Stonewall Jackson, who never found out she was a woman.

The only use of flying cats in a military engagement

Nothing was sacred to King Cambyses II of Persia. The historian Herodotus writes that he shamelessly "opened ancient tombs to examine the dead bodies." That's the kind of guy we're dealing with here.

But Cambyses II really hit bottom when his armies laid siege to the ancient Egyptian city of Memphis in the sixth century B.C. The Egyptians held cats to be sacred—so much so that when a kitty died, the bereaved owner ritually shaved off his eyebrows. Knowing this about the Egyptians, Cambyses ordered his troops to round up all the live cats they could find and fling them over the walls of the city. Inside, the Egyptians watched in horror as the divine creatures hurtled helplessly through the air and splattered on the ground like water balloons. To stop the defilement, they surrendered.

(What would the Egyptians have thought had they lived to see an auction held by Leventon & Co. of Liverpool, in 1890? Some 180,000 mummified cats plundered from an Egyptian burial ground near Beni Hasan were put up for bidding. The auctioneers thought they might command a nice price as a novelty item, but they wound up giving away the cats for about ten dollars a ton.)

The only country with compulsory military service for women

Being female won't get you a draft deferment in Israel. Service in the Israeli Defense Force is compulsory for men *and* women eighteen and older.

Even so, the terms of conscription are easier for women than for men, and a woman's chances of actually being drafted are only about fifty-fifty. As a rule, female soldiers do shorter hitches than their male counterparts; married, orthodox, or undereducated women, as well as female immigrants over the age of nineteen, are exempt altogether. (Legally, a woman deferred on religious grounds is expected to put in some sort of alternative service, much like conscientious objectors in the United States. But the requirement is rarely enforced.)

When an Israeli woman does get called up, she is put through five weeks of basic training and then assigned to the Women's Army Corps as a driver, nurse, radio operator, flight controller, or some other noncombat worker. The last time an Israeli woman carried a gun in combat was during the War of Independence between 1948 and 1949.

The only college in the Colonies not to shut down during the American Revolution

Not surprisingly, the American Revolution had a devastating affect on education at all levels in the Colonies. As historian Allan Nevins observes, "Teachers enlisted, funds were appropriated to military purposes, and interest in cultural affairs flagged. Charity schools were usually the first to close, but private and even town schools soon followed them."

Higher education, too, was interrupted. All the Ivy League schools, including Harvard, Yale, and Princeton, as well as other institutions of higher learning, shut their doors for the duration.

Not Dartmouth, though. Named for its chief sponsor, the second Earl of Dartmouth, the Hanover, New Hampshire, school was chartered in 1769 by King George III principally for the purpose of educating Indian youth. But the Indians quickly lost interest, and Dartmouth's first graduating class, consisting of four men, was entirely Caucasian.

Charged up with the enthusiasm that often attaches to new ventures, Dartmouth remained open throughout the Revolution. It survived the war in sound shape, and by 1791 its graduating class had grown to forty-nine.

The only soldier to serve in three centuries

In 1699 a Dijon teenager named Jean Theurel ran away from home to enlist in France's Touraine Regiment in the war against the Netherlands. He took such a liking to military life and fought so valiantly that he decided to make a career of it.

Decorated for his exploits against the Dutch, Theurel

went on to fight in every major French war in the eighteenth century, from the War of the Spanish Succession to the Revolution. He was personally promoted to the rank of captain by King Louis XVI in 1777. Theurel was over ninety at the time.

Rebuffing suggestions that he retire, Theurel remained in the French Company of Paris and continued to draw officer's pay well past the dawn of the next century. It was Napoleon who finally ordered the centenarian from Dijon mustered out of the service, awarding him a yearly pension of fifteen hundred francs. Theurel died 5 years later, his age unofficially recorded at 120 plus.

The only known shoot-out between earthlings and aliens

The annals of ufology are filled with tales of encounters—close, distant, and otherwise—with alien spacecraft. But only once has such a meeting erupted in gunplay.

It happened in the tiny farm community of Kelly, Kentucky, in October, 1955. Mr. and Mrs. Gaither McGehee, their two sons, and a neighbor were sitting on the porch of the McGehee house when they saw an eerie light across a field, accompanied by a loud noise.

According to accounts they gave the local sheriff, a cadre of little green men surrounded the house and started firing. The McGehees grabbed their shotguns and fired back. Eventually, the space midgets turned tail, retreated to their spacecraft, and flew off.

Though the McGehees' story defied credibility, it had a few things going for it. For one thing, their house was pocked with strange-looking bullet holes no earthly gun could have made. For another, the McGehees were known to be solid and sober citizens who couldn't have fabricated such an incident.

"They were very religious people," said nephew Danny McCord. As if more evidence were needed, Gaither McGehee was so stressed out by the gun battle that he took ill and died of a heart attack a week later.

The only fighter pilot imprisoned and decorated for the same act

In July 1944 Soviet fighter pilot Mikhail Devyatayev was shot down over Lvov, in the Nazi-occupied Ukraine, and taken prisoner by the Nazis. In a daring escape that even Chuck Norris couldn't have matched, Devyatayev swiped a Heinkel bomber from under his captors' noses, rescued nine other escaped POWs, and flew them safely back to mother Russia.

In recognition of his exploits, the Soviet authorities arrested Devyatayev and convicted him of treason for allowing himself to have been captured. He languished in prison until his release in 1953 under the terms of a general amnesty. Five years later his actions were redefined as bravery, and he was awarded the Gold Star, inducted into the Order of Lenin, and proclaimed a national hero.

The only U.S. Army general to have worn a velvet uniform in battle

Always the renegade, George Armstrong Custer began wearing a blue velvet military uniform sometime after the Civil War. He had already proven himself an able commander—most notably at the Battle of Bull Run—and at twenty-three he became the youngest briga-

dier general in U.S. history. Though wearing velvet
clearly violated Army dress codes, none of Custer's commanding officers ever attempted to straighten him out.

Custer, whose growing irrationality took him on a
monomaniacal campaign against Native Americans, is
best known for his suicidal surprise attack on an en-
campment of Sioux and Cheyenne at the Little Big Horn
River, in Montana, on the morning of June 24, 1876. His
men, who had just shlepped ten miles in the heat, were
in no shape for fighting; they were also ridiculously out-
numbered—266 Americans to thousands of Indians. Every one of Custer's men died in battle; the Indians had
forty-two casualties.

Custer must have cut quite a figure in his last stand,
with his long blond hair and velvet uniform. But we will
never know. When his body was recovered afterwards,
it had been bathed and stripped naked, and his hair was
cut short. He was the only American at Little Big Horn
whose body wasn't mutilated by Sitting Bull's braves.

The only World War II warplane mass-produced before a prototype was tested

On the eve of World War II, the British government
commissioned R. J. Mitchell to create a new warplane
that could go up against Hitler's Luftwaffe. Mitchell designed a highly versatile aircraft that could climb 2,530
feet per minute and reach a speed of 362 miles per hour.

It was called the Spitfire, and without bothering to
have a prototype built and tested, Britain's secretary of
state for air, Lord Swinton, ordered the plane into immediate mass production.

His act was as rash as it was unprecedented, but
Luftwaffe flyers were already darkening the skies over
London, and there was no time to lose. Flying the Spit-

fires in combat for the first time, the RAF successfully countered the German air attack and, by 1940, had won the Battle of Britain.

The only conscientious objector awarded the Medal of Honor

Well over three thousand U.S. servicemen have been awarded the Medal of Honor since its inception in 1862. Among them was one man who refused to fight.

A Virginia-born Seventh-day Adventist whose religious beliefs barred him from carrying a weapon, Private, First Class Desmond Doss served as a medic with the 77th Infantry Division during World War II. But his aversion to fighting didn't keep him from going into battle.

On Guam and Leyte, Doss was wounded twice tending the wounded under heavy enemy fire, once crawling into a cave filled with Japanese snipers to administer plasma to a wounded American. *The New York Times* reported that "among the men of the 'Statue of Liberty' Division, the name of Doss became legendary for self-abnegation, sacrifice, and the sheerest kind of courage."

During a bitterly fought battle in Okinawa in 1945, Doss scaled a jagged escarpment under heavy fire from Japanese mortars, artillery, and machine guns to rescue seventy-five wounded Americans. Refusing orders to leave the area, he single-handedly lowered each man in a rope-supported litter down from the escarpment to safety.

On October 12, 1945, the twenty-six-year-old Doss received the Medal of Honor from President Harry Truman at a White House ceremony. He remains the only conscientious objector ever to be so honored.

The only woman awarded the Medal of Honor

In 1865 Dr. Mary Edwards Walker (1832–1919), wearing a frock coat and striped trousers, was arrested in New York City for "masquerading as a man." It wasn't the first time her unconventional attire had caused her trouble.

She had taken to wearing men's clothing at the age of 16, and ever after fashionable women snubbed her, humorists derided her, politicians denounced her, and little boys hurled rotten eggs at her in the streets. One editorial writer went so far as to demand the "refeminization" of Dr. Walker: "Her trousers must be taken from her—where and how, is, of course, a matter of detail."

But Dr. Walker's transvestism was a deeply held principle. For women in those days, bondage by undergarment was very real, and she was a relentless opponent of "confining and unhygienic fashions," such as the whalebone corset, which embraced the body like a boa constrictor.

At the trial Mary asserted her God-given right "to dress as I please in free America on whose tented fields I have served four years in the cause of human freedom." As her finishing stroke, she read the text of a special act of Congress giving her permission to wear trousers in recognition of her heroic service in the Civil War. The judge had no choice but to acquit her.

Dr. Walker had indeed distinguished herself in the Civil War, serving as a nurse and later as a spy and surgeon in the 52nd Ohio Infantry Division of the Union Army. In the field she wore striped trousers, a felt hat, and an officer's greatcoat, just like her fellow officers. During the Battle of Chattanooga, she was captured by a Confederate patrol and spent four months in the notorious Castle Thunder Prison in Richmond.

For her service to the sick and wounded, President Andrew Johnson awarded her the Medal of Honor; she remains to this day the only female recipient among well over three thousand men. Then, in 1917, when Dr. Walker was 85, a government review board revoked her medal along with those of 911 other Civil War veterans on the grounds that there was "nothing in the records to show the specific act or acts for which the decoration was originally awarded." Asked to return the medal, she replied, "Over my dead body!"

True to her word, she wore the medal every day, and was wearing it when she slipped and fell on the Capitol steps, which led indirectly to her death on February 19, 1919. At her funeral it was still pinned securely to her Prince Albert coat.

The only World War II casualties in the continental United States

In the fall of 1944, Japan launched Operation Fu-Go, a relentless barrage of giant rice-paper balloons aimed at the West Coast of the United States. An incendiary bomb was attached to each of the hydrogen-filled gasbags, which were borne across the Pacific on strong easterly winds.

Many of the bombs sputtered out or detonated harmlessly over water. But at least one thousand reached the U.S. mainland, some winding up as far east as Nebraska. One exploded in a forest near Bly, Oregon, in May 1945—three months before the bombing of Hiroshima and Nagasaki—killing six picnickers.

Nearly forty years later, several female Japanese factory workers who had helped manufacture the deadly bomb sent letters of condolence to the families of the victims. Enclosed with their notes were one thousand origami cranes—a time-honored expression of peace in Japan.

The only Civil War officer executed for war crimes

Henry Wirz was the Confederate officer in charge of the military prison at Andersonville, Georgia, where Union troops were quartered in unspeakable filth and degradation, and thirteen thousand died. During a three-month military trial in Washington that generated more than two thousand pages of testimony, he was accused not merely of starving his prisoners but of performing medical experiments on them, shooting and beating them arbitrarily, and other acts of sadism.

Wirz's lawyers argued that he was a mere functionary who was acting on orders and was now being scapegoated for atrocities not of his doing. Indeed, witnesses at his trial testified they had seen Wirz "strike, kick and shoot prisoners in August 1864," when he was actually away from the prison on sick leave. Truth to tell, had Wirz's commanding officer, General John H. Winder, not died in February 1865, most likely he, and not Wirz, would have been held to account.

But the public needed to make an example of someone, and Wirz fit the bill perfectly; even President Andrew Johnson wanted him dead. He was found guilty and sentenced to be hanged in the yard of Washington's Old Capitol Prison.

Shortly before Wirz's execution date, secret envoys from the White House came to his jail cell and offered him his freedom in exchange for a signed statement that he had seen Confederacy president Jefferson Davis murdering Union soldiers. But Wirz would not lie to save his skin. On November 10, 1865, before a crowd of 250, the execution took place as planned.

"I know what orders are, Major," he said to the officer in charge of the hanging. "I am being hung for obeying them." The hanging was botched: Wirz's neck failed to break when the trapdoor was sprung, and he strangled slowly. Two companies of Union officers watched among the crowd, chanting "Remember Andersonville."

The only war ever fought over an ear

Competition between Spain and Great Britain for commercial shipping rights in the West Indies began to get ugly in the 1720s. Ship raids and seizures were frequent, and in 1731 Spanish coastguardsmen waylaid a British merchant vessel near Cuba. Boarding the ship, one of the Spaniards severed Captain Robert Jenkins's ear with a saber.

Or so Jenkins claimed when he appeared, ear in hand, before Parliament in October 1739. The lawmakers bought his story and declared war on Spain.

The War of Jenkins's Ear waxed and waned for two years, neither side able to work up much enthusiasm for it. At one point British troops attempted to capture the Spanish fort at St. Augustine, Florida, but got nowhere; Spain's assault on the British garrison in Georgia was equally inconclusive. But the War of Jenkins's Ear finally did heat up after it was absorbed into the War of the Austrian Succession.

The only war ever fought over a bucket

When brigands from the Italian city-state of Modena raided neighboring Bologna in 1325 and absconded with the oaken bucket from the town well, the Bolognese sent an army to retrieve it. What little is known today about this silly conflict derives from the equally silly poem that commemorates it—Alessandro Tassoni's twelve-canto epic, *The Rape of the Bucket.*

The only Danish war fought entirely between Mexico and France

In 1838 a French baker living outside Mexico City claimed a gang of drunken Mexican military officers had pigged out on pastries in his restaurant and then left without paying. In fact, French nationals in Mexico had been similarly victimized for years, and King Louis Philippe now demanded $600,000 in damages. The Mexican government told him to take a hike.

In response, France dispatched a naval fleet to the Gulf of Mexico in February and later blockaded the port of Vera Cruz. Tensions mounted, and by October the two countries were at war.

Casualties were heavy, and General Santa Anna lost his leg in the fighting, which Mexican journalists waggishly dubbed La Guerra de los Pasteles, or "The Pastry War." With defeat imminent, Mexico agreed to pay France the $600,000 only to be informed that the ante had been upped to $800,000—$600,000 for the pastries, $200,000 for the cost of the blockade.

But France softened and, in March 1839, withdrew its troops in exchange for a $600,000 settlement. There is no record of how much of that went to the put-upon baker.

The only war casualties caused by a fish

In the early years of World War II, the Allies decided it was only a matter of time before the Nazis began waging war with deadly nerve gas, which was already being produced in German laboratories.

So the U.S. Army Chemical Corps initiated a research

program to develop an antidote. Electric eels necessary for the study were deposited in cement-lined holding tanks at collection stations throughout South America. Two workmen were walking along a plank laid across one such pool at a hacienda in Amazonas, Brazil, when they stumbled and fell into the water. A single eel can generate a 550-volt current; the workmen were electrocuted instantly.

(Eels, incidentally, have two hearts. One is in the chest cavity—or what passes for a chest cavity in an eel. The other, a lymphatic heart, is in the tail. Strike an eel hard enough on the tail with a rock or a heavy book, and it will die of cardiac arrest.)

ISASTERS

The only composer crushed to death by the Talmud

In his day, Alkan, the pseudonym of Charles Henri Valentin Morhange (1813–1888), was hailed as "the Berlioz of the piano"—a prolific and inventive composer of keyboard works as well as a dazzling concert performer in his own right. In his prime Alkan was a popular figure in Paris salon society and an intimate of Chopin, Victor Hugo, and George Sand. But he grew morose and withdrawn in his later years, avoiding company and rarely performing in public. An orthodox Jew, Alkan was removing a Talmud from a high bookshelf in his Paris apartment in 1888 when the entire bookcase, filled mostly with copies of the Talmud, the Torah, and other Jewish scholarly works, toppled over and killed him.

Regrettably, Alkan was not the first person to be felled by a liturgical beanball. The *Times* of London reported in its edition of October 6, 1886, that the Very Reverend Dr. J. B. Kavanagh, of the Roman Catholic parish church, in Kildare, was raising a chalice at the conclusion of an early morning mass when a marble cherub hanging over the altar broke off and fell on his head.

"He fell back heavily, murmured the words 'My

God,' twice, and became insensible," the *Times* said.
Never regaining consciousness, he died a few days later.

The only documented automobile accident in the eighteenth century

Nicolas Joseph Cugnot, a French army officer and engineer, became the world's first motorist when he designed, built, and operated a three-wheeled steam-driven
tractor in 1769. Its main purpose was hauling cannons,
but the vehicle could carry four passengers at a cruising
speed of about three miles per hour.

Though his *fardier* was difficult to steer, contempo-
rary observers report that Cugnot occasionally took it for
joyrides through the streets of Paris, careering wildly
and sending pedestrians scurrying for safety. After
knocking over a wall, he was reportedly jailed for reckless driving.

Presumably, Cugnot's vehicle was totaled in that mishap. He later built a much larger version, which is displayed at the Conservatoire des Arts et Métiers in Paris.
Its chassis was made from hand-cut timbers, and a coal
bucket was placed conveniently next to the driver's
bench. It was probably never driven.

The only casualty of the Three Mile Island disaster

Despite its grave environmental implications, no
deaths or injuries—not even a nosebleed—resulted directly from the 1979 radiation leak at Three Mile Island,
Pennsylvania. A couple of three-headed cattle, perhaps,
and maybe an orange sheep or two, but no real casualties.

In a two-page ad in *The Wall Street Journal*, Dr. Edward Teller, the father of the hydrogen bomb and one of nuclear energy's most passionate defenders, said, "I was [in Washington] to refute some of the propaganda that Ralph Nader, Jane Fonda, and their kind are spewing to the news media. I am 71 years old and I was working 20 hours a day. . . . I suffered a heart attack. . . . I was the only one affected by the reactor. No, that would be wrong. It was not the reactor. It was Jane Fonda."

The only good news to come out of the 1989 Exxon oil spill

"Three-quarters of [the oil] was contained within the ship," White House Chief of Staff John Sununu told reporters after the *Exxon Valdez* spilled 250,000 barrels of oil into Alaska's Prince William Sound. "There's been very little reporting on that."

The only airplane collision with the Empire State Building

On the morning of July 28, 1945, Manhattan office workers watched in horror as a twin-engine B-25 U.S. Army bomber emerged from the fog and flew among the rooftops for several minutes, struggling to gain altitude. At 9:49, the plane slammed into the seventy-eighth floor of the Empire State Building, 1,050 feet above Fifth Avenue, killing the pilot and his two passengers, as well as ten office workers in the building. Many people who only heard the impact from afar thought New York had been bombed by Japan.

No one knows for certain what caused the plane, en route from Bedford, Massachusetts, to Newark, New Jersey, to crash. Some speculate that the pilot, Colonel William F. Smith, Jr., confused by the fog, mistook Manhattan for New Jersey and began his descent prematurely.

Its wings sheared off on impact, the aircraft tore an 18′ × 20′ hole in the side of the building. When the gasoline tanks exploded, one of the engines flew across the seventy-eighth floor and out the other side, landing on a twelfth-floor rooftop, where it ignited a fire that destroyed the penthouse studio of sculptor Henry Hering.

The only baseball player ever killed during a major league game

The New York Yankees trailed the American League–leading Cleveland Indians by only a half game when the two teams met at New York's Polo Grounds on August 16, 1920. Cleveland shortstop Ray Chapman led off the fifth inning against Yankee pitcher Carl Mays, and the first pitch slammed into Chapman's unprotected head—no helmets in those days—fracturing his skull.

The report was so sharp that many fans assumed the ball had struck Chapman's bat. In fact, the ball rolled back to the mound, and Mays tossed it to first for the putout, only to discover that the batter had collapsed at the plate. Chapman was carried off the field by teammates and rushed to St. Lawrence Hospital. He died the next day.

Fans and opposing players came down hard on Mays, who had never been especially popular and was known not to be squeamish about brushing back batters who crowded the plate. There was talk of having him banished.

But Mays had cooperated fully with police, visited Chapman in the hospital and, according to the Washington *Star*, "was overcome with grief when the news [of

Chapman's death] was told to him." He had not acted irresponsibly in any way, nor, he insisted, had he deliberately thrown at Chapman.

"Hell, I threw him a curveball," he later said. "You don't throw a curve when you're trying to hit somebody."

The only NHL player killed during a game

In the first period of a 1968 home game against the Oakland Seals, Bill Masterton, of the Minnesota North Stars, was bodychecked by Larry Cahan and Ron Harris of Oakland. He fell backward and struck his head on the ice. Never regaining consciousness, he died of head injuries a few days later.

Those who were there, including Minnesota coach Wren Blair, agreed that Masterton had been checked hard but cleanly and that Cahan and Harris were in no way to blame. It was a tragic accident and nothing more.

"He hit the ice so hard that I'm sure he was unconscious before he fell," said Blair. No penalties were called on the play.

Prior to the Masterton incident, the last professional hockey player to die on the ice was Owen McCourt. That was in 1907, ten years before the NHL was founded.

The only person in North America ever beaned by a plummeting meteorite

When you consider how many thousands of meteors have plunged to earth from outer space, it's extraordinary that so few have done any real damage. In October 1973, a calico cat named Misty was grazed by flying shards of a meteorite that crashed through the roof of a garage near Canon City, Colorado. And a young girl was struck by what may or may not have been a meteor in Tokyo in the 1930s. But the only documented assault by meteorite in this country occurred in Alabama in 1955.

On the evening of November 30, a violent but unseen explosion prompted a three-state search involving thirty-five airplanes. Nothing turned up, but the Alabama state geologist suggested that the noise could have resulted from an exploding meteorite.

Evidently, he was right. Mrs. Hewlett Hodges, of Sylacauga, Alabama, was napping on her living-room sofa when a nine-pound meteorite crashed through the roof, ricocheted off a dresser, and grazed her arm and hip. While Mrs. Hodges spent a few days in the hospital recovering, U.S. Air Force geologists analyzed the space rock, which they returned to her upon her release.

She immediately made plans to auction it off to the highest bidder but was sued by her landlady, Mrs. Birdie Guy, who claimed the meteor was rightfully hers.

"This has been settled in the Supreme Court before," she said. "The Court said that a meteorite belongs to whose land it fell on."

The only unintentional denture transplant

According to *The New England Journal of Medicine*, a Los Angeles bartender saved the life of a man having a heart attack by administering mouth-to-mouth artificial respiration. But in the process, he dropped his dentures down the victim's throat.

Paramedics arrived to take the sixty-year-old patient to White Memorial Medical Center, where doctors inserted tubes in his throat to aid his breathing. Even after the tubes were removed, however, the patient complained of a bad sore throat, and within days he was running a high fever and suffering neck pains as well. X-rays revealed a dental bridge lodged just above his windpipe.

"The patient made a rapid recovery after removal of the foreign body," his doctors reported in the *Journal*.

The only time José Serebrier conducted with a baton

. . . he stabbed himself with it.

During a 1975 concert in Mexico City, Uruguayan conductor Jose Serebrier accidentally stabbed himself through the hand with his baton.

While musicians and chorus members gasped, blood gushed from the wound, staining his white tuxedo shirt and spattering their shoes. "The baton broke into pieces," the conductor later said. "One piece was sticking through my hand. Ironically, I never use a baton. But I decided to use one for this performance because I thought it would help me achieve greater musical control."

The only self-inflicted death by baton

José Serebrier (see **The only time José Serebrier conducted with a baton,** above) wasn't the only conductor to impale himself on the point of his baton. Three centuries earlier, Jean-Baptiste Lully (1632–1687), court composer and conductor to King Louis XIV, accidentally pierced his foot during a performance with a pointed cane that he used to keep time. Gangrene and blood poisoning set in, and he died.

The only U.S. town ever nuked

Walter Gregg and his family should have gone shopping or taken in a movie on the afternoon of March 11, 1958. Instead, they hung out at home and were around to see their house demolished by an atomic bomb.

It happened when the bomb bays of a U.S. Air Force B-47 en route from Georgia's Hunter Air Force Base to West Germany accidentally opened and an atomic warhead fell out. The bomb crashed through the Greggs' roof, outside of Florence, South Carolina, obliterating the house and gouging out a thirty-five-foot-deep crater in the backyard. Luckily, the explosion was nonnuclear. What detonated was the TNT in the bomb's trigger device.

Gregg and his wife, as well as their three young children and a cousin, were all slightly injured by flying debris. Five other houses and a church were also damaged, and a motorist on Route 301 said the force of the blast turned his car around.

Five months later, the Air Force paid an out-of-court settlement of fifty-four thousand dollars to the Greggs. Meanwhile, you can still buy T-shirts in nearby Florence that say, "We were the town that got nuked."

The only survivor of the 1902 eruption of Mount Pelée in Martinique

On the morning of May 8, 1902, Mount Pelée, a long-dormant volcano on the Caribbean island of Martinique, erupted with cataclysmic fury. The old trading port of St. Pierre vanished under a layer of burning ash and lava within forty-five seconds; all twenty-eight inhabitants perished.

All but one, as it turned out. Three days after the eruption, rescuers heard cries from under a pile of rubble where the town's prison had stood. Digging through the wreckage, they found a prisoner holed up in a subterranean cell. He seemed in good health, but for some minor burns suffered when the air around him overheated. He had no idea what had happened, and he was annoyed at not having been fed or attended to in several days.

There was no place to confine the prisoner. But since he wasn't in for anything serious, his rescuers turned him free. He later moved to the United States, where he capitalized on his survival by allowing himself to be exhibited in a circus.

The only dog killed by a pizza—*without* eating it

It started out as just another fast-food meal. But it ended in indigestion and tragedy.

Joyce and David White, of Berlin Heights, Ohio, heated up a pizza one evening in 1986 but neglected to read the "best if served by" imprint on the box. The pie, it turned out, was labeled edible until seven days after April 18—or April 25. The Whites didn't eat it till April 26, and after a few bites, they became violently sick. So they jumped in the car and raced out of the driveway to get to a doctor.

In their haste, they ran over their dog, Fluffy.

The distraught couple slapped the manufacturer of the pie and the Pick & Pay grocery where they bought it with a $125,000 lawsuit. Had the pizza not been "spoiled, rotten, rancid and moldy," they claimed, they never would have gotten sick—and Fluffy would still be alive.

The only drowning directly attributable to a dog

Two boys, Bellis and Jones, were rowing in the Mersey River near Tranmere, England, when their boat capsized, according to the Times of London of December 8, 1869. Bellis couldn't swim; Jones could. But Jones was unable to rescue Bellis, because every time he approached him, he was bitten by Bellis's dog, who had climbed on his master's back. Finally, Bellis drowned.

The only major vegetable-oil spill

According to the Smithsonian Center for Short-Lived Phenomena, more than six thousand gallons of oil leaked into the Rouge River, just outside Detroit, in the winter of 1973. When ecologists analyzed the spill, they discovered it was 100 percent pure vegetable oil, used in the manufacture of potato chips. It had escaped from a faulty storage tank at the nearby Frito-Lay plant.

Since the river was frozen, much of the oil accumulated in a huge slippery puddle on top of the ice and was easily collected with little ecological damage. In fact, the oil had been oozing its way across Frito-Lay's executive parking lot in an inch-thick slick for several weeks: Walking to and from their cars, the oblivious potato-chip execs had sloshed through the oil twice a day without complaint. The minidisaster was discovered by a police officer strolling near the river.

The only major literary figure killed by a plummeting tortoise

The father of Greek drama, Aeschylus (525–456 B.C.) was warned by a soothsayer that he would be fatally struck on the head by a falling object. Rather than accept his fate, he took refuge in a wheat field where he was fatally beaned by a tortoise dropped from the talons of a soaring eagle. The eagle had presumably mistaken Aeschylus' bald head for a rock on which to break open the tortoise's shell to get at the meat.

Admittedly, few serious historians buy into this version of Aeschylus' passing and regard it as just another shaggy-eagle story. Some believe the Greek rhetorician Aelian, who lived about two centuries after Aeschylus, made it up. Sir Thomas Browne used it in his *Pseudodoxia Epidemica* (1646) to pick holes in Copernicus' theories: If the earth did rotate, as the astronomer insisted, the tortoise would have missed its target.

CRIME AND PUNISHMENT

The only person in U.S. history ever convicted of cannibalism

What Alferd Packer did in the winter of 1874 was unpardonable: On a grueling trek across the Rockies, he ate most of the Democratic party of Colorado's Hinsdale County. For that unconscionable breach of good taste, Packer was hustled off to the Gunnison State Jail later that year, the only person in American history ever to be tried for and convicted of cannibalism.

In all fairness to Packer, who was roundly reviled as a "mad hyena," a "voracious, man-eating son of a bitch," and "the Colorado Cannibal," his gourmandism was no mere dietary caprice. It happened this way: On February 9, 1874, he set out on the seventy-five-mile hike across the Rockies with five mining companions. Sixty days later, Packer arrived alone at his destination, the Los Pios Ute Agency. He was bearded, filthy, and missing his right thumb but otherwise in unaccountably robust health for a man who had just weathered two hellish months in the mountains, where food was scarce and the mercury often dipped to fifty below.

"Where are your companions?" the Los Pios regulars asked. Packer avoided their questions and their stares.

Finally, he confessed that fellow traveler Shannon Wilson Bell had slain the others in the party and that he in turn killed Bell in self-defense. Then, to stay alive, he roasted and devoured the flesh of his dead companions. "It tasted like jerked beef," he said.

There are those who feel the Democratic judge who heard Packer's case wasn't altogether impartial. "There were only six Democrats in all of Hinsdale County, and you, you S.O.B., you ate five of them," he said. Packer served seventeen years in the Gunnison jail, a model prisoner in all ways who spent his idle moments tending his beloved plants and weaving horsehair belts. He died a free man at age sixty-five in 1907.

In 1968 a group of students at the University of Colorado established the Alferd Packer Memorial Grill, and lobbied to turn Alferd Packer Day into a national holiday. That hasn't happened—yet—although you can still wolf down a Packerburger with onions at the grill between classes. (Packer himself would have passed on the dish: He turned vegetarian after his release from jail in 1903). Colorado alumni have also organized a nationwide network of Packer Clubs. Their motto: Serving his fellow man since 1874.

The only emergency police call placed by a tomato

After repeatedly receiving calls over the 911 police-emergency line, sheriff's deputies in Blacksburg, Virginia, converged on the home of Linda and Danny Hurst, guns drawn, ready for action.

But the house was empty—no Hursts, no thieves ransacking their closets and drawers. The culprit was a tomato left to ripen in a hanging basket. Eventually, it grew mushy and began to drip juice on the Hursts' answering machine, shorting out the dialing mechanism and triggering the phantom 911 calls.

The only mail service organized and run by criminals

In May 1923 bandits waylaid the Blue Express, on China's Tientsin-P'u-k'ou railway line, and took 120 passengers captive, herding them into a hideout in the nearby Pao Tzu Ku Mountains.

With the captors' consent, the American Red Cross arranged for the shipment of mail to and from the hostages. The bandits themselves printed and sold stamps and oversaw the delivery service.

The stamps, in five- and ten-cents denominations, carried a crude depiction of the mountains and the legend "Pao Tzu Ku Bandit Post." The service was suspended in mid-June following the release of the hostages.

The only bail ever set that exceeded the national debt

In 1990 a Birmingham, Alabama, district-court judge with a reputation for excessive leniency silenced his critics by setting bail for a theft suspect at nine trillion dollars.

According to Birmingham mayor Richard Arrington, Judge Jack Montgomery had frequently set ludicrously low bond for repeat offenders. In the case of one theft suspect who had been arrested six times in as many months, the judge had never set a bond higher than five thousand dollars. Given the man's history, the mayor argued, bail should have been much higher.

Judge Montgomery obliged. When the suspect came before him a seventh time on charges of theft, he set bail at nine trillion dollars—a bit less than triple the national debt.

"This is so he doesn't get in any more trouble," he explained.

The only U.S. lawmaker censured for inserting obscene descriptions into the *Congressional Record*

Ever since the U.S. House of Representatives first convened in 1789, its members have censured their own for various wretched excesses at least two dozen times. But only one representative has been both censured *and* censored, and that was Thomas Blanton of Texas, who, in 1921, was accused of reading the text of an obscene letter into the *Congressional Record*.

"Foul and obscene matter, which you know you could not have spoken on the floor, and . . . which could not have been circulated through the mails in any other publication without violating the law," intoned House Speaker Frederick H. Gillett, "was transmitted as part of the proceedings of this house to thousands of homes and libraries throughout the country, to be read by men and women, and, worst of all, by children, whose prurient curiosity it would excite and corrupt." While nothing could be done about the mailed copies, all bound editions of the offending publication were seized, edited, and reprinted minus Blanton's ribaldry.

Strangely, Blanton's colleagues seemed more disturbed than his constituents, for he was reelected the following year and remained in office until 1937. His major achievement—apart from getting scolded for talking dirty in print—was the drafting of a landmark reform bill abolishing free baths and shaves for members of the House.

The only American serviceman court-martialed for abusing a potato

This would have made a great *M*A*S*H* episode: During a KP stint at Fort Meyer, Virginia, in 1959, Private Andrew God, Jr., was caught lopping the eyes off potatoes when he should have excised them surgically with the point of his knife. For such profligacy, the soldier was busted on charges of having "willfully suffered potatoes of some value, the military property of the United States, to be destroyed by improper peeling." (A second serviceman, Specialist, Fourth Class Eugene J. Jaskiewics, was also charged with tuber abuse but waived his right to a trial and accepted a sentence of two hours' hard labor for two weeks.)

At his trial, God pleaded self-defense. "You can't jab a potato with a knife and dig into it," he said. "If the knife slips, you've got it in your hand." The court bought his explanation, and the charges were repealed.

The potatoes were not.

The only crime specifically mentioned in the U.S. Constitution

Nowhere in the Constitution is there a single reference to murder, armed robbery, insider trading, or fishing out of season. The reason behind this is that for the most part crime and punishment were left to the states to worry about; treason, however, is by definition a *federal* offense.

But the fresh memory of England's tyranny gave the framers of the Constitution pause; they did not want the new government to use its power to prosecute treason as a means of squelching *any* dissent—or to jail those who had only advocated rebellion but not participated in it. For that reason, they defined the crime very specifically. According to Article III, Section 3 of the Constitution, "Treason against the United States shall consist only in levying war against them, or in adhering to their enemies, giving them aid and comfort. No person shall be convicted of treason unless on the testimony of two witnesses to the same overt act, or on confession in open court."

The only umpire banished from baseball for life for dishonesty

When the Detroit Wolverines began the 1882 season with a string of unlikely losses, team owner William G. Thompson suspected they weren't playing on a level field. So he hired a private detective to trail umpire Dick Higham, who had officiated at twenty-six of the Wolverines' twenty-nine games. The detectives found what they were looking for: letters, written by Higham in easily deciphered code, telling local gamblers when to bet against the Wolverines. Higham, it turned out, had been tipping off gamblers by wire and mail since the beginning of the season, and also betting heavily on the games he umpired.

Ironically, Higham had been hired as an umpire after a five-year tenure as a catcher with the Chicago White Stockings and other teams, during which he'd been suspected of throwing games. Following his expulsion from baseball, he took up yet a third career.

He became a bookie.

The only grade-schooler ever arrested for bank extortion

A ten-year-old girl was arrested in Cordele, Georgia, in 1986, for extorting money from banks by phone, in violation of federal banking laws.

According to United Press International, the girl was nabbed by police while she was attempting to shake down a local bank from her bedroom phone. She told her victims she was nineteen and heavily armed and warned them not to call the police. One did.

"I believe this is the youngest female I've ever arrested for a felony offense," said arresting detective Tommy L. West. "It was weird."

OVERACHIEVERS

The only person ever to swim the Mississippi River lengthwise

"My uncle was an engineering genius," begins an old joke. "He was the first person ever to build a bridge across the Mississippi River." Pause. "Lengthwise."

A twenty-seven-year-old factory worker from Clinton, Oklahoma, named Fred P. Newton did the next best thing. In 1930 he swam the Mississippi lengthwise—or most of it, anyway. The 1,826-mile journey remains the longest swim ever recorded. More remarkably, he undertook the feat purely on a whim. He had no organized backing, assistance, or promise of reward.

Slathering his entire body with a protective coating of petroleum jelly, Newton waded into the Mississippi at Ford Dam, near Minneapolis, on July 6. He hoped to complete his watery marathon before the first frost, but weather conditions, stomach cramps, and occasional encounters with river barges forced him to make more stops than he'd anticipated; at times the water temperature fell as low as 47°F.

It was December 29 when Newton finally clambered ashore at the Carrollton Avenue bend of the river, in New Orleans, somewhat dazed and shaking with cold.

According to *Significa*, by David Wallechinsky, Irving Wallace, and Amy Wallace, three police officers and a small crowd of curiosity seekers were on hand to welcome the swimmer. He had spent more than 740 hours in the water.

The only transpacific flight in a hot-air balloon

Richard Branson, the zillionaire chairman of Virgin Atlantic Airways, and Per Lindstrand, a Swedish pilot, were far from the first to cross the Pacific in a balloon; it had been done a few times, as early as 1981, but always in a *helium* craft. No one had ever gone the distance on hot air.

The men lifted off from Miyakonojo, Japan, on January 15, 1991. Had their trip aborted then and there, they still would have rated a mention in the record books for having launched the biggest balloon ever—196 feet high. They also set a speed record along the way, clocking 198.8 miles per hour. And they surpassed the hot-air long-distance record they'd set on an Atlantic crossing in 1987, covering 6,761 miles by the time they touched down 150 miles west of Yellowknife, in Canada's Northwest Territories.

Yellowknife, however, was hundreds of miles from the California coast, where they had intended to land. Strong winds, they explained, pushed them far off course.

The only person to cross the United States on a unicycle

On a dare from Robert Ripley (of *Believe It or Not!* fame), Walter Nilsson, "King of the Unicycles," set out from New York City in 1934 atop an eight-and-a-half-foot unicycle, bound for the West Coast. Accompanied by a Ripley associate (who drove alongside him in a car),

Nilsson pedaled through blinding rains, a Nebraska hailstorm, and the devastating heat of Death Valley. It took the thirty-three-year-old actor turned cycling phenom 117 days to cross the continent—3,306 miles—and he did it without falling once, wheeling into San Francisco to the cheers of thousands, who mobbed him like a second Lindbergh.

Ripley publicized the journey as "the most unbelievable feat of the year." But the strain of the trip left Nilsson with hemorrhoids and back pains that harried him the rest of his life.

The only winner of two unshared Nobel Prizes

In the early 1940s, Linus Pauling's investigation of the biochemical structure of the blood components known as globulins led him to create the first synthetic antibodies. Later, he helped solve the puzzle of infantile paralysis and sickle-cell anemia, and contributed landmark theories on the structure of proteins. For his research "into the nature of the chemical bond and its application to the structure of complex substances," Pauling was awarded the 1954 Nobel Prize in chemistry.

Though a lifelong pacifist, Pauling worked for the National Defense Research Commission during World War II, developing rocket fuels and aviation components. But after the war, he wrote and spoke out prolifically against the bombing of Hiroshima and Nagasaki, publicized the dangers of radioactive fallout, and lobbied for an end to nuclear testing.

Pauling's peace initiatives won him as many foes as friends. In the United States, he was labeled pro-Soviet and, until his 1954 Nobel, even had difficulty getting his passport renewed. (Ironically, some of his early structural theories were banned in Stalinist Russia for being un-Marxist.)

Famous only children:

1. Clark Gable, actor
2. Vivien Leigh, actress
3. Elton John, singer
4. Robert Louis Stevenson, writer
5. Emile Zola, novelist
6. Roger Staubach, quarterback
7. Frank Sinatra, singer
8. Eleanor Roosevelt, First Lady, U.N. ambassador
9. Lillian Hellman, playwright
10. Van Cliburn, pianist
11. Bruce Felton, author

But a test-ban proposal he drafted became the foundation of a 1963 testing moratorium signed by the United States, Great Britain, and the Soviet Union, and that year Pauling received the 1962 Nobel Prize for peace. He had "campaigned ceaselessly," said the Nobel Prize committee, "not only against nuclear weapons tests ... but against all warfare as a means of solving international conflicts."

The only snowball collection

Although he lives in the New York City bedroom community of Hartsdale, Stuart Himmelfarb keeps his snowball collection in a freezer in his parents' house in the Bronx. His wife Beverly, he explains, wants no part of it.

A luggage distributor, Himmelfarb began collecting

snowballs as a child, storing them under slabs of meat in the family freezer. All those early specimens have since been lost; his current collection, which numbers about thirty pieces, is maintained in plastic bags and plastic baseball holders. Each is tagged according to blizzard of origin.

Himmelfarb's holdings include a snowball from the biggest New York City February blizzard on record (February 6–7, 1978), another from a rare early April teninCher that snowed out opening day at Yankee Stadium in 1982, and a walnut-sized remnant of what many New Yorkers still snidely refer to as the Lindsay blizzard of 1969.

That storm wound up dumping more than a foot of a snow on an ill-prepared metropolis, Himmelfarb recalls, despite Mayor John Lindsay's cavalier—and much-regretted—prediction that it would come to nothing. On the fifteenth anniversary of the Lindsay blizzard, Himmelfarb hosted a reunion at which white food was served almost exclusively—cottage cheese, cream cheese, marshmallows, vanilla ice cream, and a tuna and whitefish snowman. The only nonwhite food on the menu: snow peas.

The only woman to go over Niagara Falls in a barrel and survive

If such things must be proven, schoolteacher Anna Edson Taylor established once and for all, in front of a thousand witnesses, that a woman can be as reckless as a man.

On the afternoon of October 24, 1901—her forty-third birthday—the ex-schoolteacher squeezed into a four and a half by three foot wooden barrel, well cushioned within and fitted with a rubber hose that allowed her to breathe. A boat towed her out into the turbulent Niagara River. Then, at exactly 4:05, the line was cut and the barrel shot downstream, bobbing crazily. At 4:23 it reached the brink of Horseshoe Falls, on the Canadian side, seemed to pause for a moment, and then plummeted 176 feet into the eddies below.

When the barrel was recovered, it had to be sawed apart to extricate the dizzy daredevil. She had been knocked unconscious, and blood was pouring from a gash in her forehead. Later, she warned others "not to attempt the foolish thing I have done."

Ms. Taylor, who hoped her feat would bring her fame and fortune, died penniless in the Niagara County Infirmary in 1929. She was buried between two other Falls jumpers in a Niagara Falls, New York, cemetery.

In 1980 the Bay City, Michigan, Chamber of Commerce sued to have Ms. Taylor's remains exhumed and reinterred in Bay City, where she had taught grade school, and where her barrel was built. An ugly legal battle ensued, but the move was successfully blocked in court by a group called The Remaining Friends of Annie Taylor.

The only person to have been both a dwarf and a giant

Born in Graz, Austria, in 1899, Adam Rainer stood just three feet ten inches by the time he reached twenty-one, when a bizarre glandular shift sparked a violent growth spurt. *The Guinness Book of World Records* reports that at thirty-two, the ex-dwarf was over seven feet tall, and at the time of his death at age fifty-one, he was seven feet eight inches. Medical authorities adjudged him history's only dwarf turned giant.

The only two-faced man

The scion of one of England's most aristocratic families, Edward Mordake had everything going for him—wealth, erudition, musical ability, and good looks twice over. The sad fact is that Mordake was born with two faces—a normal one in front and a kind of emergency-backup face on the back of his head, with eyes that apparently could cry, laugh, and track movement, as well as a nose, ears and lips. In *Anomalies and Curiosities of Medicine,* George Gould calls Mordake's case "one of the weirdest as well as most melancholy stories of human deformity."

Not surprisingly, Mordake spent his short life in total seclusion, refusing to leave his room, receive visitors, or even entertain the possibility of double dates. Though no one ever heard the posterior mouth speak, it gibbered and drooled continually. And Mordake told his doctors that his "devil twin" kept him awake at night babbling "forever of such things as they only speak of in hell. . . . For some unforgiven wickedness of my forefathers, I am knit to this fiend—for a fiend it surely is."

Inevitably, Mordake went mad and took his own life at twenty-three. He left a note asking that his second face be destroyed "lest it continue its dreadful whisperings in my grave."

The only woman to give birth to bunnies

This story is a blatant hoax, we admit it. But for a brief period in the eighteenth century, thousands of Britishers believed it was true—or wanted to, anyway.

On April 23, 1726, a London tailor's wife named Mary Toth reported to the police that she had been vio-

lated by a mammoth rabbit. Five months later she went into labor, and with one of England's foremost physicians, John Howard, in attendance, gave birth to five rabbits.

Though strange things were often believed to happen on April 23—Saint George's Day—the reports of Mrs. Toth's singular issue were greeted with skepticism and disdain. But when Nathaniel St. Andre, anatomist to King George I, arrived at Mrs. Toth's bedside to conduct a formal inquiry and another two rabbit babies popped out, he was convinced. So were a growing a number of English sensation seekers.

Nonetheless, many of St. Andre's colleagues remained wary, and Sir Richard Manningham, of the Fellowship of Royal Surgeons, hinted that unless Mrs. Toth spoke the truth, she would be tortured.

Finally, she told all. For reasons never made clear—a morbid desire for publicity, perhaps—she had faked the whole thing, even arranging to have her husband sneak in the rabbit babies at the right moment. There had been no rape, no pregnancy, and certainly no giant rabbit.

The only documented case of quindecaplets

At a Rome clinic in 1971, Dr. Gennaro Montanino reported having removed 15 fetuses—10 females, and 5 males—from a 35-year-old woman. Each was perfectly formed and weighed under five ounces.

A more garish—though clearly unconfirmed—tale of multiple birth is that of Countess Margaret, wife of Count Hermann of Henneberg. According to the sixteenth-century Polish historian Martin Cromerus, a peasant woman carrying twin babies in her arms asked the countess for alms; the countess not only told her to get lost but suggested that the two babies had different fathers. In revenge, the spurned woman prayed for the countess to deliver one baby for every day of the year.

On Good Friday, 1278, at age forty-two, Countess Margaret reportedly gave birth to 365 children—182 girls, 182 boys, and 1 hermaphrodite. They were baptized in two enormous brass washbasins by the Bishop of Treras, who named all the boys John, and the girls Elizabeth.

The name of the hermaphrodite is unknown.

The only eleven-year-old admitted as an undergraduate to Harvard

Boris Sidis, a Russian-born professor of abnormal psychology, believed that geniuses are made, not born. When his son William James Sidis (named for the famous Harvard psychologist) was just six months old, Boris turned the nursery into a laboratory, dangled alphabet blocks over the crib, hypnotized the child, and began to teach him to read. By age three, baby William was composing stories in English and French on the typewriter. By five he had mastered Latin and Greek, authored a treatise on anatomy, and developed a method for calculating the day of the week on which any date had fallen in the past ten thousand years.

In 1908, at the age of nine (and having recently proposed a new way of computing logarithms), the wunderkind was presented for matriculation at Harvard. But the admissions committee, while conceding his academic qualifications, deemed him still too immature for college life. So young Sidis waited, and shortly after his eleventh birthday he became the youngest Harvard freshman in history.

During his freshman year, he astounded the science faculty with a lecture on "Four-Dimensional Bodies." His teachers foresaw a brilliant future for the boy—but then something came unhinged. Sidis suffered a nervous breakdown and was institutionalized. He returned to school, graduated magna cum laude at sixteen, and briefly held a professorship at a university in Texas.

Then he suddenly gave up all academic and intellectual pursuits and became a legendary underachiever. He made every effort to hide his past accomplishments, took only menial jobs, and refused promotions. He occupied his powerful intelligence with three subjects to the exclusion of all others: the culture of the Okamakammessett Indian tribe, the submerged continent of Atlantis, and—most obsessively—streetcar transfers.

He collected thousands of transfers from all over the world, carefully preserving and cataloging each one. He haunted airports and train stations, hoping to pick up rare transfers from travelers from distant cities. And, at his own expense, he published the encyclopedic *Notes on the Collection of Transfers*, which sold fewer than fifty copies. Sidis maintained that the greatest achievement of his life was a fifteen-hour continuous journey on the streetcars of New York, during which he acquired forty transfers—riding the entire distance on a single fare.

In 1937 *The New Yorker* ran a "Where Are They Now?" story about his strange life. Sidis sued on the grounds that reminding the public of his childhood as a prodigy made it impossible for him to get work as a clerk or dishwasher. He had become "an ordinary man," he claimed, and was willing to take an intelligence test to prove it. The judge would not agree that Sidis was ordinary in any sense of the word, and the case was dismissed.

Once, a reporter cornered him late in life and asked how he felt about the prediction of Daniel F. Comstock, back in 1910, that the little boy who lectured on the fourth dimension would "grow up to be a great mathematician, a leader in the world of science." "It's strange," said Sidis. "But you know, I was born on April Fools' Day."

The only passenger to fall out of—and back into—an aircraft in midflight

In the closing months of World War I, a Canadian fighter pilot named Makepeace was attacked fifteen thousand feet over Germany by German aerial gunners. To get away, he took the plane into a sudden nosedive, catching U.S. Army captain J. H. Hedley, sitting behind him, by surprise.

Hedley was sucked violently upward out of the plane like a champagne cork; Makepeace, meanwhile, kept plummeting. But as the aircraft leveled out hundreds of feet below, Hedley, who had apparently been caught in a powerful downdraft caused by the plane's descent landed with a thud on the rear of the fuselage. He scrambled back into the plane and stayed put until Makepeace was able to land safely behind Allied lines.

The only person to walk backward from Santa Monica to Istanbul

When they finally get around to dedicating a pedestrians' hall of fame, Plennie L. Wingo will rate an entire wing. On April 15, 1931, he left Santa Monica, California, bound east while looking west. He arrived in Istanbul, Turkey, on October 24, 1932, having traversed an eight-thousand-mile route across two continents, walking the entire distance backward. For hindsight he wore a pair of specially designed reflective glasses.

Then, in 1977, at the age of eighty-one, Wingo celebrated the forty-fifth anniversary of his marathon reverse promenade by hiking backward from Santa Monica to San Francisco. The 452-mile trek took him a leisurely 85 days.

The only municipal rapid-transit system built in total secrecy

On a moonless night in February 1868, Alfred Ely Beach, publisher of *Scientific American*, stood in the basement of Devlin's Clothing Store, beneath the corner of Broadway and Warren Street in lower Manhattan. With him were a team of workmen bearing picks, shovels, wheelbarrows, and a hydraulic boring tool. He chalked a spot on the wall, and the most daring excavation project of its time began.

It was a project Beach had first envisioned nearly

two decades earlier. "My plan," he had written in 1849, "is to tunnel Broadway through its whole length with openings for stairways at every corner . . . laying down a double track . . . the whole to be brilliantly lighted with gas. The cars . . . will stop every 10 seconds at every corner."

Although Beach was a highly regarded publisher and patent attorney, respectable people sneered at his underground tunnel and deemed it the stuff of a madman's dreams.

But their scorn was unjust, for if any city in the world desperately needed a subway system, it was traffic-choked, midcentury New York. Beach himself knew the situation firsthand: although his law office and apartment were scarcely two miles apart, he was nearly an hour getting home each night.

Beach was not a man to be scorned. An inventor's inventor, he had created, at the age of twenty-one, the world's first working typewriter and demonstrated it at London's 1856 Crystal Palace Exposition.

But neither his typewriter nor his other inventions provided him with much income. It was from his publishing career and law practice that he earned his living. In addition to his stewardship of *Scientific American*, Beach also ran the *New York Sun* for a while and established an additional two dozen publications.

By the late 1860s, Beach realized that a *horse-drawn* subway would be dangerously impractical and turned his thoughts to manmade locomotion. It quickly became obvious that of all the alternatives, pneumatic power was by far the most desirable.

Obvious too was the need to build his experimental subway under cover, considering the public's cynicism. So Beach applied for no charter and asked for no assistance. The workmen who followed him to Devlin's basement that night in 1868 were sworn to absolute secrecy.

Night after night they returned to the lengthening tunnel via the basement, digging and scooping farther and farthor into what surely must have seemed a Dantean nightmare. It took fifty-eight nights to bore through to Murray Street, the northern terminus of the Broadway tunnel. Assembling the 220-passenger railroad car that would shuttle its length and outfitting the station took another two years and $350,000 of Beach's money.

The day of the unveiling was February 26, 1870. A master of public relations, Beach invited the press, the city fathers, and a throng of VIPs, regaling them with a sumptuous buffet lunch and, of course, test rides on his pneumatic marvel.

Unlike present-day subway trains, Beach's single cylindrical car, which could accommodate twenty-two passengers, fit the nine-foot-wide tunnel with an almost coital snugness. A mammoth fan at one end literally blew the car the tunnel's length at about ten miles per hour. Approaching the opposite end, 312 feet away, the car tripped a wire that reversed the blower, causing it to inhale the car back to its starting point.

The visitors were as impressed with the furnishings as they were with the train itself. The car, upholstered in dark leather and red velvet, would please a sultan. The walnut-paneled waiting room that ran half the length of the tunnel was appointed with mirrors, costly divans, paintings, a fountain, and a grand piano.

But Beach's experiment in below-the-ground transportation was only that—an experiment. What he really wanted was to extend the tunnel five miles north to Central Park and to add several cars. Running at full throttle, he claimed, the subway would skate along the rails at a mile a minute and carry twenty thousand passengers a day.

The physical obstacles blocking Beach's way were

nothing compared to the political obstacles. In 1870 all transportation companies in New York, large and small, were under the thumb of Boss Tweed, the most powerful man in the state. When Beach took his case to the state capital in Albany, Tweed viewed it as an insurrection and squashed it by pushing through a bill of his own that called for a public outlay of as much as sixty-five million dollars to erect an elevated tramway.

Never giving up, Beach continued to campaign for passage of his Beach transit bill. Finally, in 1872, with Tweed in jail and a more public-spirited governor in Albany, Beach got his go-ahead.

But his subway was never built. It had been three years since the inventor's initial triumph, and public enthusiasm for the subway had faded. Beach himself had his doubts. The panic of 1869 had dried up many of the private funding sources he would have needed. And real-estate magnates were ranting vigorously against the project, convinced that once the digging began, Trinity Church and the surrounding towers of lower Manhattan would topple like dominoes.

In the following years, Beach turned his efforts to other matters—his publications, his philanthropic endeavors, his religion. By the time of his death in 1896, he had long since vanished from sight. But in 1912 workmen building a for-real subway system for New York unsuspectingly broke through the brickwork of Beach's tunnel and uncovered station, tracks, and train in one of the most unusual archaeological finds of the day. Today Beach's tunnel is part of the city's City Hall subway station.

The only person buried standing up in Westminster Abbey

While Ben Jonson was still the rage of the London stage, King Charles I promised him personally that he could be buried in any spot he chose in Westminster Abbey. Jonson picked out a location on the north side of the nave, but after he died in poverty, on August 6, 1637, the site turned out to be barely eighteen inches square.

Rather than break his word, Charles ordered Jonson's coffin interred vertically, feet first. The inscription "O Rare Ben Jonson," engraved on the tomb marker, is sometimes interpreted as a comment on the dramatist's unique burial posture—and not his lyrical gifts.

POSTSCRIPT: *NONE* OF A KIND

While there has been one—and only one—bachelor president, there has *never* been a president without siblings. Furthermore, there is not, nor has there ever been, even one

American buried in Westminster Abbey.

fair ball hit out of Yankee Stadium.

Super Bowl shutout.

fur-bearing animal native to Antarctica.

monkey native to the United States.

flying snake.

resident of Iceland whose ancestors didn't come from someplace else.

Kentucky Derby victory by Man O' War.

fish that can swim backward.

true perpetual-motion machine.

World Series victory by a team that lost the first three games.

grand slam home run hit off Jim Palmer.

airplane to fly through an air pocket (since there's no such thing).

antelope native to North America (the lyrics to "Home on the Range" notwithstanding).

formal British constitution.

cure for the common cold.

U.S. telephone area code with a middle digit other than 0 or 1.

law prohibiting the destruction or defacing of U.S. currency.

witch burned at the stake in Salem, Massachusetts.

proven aphrodisiac.

movie in which James Cagney said, "You dirty rat," Charles Boyer said, "Come with me to the Casbah," or Humphrey Bogart said, "Play it again, Sam."

real river in Saudi Arabia.

Albanian word for "headache."

reference to a cat in the Bible.

turkey in Turkey.

bone in an elephant's trunk.

person excommunicated from the Hindu religion.

U.S. president who died in May.

horse that took part in the charge up San Juan Hill.

slave freed as a direct result of the Emancipation Proclamation.

English ship sunk by the Spanish Armada.

photograph of Abraham Lincoln smiling.

tooth or claw on an anteater.

Hawaiian word ending in a consonant.

igloo in Alaska.

INDEX